THE JIMI HENDRIX EXPERIENCE

ALSO BY JERRY HOPKINS

THE ROCK STORY

GROUPIES AND OTHER GIRLS
(WITH JOHN BURKS)

FESTIVAL!

ELVIS: A BIOGRAPHY

THE LAST SEX MANUAL
(WITH RON PION, M.D.)

NO ONE HERE GETS OUT ALIVE
(WITH DANNY SUGERMAN)

ELVIS: THE FINAL YEARS

THE HULA

BOWIE

YOKO ONO

THE LIZARD KING:
THE ESSENTIAL JIM MORRISON

THE JIMI HENDRIX EXPERIENCE

BY JERRY HOPKINS

WITH A DISCOGRAPHY BY STEVEN SZEP

PLEXUS, LONDON

Copyright © 1983 by Jerry Hopkins, 1996 by Haku 'Olelo
Published by Plexus Publishing Limited
55a Clapham Common Southside
London SW4 9BX
First Printing 1996

British Library Cataloguing in Publication Data

Hopkins, Jerry
    The Jimi Hendrix experience
    1.Hendrix, Jimi, 1942-70 2.Rock musicians - United States
    - Biography 3.Guitarists - United States - Biography
    I.Title
    782.4'2'166'092

ISBN 0 85965 202 5

Published by arrangement with Arcade Publishing, Inc.
Printed in Great Britain by Bath Press Ltd.

    The author gratefully acknowledges permission from the following sources to reprint
material:
    Bella Godiva Music, Inc., for permission to quote lyrics from "Angel," "My Friend,"
"Crosstown Traffic," "Electric Ladyland," "Voodoo Chile," "Rainy Day, Dream Away,"
"1983," "Room Full of Mirrors," "Machine Gun," "Dolly Dagger," and "Killing Floor." No
part of the above songs may be used commercially without the expressed written permission of Bella Godiva Music, Inc.
    CBS Songs, for permission to quote lyrics from "Wild Thing" by Chip Taylor, published
by Blackwood Music, Inc.
    Chappell Music Company, for permission to quote from the following songs by Jimi
Hendrix: "Foxy Lady" and "Purple Haze" © 1967, 1968 by Yameta Co., Ltd.; "Fire" and
"Are You Experienced?" © 1967 by Yameta Co., Ltd.; "Little Wing" © 1968 by Yameta Co.,
Ltd.; "If 6 Was 9" © 1968 by Yameta Co., Ltd.; and "Bold as Love" © 1964, 1968 by Yameta
Co., Ltd. All rights controlled by Unichappell Music, Inc. International copyright secured.
All rights reserved. Used by permission.
    Devon Music, Inc., for permission to use lyrics from "My Generation," words and
music by Peter Townshend, © 1965 by Fabulous Music, Ltd., London, England. TRO-
Devon Music, Inc., New York, controls all publication rights for the U.S.A. and Canada.
Used by permission.
    GPI Publications, for permission to reprint material from the *Guitar Player* magazine
"Hendrix Special" by Don Menn, published by GPI Publications.
    The Estate of Jimi Hendrix and James A. Hendrix, his father, for permission to reprint a
poem by Jimi Hendrix. No part of said poem may be used commercially except by the
express written consent of James A. Hendrix.
    Warner Bros., Inc., for excerpts from *The Jimi Hendrix Story* © 1973, Warner Bros., Inc.
All rights reserved.

10 9 8 7 6 5 4 3 2 1

INTRODUCTION

It was a story made for the movies. Not the story of Jimi Hendrix's life but that of his death, and what happened nearly a quarter of a century after it. It could only be a true story. If someone wrote it as fiction, as a novel or a screen-play, no one would believe it.

Even during Jimi Hendix's lifetime, there is evidence to show that the guitarist was abused by his professional representatives. There's nothing new about that; it's an entertainment business cliché. So, too, during the time fol-lowing his death the rip-offs continued, until finally Jimi's father, his sole heir, employed a black lawyer in Los Angeles to sort out and handle his increasingly complex affairs. All went well, or seemed to, until 1993, when Al Hendrix, a seventy-two-year-old retired gardener, went to court claiming that the California attorney had taken his son's musical legacy and sold it to the highest bidder. Leo Branton Jr., the Los Angeles lawyer who had represented the Hendrix estate for more than twenty years, was accused of getting the elder Hendrix to sign away his son's musical copyrights to several offshore companies—neglecting to say that he, the lawyer, had an interest in those firms. For the Jimi Hendrix catalog of songs and recordings, released and unreleased, Al Hendrix reportedly was paid $500,000, plus a modest annual annuity. The offshore companies then negotiated a sale to one of the largest American musical conglomerates, for as much as $75 million.

Then—and this is where the story gets good—a longtime Jimi Hendrix fan came to the rescue, providing Al Hendrix with the money to fight back. That man was Paul Allen, a lifelong Seattle resident and cofounder with Bill Gates of Microsoft, owner of the Portland Trail Blazers basketball team and ranked in 1995 by *Forbes* magazine as the fourth richest man in the United States.

What happened next—a courtroom story equal to anything novelist John Grisham might concoct—is described in the epilogue to this book.

When *Rolling Stone* magazine published a brief history of the electric guitar, the tall, thin performer who played the guitar upside down (to accommodate his left-handedness) was placed "in a class by himself," a mammoth talent whose "pioneering use of effects like phasing, wah-wah and fuzz tone have become part of the rock guitarist's vocabulary."

Other publications in the field agreed. Said *Guitar Player* in 1975, "*GP* has never before devoted an entire issue to the life of a particular guitarist, but now is a good time to start. Jimi's contribution to our instrument is so wideranging, so massive, that fully five years after his death our offices continue to receive almost daily requests [for information] about his music, his technique, his equipment. Clearly no other electric guitar player has had the influence of this man."

Another twenty years has passed, and his stature has grown exponentially. Quite simply, Jimi Hendrix was one of the most significant musical contributors not just to our time but to all time. In only a few years he defined the spectrum of the electric guitar—or, rather, redefined it—and influenced thousands of guitarists, many of whom went on to become worldwide stars. There are things he did on the guitar that no one yet can explain or duplicate, not even given the sophisticated electronic assistance that's been developed since his death.

Cynics call the death of a rock star at the peak of his career "a good career move." Even Jimi himself, two years before he died, said, "It's funny the way most people love the dead. Once you're dead, you're made for life." Sadly, there is some truth to this. In the years since Jimi's death due to an apparent barbiturate and alcohol overdose at age twenty-seven, his music and life story have been one of the most consistently revered and heavily trafficked natural resources in contemporary cultural history.

During his four-year recording career, only seven albums were released, including two weak recordings thrown into the marketplace from his formative years to capitalize on his later success and a compilation of previous hits—in other words, only four that he really cared about. By 1996, another dozen were put in the shops officially, and an incredible 132 albums and singles and 238 CDs appeared on the illegal, or bootleg, market, a figure that rises weekly.

While it's arguable that much of this material would never have been released if Jimi were alive, his record companies report that he is one of their most consistent bestsellers, accounting for more than three million units a year. In other words, Jimi Hendrix is selling more music now than he did when he was alive. "Once you're dead, you're made for life."

In 1991 he got his star on the Hollywood Walk of Fame, and a year later he was selected for a Lifetime Achievement Award at the Grammy Awards and inducted into the Rock and Roll Hall of Fame. "Of all those named to the Hall of Fame," Jann Wenner, the founder-editor-publisher of *Rolling*

Stone, who godfathered the Hall of Fame, told me, "Jimi was the only shoo-in. When he was nominated, we knew he was as good as in."

In twenty-five years, at least twenty-five books about Jimi have been published, putting him in the rock and roll library behind Elvis Presley and the Beatles in numbers, but ahead of everyone else. (Another thirty to forty books about the 1960s are substantially about him or feature him.) Since his death, there have been eleven fan magazines, six of which still are published regularly in the United States, Ireland, England, France, and Brazil; one of these also is translated into Japanese.

A $60 million Hendrix museum is under construction in Seattle, also bankrolled by Microsoft cofounder Paul Allen, and a recording studio Hendrix owned, Electric Lady, has been turned into a small museum in New York. Wrangler Jeans has used one of his songs, "Crosstown Traffic," in its most successful commercial; other songs have promoted Pepsi Cola and Nike running shoes. A magazine and uncounted boutiques and discotheques, in addition to a line of underwear, have been named for his song "Foxy Lady." The U.S. Army, which counts Jimi as an alumnus—he was a paratrooper—included "Voodoo Chile" in a 1991 concert in Panama beamed to General Manuel Noriega, part of a message to come out of his hideaway with his hands up. There have been half a dozen filmed documentaries, and as this book goes to press, Touchstone Films, part of the Walt Disney empire, is preparing a feature film starring Laurence Fishburn in the title role.

A group of contemporary rock bands have recorded Jimi's songs for an authorized tribute CD and cassette, and several bootlegs have gathered other recorded covers by Eric Clapton, Sting, Stevie Ray Vaughan, Aerosmith, the Red Hot Chili Peppers, Rod Stewart, and Led Zeppelin. Dozens of private archives were begun. One of his guitars, a gift to one of his original sidemen, sold at auction for $350,000, and other memorabilia, including clothing and handwritten lyrics and other scribblings, have been offered by the world's leading auction houses. Hundreds of thousands of posters and Hendrix pendants and T-shirts and buttons and busts and coffee cups and other pop kitsch are sold each year worldwide, authorized and otherwise.

Another yardstick of success is how much legal activity has surrounded, and assaulted, the earnings. No one has kept track, but one attorney estimates the number of lawsuits at "more than a hundred," ranging from paternity claims to demands for past royalties due. The legal record of the suits between Al Hendrix and Leo Branton et al. by 1996 includes approximately 2,000 docket entries, filling fifty-one volumes; court clerks in Seattle got so many inquiries that they committed the case number to memory. In 1996 the opposing parties were still fighting over the division of the spoils, and the file continued to grow.

Why such adoration? And greed, and all the rest?

Besides the fact that the music is as exciting as it was twenty-five years ago, there is inevitably the Hendrix image to be reckoned with. This gets us back to the guitarist's own appraisal about achieving immortality on earth by leaving it. "Live fast, die young and make a good-looking corpse" is the way writer Willard Motley put it in his novel *Knock on Any Door.* Jimi did that, flashing through the psychedelic 1960s, setting much of that decade's style, becoming what one writer called "the Cassius Clay of Pop," another "the flower generation's electric nigger dandy—its king and golden calf."

Jimi was the perfect hedonist, a superstar with uncounted dollars to play with, leaving his business affairs to the management of others, dedicated only to making good music and having a good time. This took him along strange paths—into a pharmacy of mind-changing drugs, from continent to continent, and to the study of voodoo, space travel, Eastern religions, and psychic phenomena. Behind him he left a phosphorescent wake bobbing with burned-up guitars and burned-out friends, landmark concerts and recordings, and a musical reputation that grows stronger and a personal myth that becomes more outlandish every year. The Jimi Hendrix story is one of a human spun wildly and beautifully beyond the bounds the rest of us know.

Jimi was also a classic innocent, and as a consequence a target and victim. In 1975 *Rolling Stone* commissioned me to investigate reports that Jimi's estate was being plundered by what the editors eventually called "a calculating band of lawyers, promoters, cons and other vultures." I went to Seattle, Los Angeles, and New York to research that article, interviewing twenty-five or thirty people, including, Jimi's father, the guitarist's friend and longtime road manager, Gerry Stickells, and enough attorneys and accountants to make my head spin. The result was "A Piece of the Rainbow," which *Rolling Stone* subtitled "A Scandal of Lawsuits and Laundered Money." When it was published in 1976, Jimi's bass player, Noel Redding, called to say that I had "barely scratched the surface."

Much more of the story is told here. A few individuals, of course, refused to be interviewed, among them one of Jimi's attorneys, Henry Steingarten, who told me that he didn't think he had any information that would be of assistance, and the president of Reprise Records, Mo Ostin, who said, "It's something I feel uncomfortable about. I don't want to get into an interview situation that I'd regret later." Others, involved in recent lawsuits, never returned my calls.

But many, many more did talk, several for the first time, including Jimi's father and brother, Al and Leon Hendrix, who gave me opposite but not opposing views of Jimi's childhood. Barbette Andreadakis, Jimi's manager's housekeeper, and Jerry Morrison (not his real name), the manager's aide and confidant, offered a revealing backstairs look at Jimi's business operations. Jerry also told me an amazing story never even hinted at during Jimi's lifetime: a kidnapping by the Mafia. A Beverly Hills attorney, Mickey Shapiro, who was suing the Hendrix estate for his client Noel Redding, provided photocopies of all the documents in the files of an offshore trust company controlled by Jimi's manager into which millions of dollars had disappeared. Jim Fricke, chief curator of Paul Allen's museum in Seattle, made his vast files and visuals available.

Besides those already mentioned, I talked, corresponded, and exchanged cassette tapes with Bill "Hoss" Allen, Marshall Brevitz, the Chambers Brothers (Joe, Julius, Lester, and Willie), Stan Cornyn, George Costa, Pat Costello, Larry Dietz, Danny Fields, Dick Fontaine, Frank Forrest, Don Friedman, Steve Gold, Jerry Goldstein, Michael Goldstein, Nigel Gordon, Leo Harmon, Pat Hartley, Sharon Lawrence, Arthur Lee, Mark McLaughlin, Terry McVay, Ron Merions, Buddy Miles, James Oliver, Ray Paret, the Plaster Casters, Mike Quashie, Noel Redding, Shimon Ron, Ellen Sander, Don Schmitzerle, Andy Stern, Gary Stromberg, Dr. Stephen Tenby, Rae Warner, and Elmer Valentine.

Guitar Player magazine provided tapes of interviews with Eric Barrett, Mike Bloomfield, John Hammond Jr., Eddie Kramer, Ken Shaffer, and Gerry Stickells. *Rolling Stone* made available its files, a desk, and a telephone. Three early books were helpful: David Henderson's *Jimi Hendrix: Voodoo Child of the Aquarian Age;* Curtis Knight's *Jimi: An Intimate Biography;* and Chris Welch's *Hendrix: A Biography*. So, too, was a transcript of the Warner Bros. documentary *The Jimi Hendrix Story,* provided by Warner Bros., and the unpublished manuscript of a history of Warner Bros.–Reprise Records, provided by its author, Ellen Pelissero.

For this update of the book, I interviewed Leo Branton Jr., Alan Douglas, Ed Howard, Kenny Hagood, Steve Weiss, Leon Dicker, Maxwell Cohen, Barry Reiss, Mickey Shapiro, Jack Hammer, and Jim Fricke, chief curator of the Experience Music Project museum in Seattle.

Further thanks go to Timothy White, editor in chief of

Billboard magazine; Steven Rodham, publisher of *Jimpress*, one of the best of the current crop of fan magazines, who provided back copies and answered many questions; and my brother Jack Hopkins, who is, in one of those great coincidences that make life interesting, a court reporter for the *Post Intelligencer* in Seattle. He made his home available and assisted with legal research.

Finally, it is traditional for authors to thank their agents. In twenty-six books, I never had one I wanted to acknowledge publicly. This time, it's different. Patricia Butler gets much of the credit for this book's existence.

THE JIMI HENDRIX EXPERIENCE

CHAPTER

1

$\mathbf{H}$is daddy was a tap dancer and his mama was a party girl.

His father, James Allen Hendrix, learned to tap-dance from his older brother and learned acrobatic dancing from his mother, who had been a dancer in a traveling vaudeville troupe. Born and raised in Vancouver, British Columbia, his great-grandmother was a full-blooded Cherokee (which made Jimi one-sixteenth Cherokee). As a teenager just over five feet tall and decked out in a zoot suit of the time—ballooning pants tapered tight to the ankle, a jacket that hung to his knees—Al became a prominent figure in the Pacific Northwest in the late 1930s, first at high school dances and then in front of visiting jazz bands. Once he even got to dance with the great Louis Armstrong's orchestra.

Eventually Al worked in several Canadian nightclubs, and the way he remembers it, he was able to make more money in one night dancing than he could make in a week of hard labor. But it wasn't any good. The dance nights came infrequently and his wardrobe and travel costs often consumed all the profits. So in 1940, soon after his twentieth birthday, Al Hendrix hung up his zoot suit and moved to Victoria on Vancouver Island, where he tried to get work on the railroad. He was rejected, he says, because of his height, and after a week or so shining shoes, he moved again, this time to Seattle, where he slept in boxcars and open fields until he found a menial job in an iron foundry.

Al still loved music, and he attended dances regularly, looking for a partner who could keep up with him. In September 1941 he found one. Her name was Lucille Jeter and she was only sixteen years old. Barely five feet tall and fragile—the effect of having pneumonia as an infant—she was, nonetheless, a local jitterbug champion. Al remembers that on their first date he took her to hear the jazz pianist Fats Waller. Soon after that they started "running around together," becoming popular figures at dance contests throughout the central Seattle area.

At the time, Seattle was an "open" city. There were only 4,000 or so blacks—then called Negroes—in a population of 368,000. But the large number of Orientals gave the city a tolerant racial attitude. Nonwhites were discriminated against in some better hotels and in many cheaper bars and restaurants, but there were no rigidly segregated neighborhoods.

With the coming of World War II, soon after Al and Lucille began dating, Seattle changed. Many Japanese-Americans were moved into detention camps, while large numbers of blacks arrived in "Freedom Trains," so called because of the thousands of new jobs being offered by an exploding defense industry. No longer was it unusual to see a black face on the street, and predominantly black neighborhoods developed.

Al continued to work at the foundry, suffering a hernia in early 1942. "Lucille brought me candy and stuff to the hospital," Al says. "Then after I got well, I got drafted into the army, so we jumped up and got married. That was in late March of '42."

The first child was on November 27, at 10:15 A.M., in Seattle General Hospital. Al was two thousand miles away in Georgia and unable to get home. So without him to consult, Lucille named the baby Johnny Allen Hendrix.

The labor had been long and difficult for Lucille. Consumptive since early childhood, her small body was by now being wracked by tuberculosis, and she was told by her doctors to rest for at least two months. But she ignored all medical advice. She went dancing. She also began drinking heavily, and when her son was just seven months old, she was sent to a Seattle hospital for a long recovery.

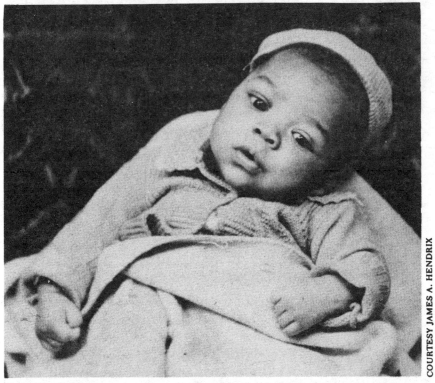

Jimi Hendrix, born Johnny Allen Hendrix, at three months

Johnny was given to a woman friend in Seattle, and when that friend died, the woman's sisters took the boy to California, where they cared for him in a small house in Berkeley. Al Hendrix's regular army allotment check continued to go to his wife, but he says that he also sent money to the two women. Al says he doesn't remember their names today, only that when he was mustered out of the service in Seattle in 1945, he took the first train south to meet his son.

At the time, Al wasn't sure where his wife was. Returning to Seattle with Johnny, he finally found her, partying. They argued and agreed to get divorced.

It was also agreed that Johnny would stay with Al, who was by now living with his sister-in-law and her three children in the low-rent Ranier Vista housing project in central Seattle. This was a federally funded section of one-story duplexes on a hillside near Lake Washington. The neighborhood was pleasant and green from the frequent rain, but there was no avoiding the grimness of poverty. Nearly all the residents of the project were black and all were poor.

As soon as he could, Al found new lodging for himself and his small son in a boarding house on Tenth Avenue. At the same time, he took the necessary legal steps to change the boy's name from Johnny Allen to James Marshall—for the brother who had taught him to tap-dance and who died when Al was young.

Today Al remembers: "I wasn't divorced yet, I was in the act of *gettin'* divorced. All I had to do to get the divorce was pay twenty-five more dollars, but all I was makin' was twenty dollars a week, my rockin' chair money from the government. I sure wish I'da did it at the time, but Lucille talked me out of it. So I let it go."

Lucille moved back in with Al in 1946, and for the next three years the relationship was, as Al puts it, "on and off." Then in 1948 a second son was born who was named Leon.

In 1949 the Hendrixes separated again, amid much

Jimmy, legally renamed by his father, at age four

drinking and shouting and tears. Al generally was a quiet man, passive, reluctant to fight, giving some the impression of being henpecked. But he had a temper that simmered, then erupted. And Lucille, whose voice was as big as she was small, tested and taunted her husband constantly, often disappearing for several nights at a time.

Jimmy—later he was to change the spelling to Jimi—was seven and Leon two when Al sent them to live with his sister Patricia and her husband, Frank, in Vancouver for the summer. When summer stretched into fall, Jimmy was en-

Jimmy, right, and his brother Leon in 1951

rolled in the Dawson Street Annex Elementary School that Al attended when he was a child. In all, Jimmy and Leon remained with their aunt and uncle and their son, Bobby, who was five, for more than a year. For the boys it was a happy time, marked by the small, ordinary events of childhood in a peaceful home and warm environment. In the afternoons the three boys freely explored the neighborhood, playing in a large sawdust pile, walking along the small boat docks on the river, going to Saturday movies, where Buck Rogers was a favorite. There was even a lady in the neighborhood they called "Betty Crocker" because she fed them chocolate cake.

Surely they missed their mother, but Al visited them on weekends about once a month, and the serenity that prevailed must have given them a sense of security they hadn't experienced in Seattle.

Just before Christmas in 1951 the boys returned home to find their mother and father together again in a house near 26th Avenue and Washington Street. It was in the same central city area and at first it felt good to the two boys. Christmas was especially memorable.

"We had a tree, we got presents and Mom and Dad were laughing together, turning the little hand crank on a toy steam shovel," Leon says. "But then they started fighting again.

"I was four and Jimmy was ten, a third-grader at Leschi Elementary School. Every day was about the same. I'd wait for Jimmy to get home from school and then we'd play outside. Mom would invite friends over and they'd drink. Then Dad would get mad. It happened over and over and over again, and so finally they got divorced, after arguing about it for almost six years.

"I remember one night when she didn't come home and my dad went looking for her. Dad put me and Jimmy in the back of the Pontiac and we went along. He found her with

Jimmy's 1955 class picture, Leschi Elementary School, Seattle.
Jimmy is the third from the left in the second row from the bottom

some guy, but she came out and got in the car and we left. I remember driving down Jackson Street and Dad shouting at her: 'Act right! Grow up! Behave y'self!'

"She kept bugging him back. She was really drunk. Mom got mad and reached over there with her foot and hit the gas and then the brake. The car jumped forward and then stopped short and me and Jimmy flew into the front seat. Now Mom was crying and telling us she was sorry. She helped us get into the back seat again and hugged us and loved us up. That was the most love I ever got from her. Probably Jimmy, too.

"Dad must've loved Mom a lot. Even when we talk about her today, he cries. He talks about her for hours, then gets mad and says I look just like her. He won't show us pictures he has of her. She was beautiful. She had long reddish hair and light skin. But what I remember is my dad always arguing with her.

"After Mom left, Dad hired an old Filipino lady who got room and board to cook meals and take care of us. She was really mean. She whipped me all the time. She gave me and Jimmy catsup sandwiches to eat and we told Dad and she gave us a whipping for telling on her."

Leon recalls that eventually the woman was fired and "we moved to one room on Terrace Street. We weren't allowed to cook in the room, but Dad had a hot plate anyway, and the bathroom was down the hall. We had a dog named Prince, and dog food cost nine cents a can. That was a big item in the budget, so Prince got half a can a day. We all shared one tea bag. We got a whipping if we left a light on, because it was wasting money."

Al had had only an eighth-grade education, so he went back to school under the G.I. Bill, first attending classes at Edison High and then at the Y.M.C.A. At the same time, he was working six nights a week as a janitor at the Pike Street Market, where fish and meat and fresh produce were sold in open stalls. Al managed to take home a lot of vegetables, given to him by friendly farmers.

But it just wasn't working. Money was so short, Al usually walked the five miles to his class because he couldn't afford the bus.

"That Christmas we had before Mom left was the last one," Leon says. "After that, at Christmas and at birthdays, there were no presents. Dad said there wasn't any reason to celebrate—it was just another day. The truth is, there wasn't any money for presents."

After a while Al stopped going to class and moved his family into another small house in the same neighborhood, near the corner of 26th Avenue and Yesler Street. He also changed jobs again, now taking a job pumping gas for City Light and Power.

"We were pretty much taking care of ourselves," Leon says. "Dad had to be at work at three-thirty in the afternoon and we got out of school at three-ten and we'd always be late getting home, so we didn't see him. He made cheese sandwiches and left them in the refrigerator for us for dinner. He got off work at midnight, got home at one A.M. and in the morning he'd be so tired, sometimes he'd burn our breakfast.

"Meanwhile we was playing outside alone until ten o'clock at night. Neighbors complained to the county welfare department about that and they came to see Dad. Dad told us to stay indoors. He said if we played indoors we wouldn't get into trouble.

"Lot of times me and Jimmy got in trouble at school. Nothing serious, the usual stuff. Sassing a teacher. Sometimes Jimmy cut class. And Dad would have to come to school to talk to the principal, and so he'd be late for work. They took that for a while, then they fired him.

"Things got real rough after that. For a long time he couldn't find work. They cut off the electricity, so he bought milk each day and put it in cold water in the sink. He collected electrical wire and burned off the rubber insulation in the furnace and recycled the copper. We ate horsemeat hamburger two or three times a week.

"Then one day Dad told me to come with him. He put the toothpaste in one back pocket, picked up an extra pair of pants and took me to this house. Dad said they were friends of his. The next five years, until I was twelve, I was in seven of those houses—foster homes."

When Leon went into the first of those homes, Jimmy was thirteen, a gangly adolescent with feet and hands so large he seemed much bigger than he actually was. He was also uncommonly shy, given to sitting in fear when in the presence of most adults and all strangers. He seemed always to be wondering where to put his big hands. He seldom made friends, and now his brother was gone. He stuttered, had trouble finding words to express what he thought and felt. The poverty and insecurity, more than a dozen homes in half that many years, and the lack of mothering—all were taking a terrible toll.

Especially the lack of mothering.

For years afterward, perhaps for all the rest oɪ his life, Jimmy dreamed about Lucille. In an interview in 1969, when asked about his dreams, Jimmy remembered one in which "my mother was being carried away on this camel. And there was a big caravan and she was saying, 'Well, I'm gonna see you,' and she was going under these trees, and you could see the shade—you know, the leaf patterns—crossing her face. You know how the sun shines through a tree, and if you go under the shadow of the tree the shadows go across your face. Well, these were in green and yellow. Shadows. And she was saying, 'Well, I won't be seeing you too much anymore, you know.' And I said, 'Where are you going?' "

Of course, it wasn't all depressing. Al Hendrix disagrees with Leon and remembers a Christmas when both boys received train sets, another occasion when Jimmy got a bicycle. Al also talks about the season Jimmy played Little League baseball and the two years in his adolescence when he played sandlot football. A series of photographs in 1956, when Jimmy was thirteen, show the youngster proudly wearing the uniform of the "Fighting Irish," posing with his coach and roughhousing happily with his proud father in their living room.

And there was music. Al says it all started when Jimmy asked him to show him how to play the spoons and also to show him some dance steps.

"He wasn't much of a dancer," Al says. "He didn't have too much dancing ability. But his hands were good. So when I was doing some yardwork, cleaning garages and such as

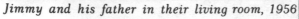

Jimmy and his father in their living room, 1956

Jimmy and his father with their dog Prince and their cat Whitey

that, and I found a ukulele, I took it home. I had to get some strings for it. He was about twelve, maybe younger. This was around 1955. He'd play that ukulele, sometimes right-handed, sometimes left-handed. I guess he figured he'd do better left-handed, and that's what he did.

"When he got good on that, he bought a guitar, an ordinary acoustic guitar, from a friend of his for five dollars. I gave him the money and he went out and bought it. I got myself a saxophone at the same time, although I never played one before. We were learning together. We just made a lot of noise, mainly. We entertained ourselves. Then I got behind in the payments and had to let the sax go back. Sometime after that I got a few dollars ahead and got him an electric guitar. I couldn't afford an amplifier, so he'd practice at home and then go off to a friend's house where they had an amp."

One of Jimmy's early musical influences, Ray Charles

MICHAEL OCHS ARCHIVES

[29]

Garfield High School

By now Jimmy was attending classes at Garfield High School, a big brick structure that towered over the neighborhood on a large grassy hill. It was a big school, with nearly two thousand students, most of whom seemed to be preoccupied with the annual Funfest, weekend dances and sporting events.

These were the placid Eisenhower years, when such TV westerns as *Wagon Train* and *Bonanza* ruled the airwaves and the most popular situation comedies included *The Donna Reed Show* and *Leave It to Beaver*. Favorite movies of the period were *Ben Hur* and *Gigi* and *Pillow Talk*. The Korean war was over and the Vietnam war had not begun. It was a time of Bermuda shorts and knee socks, crew cuts (and for Negroes, straightened, processed "conks"), the cha-cha, the Edsel, and the marriage of Grace Kelly and Prince Rainier.

Royal weddings and the cha-cha had no impact on Jimmy's life, however. For him it was merely more of the same.

Leon's first foster home was near where his father and brother lived, but others were some distance away, and Al

[30]

says he didn't see very much of his youngest son. Jimmy visited Leon occasionally, usually arriving with his guitar over his shoulder, to take him out for some candy. Once, Leon says, Jimmy bought his brother a shirt with his paper route money, earning the anger of his father, who whipped Jimmy for "spending all his money on something so foolish."

"Besides the seven foster homes," Leon says, "I shuffled around between two aunts for about a year. I think Jimmy felt sorry for me, and sometimes he came to take me home for a weekend. It was good in a way, but no treat. They were living in a rundown apartment and splitting a can of beans and Spam for dinner every night. They had two rooms and the bathroom was down the hall."

In 1958 events in Jimmy's world took an awful turn. That was when his Aunt Patricia came to Seattle from Vancouver for a visit. Jimmy didn't know it, but his mother was very ill. Lucille had remarried, but she had not stayed in touch with her sons, and Al was bitter. And now that the alcoholism and tuberculosis had her in the hospital again, he refused to see her, so he asked his sister to take Jimmy to visit her.

Jimmy's aunt had never met Lucille before, and although she tried to be pleasant, it was awkward. She remembers that Lucille looked "pretty," with a shoulder-length, pageboy hairdo. But she also recalls that Jimmy did not say much, spending nearly all the short visit staring.

It was the last time Jimmy saw his mother. Soon after that Lucille died, and Al refused to let either Leon or Jimmy attend the funeral.

Jimmy's father seldom showed his emotions, and he was a stern disciplinarian with high moral standards. If he gave little of the warmth Jimmy wanted, at least he asked no more than he asked of himself. Often he recalled his days in the army, when as an enlisted man he took orders without argument. He expected the same of Jimmy. But Jimmy resisted stubbornly or merely went along to keep his father's anger in check, then went off with his guitar. From his mother's rejection and death, and the grim home life he faced each day, music provided the perfect escape.

"The way I felt about tap dancing is the way Jimmy felt about guitar playing," Al Hendrix told David Henderson, author of another book about Hendrix, *Voodoo Child of the Aquarian Age.* "I mean it was in him to do it. He felt it. It was no job—he enjoyed it. He just picked it up all of a sudden. He had no formal lessons. He used to practice a lot. I'd come home from work and he'd be there, plunk, plunk, plunk. If I disturbed him or something, he'd go in the bedroom and he'd be there, plunk, plunk, plunking. And I'd say, 'Jimmy, sweep the floor,' or something, and he'd say, 'Okay, Dad,' and he'd do that. And after he finished doing that, he'd go back to plunk, plunk, plunking. I used to hear it constantly."

If Jimmy had no structured training, he did have the musicians available to him on the radio and on records at his friends' homes. He listened to music constantly and, in the age-old tradition, taught himself to play by mimicking what he heard and remembered. In this way, his early musical influences ranged widely, from the jazz his mother and father loved to the rhythm-and-blues and popular rock-and-roll songs that formed a part of his daily environment.

Leon remembers Jimmy picking up a broom and pretending to strum chords on it while singing early Elvis Presley songs—ballads like "Heartbreak Hotel" and "Love Me Tender." Leon says Jimmy's other early favorites included Buddy Holly, who was a white rockabilly singer from West Texas, and Chuck Berry, a black guitarist and singer-songwriter who straddled—or perhaps more accurately, tore down—the same fence that Presley did, the one separating white music (pop and country-western) from black music (rhythm-and-blues, then called "race music").

Jimmy (second from left) with the Rocking Kings in 1960

Jimmy joined several bands during his high school years, never leading them, but adding a youthful, energetic backup guitar. All of them performed the popular hits of the time. "Cathy's Clown," a hit by the Everly Brothers; "Sleepwalk," by Santo and Johnny; and Eddie Cochran's classic, uptempo "Summertime Blues" were among Jimmy's favorites. In his first group, the Rocking Kings, he also played Bobby Freeman's "Do You Want to Dance?," "At the Hop," by Danny and the Juniors, and several of the humorous Coasters songs—"Yakety Yak," "Charlie Brown," "Poison Ivy" and "Along Came Jones."

In the few photographs and posters remaining from the period, Jimmy is virtually indistinguishable from any other young black musician of the period. In one poster, tacked to Al Hendrix's basement wall and advertising the annual Seattle Seafair Picnic and Dance, Jimmy is wearing the uniform of the day: skinny black pants, a white shirt and white tie, a light jacket. His hair is in an early "conk," pasted shiny and slick to his skull.

Al points to the poster today and laughs. "Jimmy was with James Thomas and His Tomcats in that picture there. James always charged the band members five dollars for the jacket rental and Jimmy never did make any money. I remember Jimmy saying, 'Man, I'm not gonna play with those cats anymore!' I'd laugh and say he was gettin' experience. They played Vancouver one time and Jimmy was surprised I let him travel that far. The car broke down and they didn't make any money then either."

There were other problems, the most serious being the theft of his first guitar. This happened when Jimmy was playing at a local club aimed at the teenagers—no alcohol was served—and known for its showcasing rhythm-and-blues and old-time blues. Named for the famous New York jazz club, Birdland was deep in the Seattle ghetto. During a break Jimmy left his guitar on the stage. When he returned to play the next set, it was gone. He was so upset, he didn't tell his father for several months, instead borrowing guitars whenever he got a call to work. All of these guitars apparently were right-handed, so it was at this time that Jimmy began playing in his unorthodox, upside-down manner, never even restringing the instruments, learning to play from bottom to top.

"It didn't matter to Jimmy," Leon says. "He'd turn the sucker upside down and play it better than the guys who owned it."

Jimmy was also learning about amplifiers and sound equipment. In years to come Jimmy relied upon and mastered every technical piece of equipment produced that was related to the guitar. According to Leon, his fascination with that aspect of the music got its start when Jimmy rewired an old stereo record player, converting it into an amplifier.

If music was Jimmy's great escape, he found others in drugs and the thrills of juvenile larceny.

There were two popular student hangouts at the time, a delicatessen—a lunch stand owned by two brothers who later would be convicted of burglary and grand larceny—and a small cafe. Jimmy frequented both with his friends and it was there that he found and experimented with his first drugs.

James Oliver was in the crowd that Jimmy joined, at first during school lunch breaks and then after school as well. He says he and several other congregated outside the two cafes almost every day to drink cough syrup and pop occasional pills, usually Benzedrine.

"We liked that cough syrup," he says. "It had codeine in it and that's the best high except for the really heavy stuff. Half the people on that corner turned into dope fiends. I was a junkie sixteen years. Half of them guys used to hang out at the cafe are dead today. Back then, we drank the cough syrup, passing the bottle around, then went back to school and nodded out in study hall."

Jimmy was getting into trouble at school. More and more absences were reported and years later Jimmy himself told a story about getting expelled for talking back to a teacher.

"She was a good-looker," he said, "but she got me thrown out. I was talking to some chick during the lessons and this teacher got mad. I said, 'What's the matter, are you jealous?' That's the last time I saw her."

Jimmy didn't care about finishing school anyway, so the expulsion didn't bother him. Nor did he catch any grief at home.

"I dropped out of school too," his father says. "My

mother said I was just a 'visitor' at school. Jimmy was just the same. He tried to get a job as a bag boy at a grocery store. He had applications in at various places. But nothing was shaking. So I asked him to come to work with me. I was doing gardening then."

Al Hendrix enjoyed gardening. At first he worked for a brother-in-law and then, until he retired, for himself. He liked taking care of lawns and trees and flower beds, and although his tools were few and his pickup truck was old, he was proud. He tried to share that enthusiasm with Jimmy, who seldom talked and didn't seem to listen much either. The truth was, Jimmy just didn't like spending all day with his father.

Jimmy preferred to spend that time with his friends. It was with some of them that he committed his first felony, breaking into Wilner's Clothing Store to steal some sweaters, shirts and slacks. The way Leon tells the story, the next day the clothing was anonymously deposited in the "Needy Box" outside the principal's office at Garfield High.

Perhaps that was the way it happened once. Apparently there were other break-ins. In 1968 in an interview Jimmy talked about growing up in Seattle and said, "Man, when I was a kid there, I often nearly got caught by the cops. I was always gone on wearing hip clothes and the only way to get them was through the back window of a clothing store."

However "often" Jimmy participated in these late-night forays, he wasn't the instigator. His friend James Oliver says he wasn't that type.

"In the ghetto, you have guys who are always running their mouth," he says. "That's the type of guy I was. Jimmy knew all those people and he could get along with them, but he wouldn't really get involved that much. He'd just go along, y'know? He didn't rip and run like we did. He wasn't a leader. He wasn't aggressive, roughhouse, like us. He was a shy type guy. He went along because it was easy."

Even the shy followers get caught, however, and on May 2, 1961, Jimmy was one of several young men found joyriding in a stolen car. For this, Jimmy was taken into custody by the Seattle police and charged.

It seemed to have no effect, because four days later, on May 6, Jimmy was arrested by police again. Once more the charge was "taking and riding a motor vehicle without the owner's permission." This time Jimmy was jailed briefly—for seven days, Jimmy said years later—at the Rainier Vista 4-H Youth Center.

One stolen car was one thing, but two in one week was another. Eighteen years old, Jimmy was no longer a juvenile.

A few days later Jimmy stood before the judge. It didn't look good. He seemed a classic "case." Mother deceased. A father who mowed lawns. Brother in a foster home. Expelled from school and on the street and out of work. Unskilled and black and poor. Looking for trouble, stealing cars.

The judge looked at Jimmy sternly. Jimmy's head was down, but he could see the judge's eyes by looking up.

"Son," the judge said finally, "I don't really want to send you back to jail. And I don't want to see you here again."

The judge paused. Jimmy lifted his head slightly as his father fidgeted nearby.

The judge spoke again. He asked, "Have you given any thought to enlisting in the army?"

CHAPTER

2

Jimmy looked back at the judge and said, "Yes, sir. I've been thinking about being a Screaming Eagle."

The judge looked puzzled. Jimmy's father spluttered an explanation. "That's the paratroops," he said. "Jimmy wants to be a paratroop."

It was true. A friend of his had come back to Seattle a few months before, wearing the patch of the 101st Airborne Division, showing the Screaming Eagle that was the motto of the unit and its symbol of rugged manliness. Jimmy said he too wanted to wear the Screaming Eagle.

The judge said he thought that was a fine idea, and while he left the theft charges on Jimmy's permanent record, he suspended sentence with the understanding that the thin young man before him would report for military duty immediately.

Jimmy was inducted the last day of the month.

"I had to have all my hair cut off . . ."

Jimmy was in the army only a week when, in his first

letter home, he echoed every other new soldier's complaints: the loss of individuality and privacy, and the arrival of boredom and poverty.

"I've been here about a week," he wrote. "It seems I've been here a month. Time passes slow even though we do have a lot to do. How's the gardening business? I hope it's doing fine. I believe it's more expensive being in the army than living as a civilian. So far we had to get two laundry bags, $1 each, a block hat $1.75, two locks 80 cents each, 3 towels 50 cents each, stamping kit $1.75, haircut $1, shoe polish kit $1.70, shaving razor, blades and lather $1.70, insignias 50 cents. So I guess this isn't all that good financially as I first thought. $10.60. We have to pay way more than that before we're actually set for a while. We don't get paid until June 30th, 1961, so I would like to know if you can send about five or six dollars. We have to buy so much stuff right away and pay day is so far away. They only gave us five dollars when we first came and all that's gone except a dollar and a half and that isn't going to last a minute around here."

In the early 1960s Fort Ord, California, was a quiet base. It was "after the Korean war and before the Vietnam deal," as Jimmy's father, Al, puts it, and the cadre at the base routinely took companies of young men through eight weeks of basic army training without the prospect of real war ahead. This gave the experience less than a life-or-death seriousness, but it was considerably more than Boy Scout camp. For two long, steaming, summer months Jimmy learned how to live with a barracks full of other recruits, shoot a rifle, throw a grenade, march ten miles with a fifty-pound pack, make his bunk with the top blanket so tight the sergeant could bounce a quarter on it, and clean a smelly latrine.

In one letter home Jimmy boasted that he qualified as a sharpshooter with the M-1 rifle, the second highest rating. In

In the service, 1961

another, written after he finished his basic training and was awaiting his next assignment, he told his dad about all the mattresses, beds, footlockers and wall lockers he carried up and down three flights of stairs, getting the barracks ready for another cycle of trainees.

Life for Jimmy during this period was well ordered and uninspiring, and with his guitar at home in Seattle, he said, "Time is crawling by so slow it seems." The only event worth reporting, he said, was his getting stranded in San Francisco on leave when he lost his return bus ticket back to the base.

Finally, after waiting for three months for his orders, on October 31 they came through, and in an enthusiastic letter home he reported buying two pairs of jump boots, four sets of fatigues—he had to get all of them tailored to tightly hug his body, he said—and twenty Screaming Eagle patches.

"You know what that represents!" he wrote. "The 101st Airborne Division! Fort Campbell, Kentucky, yes indeedy! I wouldn't mind breaking a leg or something if I can come out wearing that Screaming Eagle patch and those Airborne wings! It's a proud outfit. The army hasn't been too bad yet, but I know it will be real soon. It will keep on being hard for about two months. Anyway, I'm prepared for the worst. I really hope I make it. Wish me luck and take it easy. Your son, James."

It was in this same letter that Jimmy revealed his plan to make army life as easy as possible once he completed his paratrooper training. He may have agreed to accept the rigors of some of the toughest training the modern army had to offer in order to win his wings, but after that he expected a soft position as a clerk.

"I signed up for clerk, administrative work and stuff like that," he wrote home, "because I really don't want to be in that infantry stuff if I can help it. When I go to Fort Campbell, all I do is go to that jump school, and if I graduate, all I will do is be sent or stationed there as a supply clerk or something, then I just have to make that one jump a month for that extra $55 a month."

Usually weeks or months passed between letters home, but this time Jimmy wrote his father again the next day, closing the letter with another burst of youthful enthusiasm: "Take it easy and when you see me again I'll be wearing the patch of proudness!" At the bottom of the letter was Jimmy's drawing of the Screaming Eagle patch.

Fort Campbell was a large post in the heart of the south, near the Kentucky-Tennessee border, only sixty miles from Nashville, home of country music, and two hundred miles from Memphis and the start of the Mississippi River delta, birthplace of the blues. For Jimmy it was like going home to his southern musical roots.

It was also an interesting time to be sent to this camp. At the end of the Korean war the United States cut back its military manpower, and Jimmy's Airborne class was the last to be sent there for training. After that, paratroopers were to be trained at Fort Benning, in Georgia. Jimmy was especially proud to be a member of the final class, and on November 13, 1961, he wrote his father again.

"Well, here I am," he said, "exactly where I wanted to go in the 101st Airborne. We jumped out of a 34-foot tower on the third day we were here. It was almost fun. We were the first nine out of about 150 in our group. When I was walking up the stairs to the top of the tower, I was walking nice and slow, just taking it easy. There were three guys who quit when they got to the top of the tower. You can quit any time. They took one look outside and just quit. And that got me thinking as I was walking up those steps, but I made up my mind that whatever happens, I'm not quitting on my own.

"When I got to the top, the jump master snapped these two straps onto my harness and slapped me on the butt and said right in my ear 'Go, *Go, GO!*' I hesitated for a split second and the next thing I knew, I was falling. All of a sudden, when all of the slack was taken up on the line, I was snapped like a bullwhip and started bouncing down the cable . . .

"While I was sliding down, I had my legs together, hands on the reserve, my chin tucked into my chest. I ran smack dab into a sand dune. Later they'll show us how to go over it by lifting our feet, of course. But my back was to it.

"Oh well, it was a new experience. There's nothing but physical training and harassment here for two weeks, then when you go to jump school, that's when you get hell! They work you to DEATH! Fussing and fighting everything you do. You have to do 10, 15 or 25 pushups. They really make the sparks fly, and half the people quit then, too. That's how they separate the men from the boys. I pray that I will make it on the men's side . . ."

There was a great innocence in Jimmy's letters home, and with that simplicity there was loneliness, a longing for someone or something familiar. In January 1962, when he wrote that he could "hardly wait" for March, when a military leave was scheduled, he asked his father to send his guitar.

"I hope that you send my guitar as soon as possible," he wrote in a letter dated January 17. "I really need it now."

Considering how much Jimmy loved his guitar, how much it consoled him, providing creative escape, it is somewhat curious that he waited so long to ask for it. Of course, Jimmy hadn't been without a guitar altogether during his first six months of service. Other young men in his barracks had instruments, which he borrowed, and well-used instruments were available at the post service club. Still, it wasn't until his own electric Stratocaster arrived that he began playing regularly.

Introduced by one of the great guitar innovators, Leo Fender, only a few years before, in 1954, the Stratocaster would become one of the all-time classics, changing both the sound and look of electric guitars for decades to come. Its contoured, solid body was perfect for the rock-and-roll/tail-fin/space-age consciousness, and its sleek vibrato capability revolutionized the sound of rock guitar.

Soon after his beloved Strat arrived, Jimmy was "discovered" by other musicians on the post. One of these was a young black musician from Nashville named Billy Cox.

"I think I was going to my company," Billy told an interviewer for the Warner Brothers documentary *Jimi Hendrix* some years later. "I had to pass Service Club Number One on the way, and I heard this guitar playin' inside. I said, 'Wow! The cat's all right!' So I stepped in and introduced myself to him. I told him I played bass and I went and checked a bass and we started jamming right off."

Jimmy met other musicians, including a saxophone-playing major named Charles Washington, who formed a small group and started booking the band into the post service clubs. Unfortunately, he says, they were fired after almost every opening night because they played "real loud."

There were other problems and, according to Major Washington, some of them could be laid in Jimmy's lap. Because he was always short of funds, Jimmy often pawned his guitar at one of the many hock shops near the base, then insisted he had to have it for the band's next job. He said he wouldn't play with any other guitar, forcing the others in the band to chip in enough to repossess it.

Jimmy also remained uncomfortably distant from the other musicians. "Jimmy in many cases was never really with us," Washington told the filmmakers. "He did a lot of concentrating on his music, and a lot of the small talk that the typical group of guys would make, sometimes he would not enter into it. Of course, we'd look over at him occasionally and there he is, staring. This is what I really meant by being on cloud nine. You didn't really get to know him that closely as far as the exact line of thinking."

The stories Billy Cox and others tell make it clear that Jimmy's best friend was his guitar. He painted his old girl friend's name, Betty Jean, on the side and began to talk to the guitar, calling it by name. He even began to sleep with the guitar. None of this was that unusual. Many guitarists have named their instruments—B. B. King is famous for his guitar, Lucille, for instance—and many have slept with them. In Jimmy's case, taking his guitar to bed with him even made great sense, as it prevented anyone from taking it from his locker and hiding it when he slept.

Nonetheless, in a barracks full of nonmusicians, this behavior seemed very odd. Consequently Jimmy was teased mercilessly by some and avoided by many more. This reaction only increased when Jimmy began walking to and from the mess hall and elsewhere on the post, picking an imaginary guitar and making strange noises.

Jimmy was beginning to notice and examine some of the sounds in his daily environment, with the idea that they might be recreated, or mimicked, on his Stratocaster. The clatter of automatic weapons on the firing range, the metallic thumps and bangs of the big airplane doors he jumped out of, the rush of wind as he whistled to earth—these and other noises of inanimate objects intrigued him. He began experimenting with his guitar, bending musical notes with the vibrato bar, trying to duplicate the sounds and work them into the popular songs he played.

Finally Jimmy won his Screaming Eagle patch, and in February 1962 he was promoted to Private First Class.

"I made it," he wrote home, "in eight months and eight days!"

But it was the music that was most important. The little combo formed with Charlie Washington and Billy Cox fell apart, and Jimmy started another, keeping Billy and picking up a drummer named Gary Gerguson and another guitarist, Johnny Jones. They called themselves the Casuals.

The Casuals—(left to right) Jimmy, Billy Cox and Johnny Jones

Playing a fairly standard selection of current hits, they began working the small, noisy roadhouses found near any military installation.

Jimmy also began visiting Nashville when he got a weekend pass, usually staying with some of Billy's relatives or with the young women they met in the bars and honky-tonks.

In the early 1960s Nashville was honky-tonk heaven, the home of Grand Ole Opry and a mecca for country music fans. But this music was totally alien to Jimmy—and to Billy too, even though he had grown up in "Music City." They didn't listen to Leroy Van Dyke and George Jones, or

Jimmy (on the left) at the Club Del Morocco, Nashville

to Patsy Cline and Flatt and Scruggs, who were some of the biggest country stars of the time, nor did they drink in Tootsie's Orchid Lounge, next to the Opry House. Their watering holes and haunts were south and east of town in the black neighborhoods, where the music was predominantly blues.

Even so, the glamour of Nashville got to Jimmy. After all, this was the first real music scene he had ever experienced. Before coming to Nashville he hadn't even seen the *outside* of a professional recording studio. There were nine studios here now and every one had an open-door policy, so Jimmy walked in to take a look.

Jimmy told Billy that when he got out of the service he was coming back to Nashville to make a record.

The opportunity presented itself sooner than Jimmy expected. At the end of the summer he broke his right ankle in a jump, and when the doctors said Jimmy would be unfit for any future jumps, he was offered a discharge based on medical "unsuitability." He took it.

Billy was mustered out at about the same time, and by fall of 1962 they were sharing a small room in "Music City."

CHAPTER

3

The three years that followed Jimmy's discharge from the army are difficult to reconstruct. From the fall of 1962, when he began scuffling for work in dark Nashville clubs, until late summer of 1965, when he quit his backup guitarist position for Little Richard and put his own band together to take into Greenwich Village, Jimmy crisscrossed the country uncounted times, playing in at least two dozen bands and in more than a hundred cities. During this time Jimmy wrote home rarely, so dated postcards and letters are few, and the performers Jimmy worked for kept poor records and have poorer memories. Thus a precise chronology is impossible to recreate. But everyone remembers the *feel* of the time, and many events and names stand out.

The first of these were in Nashville, where Jimmy and Billy Cox shared rooms over Joyce's House of Glamour on Jefferson Street, in the city's sprawling black ghetto. Within a week of arriving they met a singer named Johnny Snead, who took them into his group, the Imperials, named for a local barbershop whose owner was the band's manager. Immediately they began to work periodically in the local clubs, attracting a small but faithful following. There was even an unofficial fan club formed, called the Buttons because its founder, Sandra Matthews, was always sewing buttons on Jimmy's shirts.

In the afternoons Jimmy began hanging out around the recording studios and in the small restaurants and bars in the "Music City" neighborhood. Most of the activity here was rooted in music of the white south and Jimmy received little encouragement. Then, when he did get a break, rejection followed. One such instance came when he got a call to play a studio session for Bill "Hoss" Allen, a local radio personality who also ran a custom recording business for Starday-King Records.

"I knew Billy Cox from when he was in the army," Hoss says, "and I'd used him on weekends when he'd come to Nashville on leave. Sometime after that he told me he had a guitar player friend, so I told him to bring him in. This was Jimmy. I told him I wanted a New Orleans chink-chink-chink rhythm thing, nothing fancy. I already had a lead guitar, all I wanted was rhythm. Well, Jimmy played loud, man! I asked him to turn it down. He was ruining the whole thing. Finally I had to tell the engineer to cut him off, unplug him on the board. So then when we played it back, Jimmy was listening and he said, 'Where's my part?' He couldn't hear it because it wasn't there. I said, 'Gee, I don't know, Jimmy. Must be something wrong with your amp.' I tell you the truth, I didn't like his sound."

Another time Jimmy's hopes soared. This was when he met Steve Cropper, a young white guitarist from Memphis who had backed up Otis Redding and now was playing lead guitar in a racially integrated combo, Booker T and the M.G.s, led by Booker T. Jones. (Their first album, *Green Onions*, was released in November 1962, about the same time Steve and Jimmy met.) They started jamming to-

Jimmy, second from left, clowns on stage at the Pink Poodle Club in Clarksville, TN, 1960

gether, and Steve said he'd like to cut a couple of songs with Jimmy. At the time, Jimmy was quite capable of doing much more than perform musical carbon copies of current hits, and his guitar solos were attracting some enthusiastic response in the clubs. It was clear that Jimmy was not the average guitarist. But Steve Cropper? He was one of the best, and Jimmy was astonished.

The acetate they produced was good, but before they

could start taking it from office to office in search of a record offer, Booker T and the M.G.s hit with the title song from their album and Steve Cropper went on the road. Without Steve to "front" him, Jimmy felt depressed and lost. His band was unemployed. There was no studio work. Except for a handful of musicians and club owners and a gathering of fans, he knew no one. Finally, unable to pay his rent, Jimmy said goodbye to Billy and his other friends and hitchhiked back to the Pacific Northwest, bypassing Seattle—without even so much as a call to his father—to settle in Vancouver, where he had spent happy times as a child with his aunt.

It was there that Jimmy found his next band, the Vancouvers. This was an otherwise all-black group whose lead singer was a Chinese named Tommie Chong. (Years later Tommie Chong became the second half of the comedy team of Cheech and Chong.) Tommie, along with another member of the band, Bobby Taylor, owned the nightclub where the band played, Dante's Inferno.

It was a comfortable arrangement. Jimmy lived with his grandmother and worked with the Vancouvers on the weekends, performing Bobby Taylor's original arrangements of the popular hits of the day. Taylor was a recent graduate of the University of California's master's music program at Berkeley and so offered a higher standard of musicality than was usual for a nightclub band.

Even so, Jimmy grew bored. He loved his grandmother, but living with her cramped his style. When he didn't come home for several nights, she worried. And when he did come home, he often arrived just as she was getting up, close to dawn. Jimmy also tired of all the twist songs he was forced to play most nights. In the winter of 1962–63 the twist was the latest dance rage.

There was also something about a voodoo spell. Not much is known about it. Jimmy never shared many details, but if what is said was true, apparently he met a woman during this period in Seattle who tried to "put a spell" on him.

A few years later he told an interviewer that the woman was "trying to work roots on me. Work this voodoo stuff. Keep me there, you know. That's a scene where . . . there's different things they can do. They can put something in your food or put some hair in your shoe. She tried stuff like that, but she must have tried only halfheartedly, because I was only sick in the hospital for a couple of days."

Jimmy (at left) with another early 1960s band

COURTESY JAMES A. HENDRIX

Was it true? Or just a story? The woman was never identified nor are there any details known about the alleged hospital stay. What *is* known is that soon after the incident supposedly took place, in the spring of 1963, Jimmy left the Seattle-Vancouver area to go on the road with one of the most influential and outrageous performers in the history of rock-and-roll.

This was Richard Penniman, better known as Little Richard, a black singer and pianist whose up-tempo 1950s hits ("Tutti Frutti," "Long Tall Sally," "Rip It Up," "Ready Teddy," "Good Golly Miss Molly," to name a few), flamboyant wardrobe and makeup, and a vocal delivery punctuated with wild falsetto shrieks, theatrical moans, soaring whooos and breathless panting revolutionized the sound and style of rock. Richard was one of the first black rock performers to attract a large white audience, becoming one of the half dozen most popular performers of his time, until he was persuaded that the launching of the Russian Sputnik was a sign he should forsake rock-and-roll for the ministry.

Richard paid an enormous price for this, and by 1962, when he emerged from his retirement, the only major concert bookings he found were in Britain and on the European continent, where he was regarded as a sort of demigod. In the U.S. it was another story. There he continued to travel by plane, but his band followed along on the ground in a bus, and the dates were always in small clubs, primarily in black neighborhoods.

One night, after his umpteenth anonymous guitarist had quit, Richard wandered into Dante's Inferno and saw the skinny, left-handed guitar player from Seattle. He offered him a job. The timing was right. Jimmy said yes.

Today Little Richard says that when he first saw Jimmy he knew the guitarist was a star. More likely, Richard merely recognized a superb musician who was willing to go anywhere for little pay. After all, Richard was the only star of *his* show, and the others were what gave that star his base—individuals who were musically competent, on time, and faceless. Also, willing to put up with Richard's flaming ego. Offstage as well as on he was known to shout, "I am the king! I am the greatest! I am the prettiest!"

For more than two years, off and on, Jimmy traveled with rock-and-roll's Muhammed Ali, playing an amalgam of gospel and early rock, keeping the pant creases in his black suit as sharp as possible, his kinky hair greased into the still-popular "conk," or "process," his developing public personality in check. Little Richard may have been a has-been in the early 1960s, but he hadn't forgotten how to entertain, and Jimmy was watching closely, never interfering, never competing, but learning what made an audience twitch.

However exciting Richard may have been on stage, life on the road was much less than that. There were no new hit records. Not even when the Beatles—then taking America by fire storm—recorded some of Richard's early songs did anyone pay any attention. So Jimmy remained on the rhythm-and-blues, or "chitlin'," circuit, where working conditions were poor and payment was a sometimes thing. Often Jimmy wasn't paid on time, was given partial payment, or wasn't paid at all. At least once he left Little Richard, writing his father in 1965 from New York that "he didn't pay us for five and a half weeks, and you can't live on promises when you're on the road, so I had to cut that mess aloose."

Worse, Jimmy's days as a backup musician offered him neither challenge nor opportunity. Night after night he played the same songs the same way. Improvisation was not wanted. Showing off was forbidden. Tracks recorded in 1965 with Little Richard, released posthumously on two albums, *Friends from the Beginning* and *Jimi Hendrix-Little Richard, Together*, reveal nothing of the distinctive Hendrix style that

[55]

Muddy Waters

must surely have been developing. Even in the solo instrumental performances of three of Richard's biggest hits—"Keep a Knockin'," "Tutti Frutti" and "Lucille"—Jimmy sounds as if he were bored, playing all the notes required by the melody line, but nothing extra.

Ironically, the musical highs that did come usually occurred when Jimmy was between tours and unemployed. Once, in St. Louis, he met another left-handed guitarist, the great bluesman Albert King, who showed Jimmy how to move the guitar strings horizontally instead of vertically when fretting and shared with him his fingering style. Another time, in Chicago, Jimmy visited the Chess Records studio and watched Muddy Waters, Willie Dixon, Little Milton, Little Walter and Bo Diddley jamming. Several times on his nights off, in several cities, he listened to Ike Turner's Blues Band, and when he was in New York, he went to the famed Apollo Theater in Harlem, where he watched many other top black performers.

And then he'd go back on the road again, playing either with Little Richard or, more often now, with many other black artists, including Solomon Burke, the Isley Brothers and Wilson Pickett. Once he accompanied Joey Dee on a tour of New England, playing the twist songs he learned to loathe in British Columbia. Other times he was a member of an anonymous utility backup band on "package tours," playing for nearly every black act on the *Billboard* magazine record charts, from the Supremes to B. B. King. On one tour he even accompanied a wrestler, the flamboyant Gorgeous George.

Life on the road was grim—a series of tiny motel rooms or fitful nights aboard a crowded, noisy bus, food eaten on an irregular schedule, with performances night after night. There was no permanent address, no home to return to following a tour. There was never enough money. Jimmy couldn't even afford to have his hair styled and was forced to

T-Bone Walker, performing a trick Jimi later used

[58]

keep his "conk" in place with a comb and hot Sterno.

Nonetheless Jimmy's attitude remained positive. In all his cards home he never complained.

"Just a few words to let you know I made it to Columbia, S.C. Tell everybody hello. Love, Jimmy."

"Here we are in Florida. We're going to play in Tampa tomorrow, then Miami. We're playing all through the south. We'll end up in Dallas, Texas. My home address is in Atlanta. I hope everyone's okay. Tell Grandma in Canada hi for me. Tell Leon to be cool and go to school."

"Dear Dad, I hope everything is fine. Well, here I am again, traveling to different places. I'm on a tour which lasts about 35 days. We're about half through it now. I've been up to about all the cities in the midwest, the east and south. I'll write soon. Jimmy."

"We're in Boston, Mass. We'll be here for about 10 days. I hope everything's all right. We're right next to the ocean across the street. Jimmy."

"As you probably know, we're in California now. It was very nice today, 78 degrees, so tell everyone hello."

Slowly the Hendrix style emerged. As before, Jimmy continued to listen to the sounds of his environment, trying to imitate on his Stratocaster the rushing chatter of New York's subway trains, the high-pitched release of the air brakes on a bus, the energetic honk of a saxophone. It wasn't easy. Almost everyone insisted he stay within the rigid confines of the material as originally recorded.

More freedom came dramatically as his guitar playing took a vaudevillian turn. Not all his employers were like Little Richard. Some allowed him to get out there during the warm-up part of the show and perform some of the stunts he had seen old bluesmen use.

He played the guitar behind his head or back, shoved the neck of the guitar like an erect phallus between his knees (one of Little Richard's tricks). More remarkable, he actually played music while holding the guitar to his mouth. Some said he picked out the melodies with his teeth, others swear it was his tongue. Jimmy said he started doing this "in a town in Tennessee. Down there, you have to play with your teeth or else you get shot. There's a trail of broken teeth all over the stage."

The rock drummer Buddy Miles was only sixteen and traveling with Ruby and the Romantics when he first met Jimmy, who was playing a date with the Isley Brothers in Montreal. "He looked rather strange," Buddy recalls, "because everybody was wearin' uniforms and he was eatin' his guitar, doin' flip-flops and wearin' chains. It was really strange, man, but, oh boy, he made that band!"

One time when he was in New York he took these tricks into the Apollo and won an amateur contest. Jimmy claimed he didn't remember the song. But he did remember the prize: twenty-five dollars. It was the only money he earned that week.

By now Jimmy was establishing temporary "homes." In one card he sent home he said he was living in Atlanta in a boardinghouse. Other cards showed him living in a tiny room as Maurice James—a name change he never explained—in hotels in a seedy section of Hollywood, and in the Times Square district of New York.

Everywhere he went he made friends with local musicians, jammed with them, tried to pick up work, talked about how he was going to make it if only he got the right breaks.

As early as 1963 or 1964—no one involved is sure—when Jimmy was in Los Angeles, he met a young black musician, producer and songwriter from Memphis named Arthur Lee, who a few years later would form a successful band called Love.

"Jimmy Hendrix was one of the first long-haired black

cats I'd ever seen," Arthur says. "He had a suit like a priest, a hoodlum priest, with his hair directly in place and runned-over shoes. We became friends. He liked the way I wrote, I liked the way he played guitar, so we started jamming over near Fifty-fourth and Western.

"Jimmy was backing up Little Richard and other bands in L.A. at the time and I needed a guitar player who could play like Curtis Mayfield. You know, like on 'Gypsy Woman.' I wrote a record called 'My Diary' and Jimmy played on it. Rosa Lee Brooks was the singer."

Released on the local Revis label—named for Billy Revis, a friend of Arthur's—"My Diary" was a small hit in Los Angeles but was never distributed elsewhere. So far as is known, it is the earliest Hendrix disc.

Jimmy also made some records when he was touring with the Isley Brothers in 1964. Three singles—"Looking for Love" and "The Last Girl," "Wild as a Tiger" and "Simon Says," and "Move Over and Let Me Dance" and "Have You Ever Been Disappointed?"—were released by Atlantic Records, and a fourth, "Testify (Parts I and II)," got limited distribution on the Isleys' own T-Neck label. Although the three Isley brothers had been successful earlier with songs called "Shout" and "Twist and Shout," these new singles sold disappointingly.

And on all of them, as on the Arthur Lee song, and on the Little Richard tracks that were to follow, Jimmy played unimaginatively. However flashy his performances had become visually, his instrumental virtuosity remained hidden. It was as if Jimmy were holding back, either prohibited from showing off or saving his talent for another time.

Slowly New York became his home.

"So we got our own little crib, you know, and it was sardines and crackers on and off," Fayne Prigon told the Warner Brothers filmmakers. Fayne—or Fay, as Jimmy called her—was one of Sam Cooke's old girl friends, and when she saw him, she grabbed him. "My mom would throw in a good meal here and there. We'd get our door plugged by the hotel. We'd get thrown out. We'd pawn the guitar. We'd come back. We'd borrow guitars from people to, you know, to play, do a gig. We'd eat good for a minute, you know. It was just that, you know, on and off all the time.

"We used to go to Palms Cafe and places like Small's, the Spotlight—places around a Hundred and Twenty-fifth Street, in the Harlem scene, you know, and, ah, he'd tell them he wanted to sit in, right? And these old fuddy-duddy, rough-dried ain't-never-beens, you know, they ain't gonna give him a break, so like they just act like they don't even know that he's there. And he'd sit there with this kind of look on his face for a few minutes, you know, and he says, 'I'm gonna speak to 'em again.' You know, and I'd say, 'Hey, don't say nothin' to those cats, you know, 'cause it's obvious they don't want you, you know, to play.'

"Finally they would let him come in, you know, and play. And then they get up and really just mess up so bad behind him it was incredible, you know. And he'd be lookin' all disgusted on the stage, and he'd keep lookin' back at 'em, and then the other guys come and tell him he'd got to turn it down, you know, and take him through all kind of changes."

On one of those days when nothing seemed to be going right, Jimmy met Curtis Knight in the lobby of his run-down Times Square hotel. Jimmy was behind in his rent, and his guitar and amplifier were in a nearby hock shop. Curtis was a singer with a rhythm-and-blues group called the Squires and he was looking for a new guitarist. Curtis later wrote in his book *Jimi: An Intimate Biography* that he lent Jimi an amplifier and guitar to audition, whereupon Jimi "did things with that guitar that I had never imagined possible."

Curtis offered Jimmy a job and then took him to meet

Jimmy (left) with Curtis Knight (center) and The Squires at the Queen's Inn, New York, 1965

Ed Chalpin, a young curly-haired record promoter known for packaging old tapes and selling them at discount prices. He was, however, also interested in producing some new material, and toward this end, on October 15, 1965, Jimmy signed an agreement promising to produce, play and/or sing exclusively on records for Chalpin and Chalpin's PPX Enterprises for a period of three years. For this Jimmy received one dollar in cash and the pledge of 1 percent of the "retail selling price of all records sold for his production efforts, [and] minimum scale for arrangements he produces."

These terms were not fair—were, in fact, so unfair that when Chalpin released some of the material years later, he failed to include three of the original paragraphs when he reproduced the contract on one of the album covers. An oversight, he said, but the truth was that he was embarrassed.

At the time, Jimmy didn't care. "He would sign a contract with anybody that came along that had a dollar and a pencil," Fayne Prigon said. "Jimmy just wanted to record—you know, to make records."

If the terms of the contract were uninspiring, at least the material subsequently produced was, at the time, more or less inspired. However perfunctory Jimmy's guitar playing was on all his previous recording efforts, with Curtis Knight and the Squires he began to stretch out, experimenting in the studio with his fuzztone and playing some of the rapid-fire strings of piercing notes that later characterized many of his longer solos. Even so, Jimmy's instrumental backing is noticed not so much because of its excellence but because everything else on the recordings is so mediocre.

Much of the material was original, written and arranged by Knight. In one of these songs, obviously composed to capitalize on the trend toward "protest" songs popular in 1965, Knight virtually stole both the lyrics and the melody of Bob Dylan's "Like a Rolling Stone," which had been a big hit the previous summer. The only difference was that Curtis's version catalogued a black man's complaints.

Other originals had hardly any lyrics at all, taking the form of mostly instrumental bar boogies, punctuated by occasional git-it-on shouts and grunts.

In addition, there were a number of covers of recent hits, including the Rolling Stones' "Satisfaction," the Yardbirds' "I'm a Man" (a remake of the early Bo Diddley hit), the Beatles' "Day Tripper" and "Land of a Thousand Dances," by Cannibal and the Headhunters. As performed, all were reasonably danceable, but none was particularly memorable. Without the young guitar player from Seattle, Curtis Knight and the Squires would have gone down in musical history as no more than another bar band with a sixties New York-New Jersey following. Eventually Ed Chalpin released and rereleased this early Hendrix material on fourteen "different" albums. Attempts were made to halt distribution of the recordings, but they were mostly unsuccessful, and many were still widely available as late as 1982.

The clubs in which some of the songs were recorded were even worse than the recorded material. Jimmy performed with Curtis and his band from the end of 1964 off and on until the beginning of 1966, mostly playing in smoky discothèques and honky-tonks, where getting drunk was the order of the day—or night. Occasionally they got an "uptown" date, playing the very chic Ondine's and Cheetah in New York City. There is a surviving photograph showing Jimmy playing the guitar with his teeth, wearing a spotted cheetah "skin" shirt. But most of the places bore such names as the Lighthouse and George's Club 20, in Hackensack.

At the time, although Jimmy was unaware of it, there was a moment when he came close to being discovered by one of the all-time guitar greats, Les Paul. The way Les told the story to Don Menn of *Guitar Player* magazine, he was driving with his son Gene to Columbia Records in New York from his New Jersey home when he decided to "drive by a nightclub in Lodi, New Jersey, which usually had good talent. I stopped the car and, as usual, Gene looked in. He came back out and said, 'Father, you better look for yourself. There's a guy playing all over the guitar!'

"I went in and stood in the doorway to listen. I was really impressed by what I heard. Yes, indeed, that dude was really working his guitar over. He was bending strings, playing funky as hell. I'd never seen anyone so radical. We had to push on to New York, but we decided that after we'd done our business, we'd hurry back to the club and nail that guy.

"A couple of hours later, that's what we tried to do. When we got back and asked around, the bartender told me some black dude had come in earlier to audition, but that his playing was too crazy for them—too wild and too loud.

So he and the group he was with hadn't been hired. When last seen, the guitarist had been fooling around on the piano in the club. That's all anyone could tell us. No one there knew his name or where he could be found.

"I wanted to grab that guy, so I started a real FBI search of my own. I told my manager and my friends at Columbia that I had heard a guy that really burned, but not knowing his name or where he made his home, locating him was a real problem.

"Gene and I called musicians' locals all around New York and New Jersey. No one knew who we were talking about. Finally we decided to look in every single nightclub in north and central Jersey, and also in Harlem, uptown. But with no name and only a description of a wild man with a guitar—different from what's around, more funky, raunchy—people just looked at us.

"After running out of clubs in our area, Gene and I headed down to south Jersey. But we couldn't find that guitarist we'd seen in Lodi. We gave up and forgot about it."

In 1965 Jimmy was undergoing big changes. All of the photographs of him as a member of the Squires show him with long unkempt hair—in contrast to Curtis and the other musicians, who still wore the traditional processed "conk." More significant, Jimmy was beginning to think of himself as being more than a backup guitarist. Jimmy now was thinking about singing too.

In one of the last letters he wrote his father, dated August 8, 1965, Jimmy again talked about being out of work, but added: "I still have my guitar and amp and as long as I have that, no fool can keep me from living. There's a few record companies I visited that I probably can record for. I think I'll start working toward that line because actually when you're playing behind other people you're still not making a big name for yourself as you would if you were working for yourself. But I went on the road with other people to get exposed to the public and see how business is taken care of. And mainly just to see what's what, and after I put a record out, there'll be a few people who know me already and who can help with the sale of the record.

"Nowadays people don't want you to sing good. They want you to sing sloppy and have a good beat to your songs. That's what angle I'm going to shoot for. That's where the money is. So just in case about three or four months from now you might hear a record by me which sounds terrible, don't feel ashamed, just wait until the money rolls in because every day people are singing worse and worse on purpose and the public buys more and more records.

"I just want to let you know I'm still here, trying to make it. Although I don't eat every day, everything's going all right for me. It could be worse than this, but I'm going to keep hustling and scuffling until I get things to happening like they're supposed to for me.

"Tell everyone I said hello. Leon, Grandma, Ben, Ernie, Frank, Mary, Barbara and so forth. Please write soon. It's pretty lonely out here by myself. Best luck and happiness in the future. Love, your son Jimmy."

CHAPTER

4

Jimmy entered the place he shared with Fay carrying a package under his arm. He and Fay were broke and Jimmy had bought another record.

"Man, you better tell me who you spent our *last* five dollars on," Fay said.

Jimmy played it cute. He waggled the bag at Fay, refusing to open it, grinning and saying she had a treat in store.

"Goddammit, Jimmy! Will you show we what's in the fuckin' bag!"

Finally Jimmy pulled the record out, but he still didn't let Fay see it. He began reading aloud from the dust jacket.

"I didn't recognize anything he said," Fay told the Warner Brothers filmmakers, "so I went off and pretended I didn't give a shit. I went up to the bedroom or something and he finally came in and told me it was Bob Dylan, you know.

"I said, 'Bob Who?' "

"Bob Dylan. You never heard of Bob Dylan?"

"No, I never heard of Bob Dylan!"

"You know, and I'm sayin' what's with this weird cat, you know. Because, like, I mean, you know, Bob Dylan was really a genius in his own right, but I just couldn't get ready for it, and I figured Jimmy was so heavy into what I was into, he would never like anything like that, you know. But he just loved it to death. I wanted to get up and go to the bathroom, he would grab me by my arm, you know, like I'm going to miss this part, you know. Like, I couldn't miss it, you know. You could hear it to Forty-second Street, probably, you know. We almost got put out of the building behind Bob Dylan."

By late summer of 1965, when Jimmy and Fay had this fight—and subsequently broke up—Bob Dylan had fused folk music and rock-and-roll and was on his way to becoming the most influential poet and performer of his generation. Turning his back on his Jewish middle-class family in Minnesota—he was born Robert Zimmerman—he had hitchhiked to New York only five years earlier, when he was nineteen. His first album, largely a tribute to his idol Woody Guthrie, was released in 1962, and in the three years to follow he recorded another five, which included some of the strongest "protest" songs of the period: "Blowin' in the Wind," "Hard Rain's A-gonna Fall," "Masters of War," "Times They Are A-changin'," "Chimes of Freedom," "Maggie's Farm" and the classic anthem "Like a Rolling Stone" among them. Many of these songs were popularized by others, but there was no challenging the fact the young folk-rocker from the Midwest was the uncompromising spokesman for his time.

Jimmy was a loner, had been a loner all of his life, and the alienation and anger Dylan expressed touched him, just as they touched countless others, immediately and deeply.

Bob Dylan was not a good singer, and this gave Jimmy as much courage as the poet's anguished lyrics did. If Dylan could get away with singing in a weak and untrained raspy voice and get a record contract, Jimmy reasoned, he also had a chance. So the same week that "Like a Rolling Stone" was released, Jimmy wrote that letter home in which he talked about singing in a "sloppy" voice and decided to start looking for a job as a singer in Greenwich Village, the neighborhood where Dylan had found *his* first jobs.

"I think he was justified in his decisions, you know, like to cut on out, you know," Fay says. "And if he'd never done that, he might have been, well, I don't think it could have happened, but it's possible, you know. He could have been pikin' around for years and years and years, you know, bein' a sideman and a flunky—and he wasn't, he wasn't any of these things, you know. 'Cause it was just a matter of time, you know, all he had to do was get out of fuckin' Harlem."

Another friend, Albert Allen, who lived in the Village, offered the Jimi Hendrix filmmakers another reason for Jimmy's looking toward the downtown Manhattan section noted for its bohemians. "He was very self-conscious about himself. You know, very, very self-conscious about the things that he wore, because, you know, he was kind of different, you know, kind of freaky, especially in comparison to a lot of the brothers uptown at that time. So he was very sensitive to the places that he liked to be, and he figured that most people would tolerate him a little more down here. Because he'd just blend in with the crowd, you know, which he still didn't because he always stood out."

One of the reasons Jimmy "stood out" was that he had fallen under the influence of another outrageous black performer. This was Mike Quashie, a six-foot two-inch, 210-pound singer and dancer from Trinidad who introduced the limbo to the U.S., getting his picture in *Life* magazine in 1962 sliding on his knees under a limbo bar held only seven inches from the dance floor. He also included fire-eating and fire-walking in his nightclub act, and photographs from the period show him in wardrobe and makeup similar to that used more than a decade later by such performers as Alice Cooper and Kiss. Mike claims he was the one who gave Jimmy a lot of his ideas about voodoo and fire, as well as introducing him to the idea of tying colorful "calypso scarves" around his biceps, thighs and head.

"I was workin' the African Room," Mike says, "right across the street from the Lennox Hotel where Jimmy was stayin'. He was goin' by the name of Jimmy James and he came into the club all the time. I teased him about his vaselined hair. It was long, but he was wearin' it greased, and I'd say, 'Wha' fo', baby? You tryin' to be Nat King Cole? Wooooooo! Wha' kine nigger are you! Anyways.' "

Jimmy's rapport with this jive-talking black man was good and he always laughed when Mike good-naturedly kidded him.

"At the time I didn't know his real name," Mike says. "I only knew him as Jimmy or J.J. Sometimes I called him J.C., for Jimmy Coon. He'd come in, see my show, and I'd go see him in his hotel room, usually to buy some speed. I was into speed a long time and I give Jimmy ten, twenty dollars lots of time."

This was not remarkable. It was common in the 1960s for a musician who was unemployed much of the time to take up the slack by selling drugs to his friends and to others he met through them. Usually Jimmy bought a quantity of acid tabs and uppers at a wholesale price, then after putting aside a number for himself—enough to get stoned as often as he wanted until it was time to make another buy—he sold the rest at "retail," covering his original purchase price. In this way Jimmy sometimes paid his room rent in midtown Manhattan while looking for work downtown (where the rents were prohibitively high).

The work in the Village didn't come. Nor did any more tours or studio work. The only thing happening for Jimmy was the occasional weekend call from Curtis Knight—calls that may not have paid much but were rewarding in other ways. Curtis said that Jimmy's pyrotechnics on stage "made the girls practically come out of their dresses," so he had his pick almost every night.

"Many was the night that he would say to me at the end of the gig, 'Well, ah, Curtis, I don't think I'll be riding back to the city with you. Someone has invited me for breakfast.'"

At the same time, Jimmy met Devon Wilson, a beautiful, streetwise black girl from Seattle or Milwaukee—there is no agreement—who found her way to Las Vegas and then to Los Angeles, becoming a familiar figure on the black music scene. By the time she met Jimmy she wore a dozen or more big names on her hip, from the great jazz trumpeter Miles Davis to Jimmy's old friend, guitarist Arthur Lee. Jimmy and Devon were introduced by Buddy Miles during an Isley Brothers and Wilson Pickett tour of New Jersey, and once she was established in New York, he began taking her and her friends on his rounds.

Curtis Knight wrote in his book that "there were a number of things about Devon which Jimi felt attracted to. She was, above all, magnetic, and she was also attractive, and totally into sex—proficient, imaginative—from A to Z."

A friend of Devon's talks candidly: "She really dug him, you know. And it wasn't just the size of his meat that attracted her, like it pulled a lot of other chicks. Jimmy was big, as big as niggers are supposed to be, and that was important—Devon liked her men well hung—but she said he was also the best. She said Jimmy was gentle. He didn't push. He was, you know, real innocent. He'd been around, but he was shy, so he let Devon take the lead.

"Devon told me they were staying in one of those terrible midtown hotels, and Jimmy got it up and kept it up all night long. They were doing a lot of blow [cocaine], and it

Devon Wilson

[74]

was like his cock was frozen solid. She said she taught him a lot that night, showed him 'around the world' and a lotta the other tricks. You know, like deep throat. Devon was into that years before Linda What's-Her-Name. Devon really knew how to make a man reeelax! And Jimmy could keep it up for her. They were good, all right."

Devon also claimed she gave Jimmy his first LSD. "He liked it a lot," she told Curtis Knight. "He tried various pills with me and our relationship became one of excitement and exhilaration."

Sex, drugs and rock 'n' roll: the tripod that held up the sixties, the fuels that made the pop scene go.

In the cold early months of 1966 Jimmy straddled two worlds, two life styles. His home remained in the tawdry Times Square area, a neighborhood of big movie theaters, narrow, grimy bars and cheap, no-questions-asked hotels. Along the noisy, dirty streets Jimmy walked, bobbing and weaving from place to place.

"Jimmy would come into the African Room," Mike Quashie says, "and the owners of the place would freak. He'd have these three hookers with him. At least they *looked* like hookers, and the owners thought Jimmy was a pimp, with his wild clothes and his processed hair and his do-rag. They didn't want him in the place, didn't want that crowd at all!"

The other world Jimmy inhabited was thirty blocks to the south, in lower Manhattan, where he walked past or into at least twenty or thirty clubs in his search for work. Some, like the Village Gate and the Village Vanguard and the Five Spot on the Lower East Side, were known mostly for jazz, then featuring such performers as Cannonball Adderly, Sonny Rollins and Thelonious Monk. Others, notably those along Bleecker and MacDougal streets in the Village—including the Gaslight Cafe, and Cafe a Go Go, the Bitter

End and Gerde's Folk City—were established folk music showcases for Buffy Sainte-Marie, the Limeliters, Tom Paxton, Phil Ochs, the Chad Mitchell Trio, and the Rooftop Singers, among many more. In Greenwich Village every variety and mix of music was available. Besides folk music and jazz, there were the Lovin' Spoonful, who were fusing rock, country and jug-band instrumentation. And a group of writers from the Lower East Side—the area now called the East Village, quickly becoming a mecca for the new, rebellious bohemians—had named themselves the Fugs and were blending rock-and-roll with scatalogical poetry.

As musical lines were being blurred or erased, other lines were being drawn. Almost overnight, it seemed, a revolution had begun, summarized by two sociologists, J. I. Simmons and Barry Winograd, in their book *It's Happening:* "Look at you, blowing up whole countries for the sake of some crazy ideologies that you don't live up to anyway. Look at you, mindfucking a whole generation of kids into getting a revolving charge account and buying your junk. (Who's a junkie?) Look at you, needing a couple of stiff drinks before you have the balls to talk with another human being. Look at you, making it with your neighbor's wife on the sly just to prove that you're really alive. Look at you, hooked on *your* cafeteria of pills, and making up dirty names for anybody who isn't in your bag, and screwing up the land and the water and the air for profit, and calling this nowhere scene the Great Society! *And you're gonna tell us how to live?* C'mon, man, you've got to be kidding!"

The new life style associated with this rebellion was *against* the war in Vietnam and *for* marijuana, *against* Lyndon Johnson and *for* dancing, *against* hypocrisy and *for* ecstasy, *against* the draft and *for* meditation, *against* police and *for* sex, and nowhere were these positions better demonstrated, explained, shouted, chanted, cried, crooned, cajoled and ordered in frustration and in rage than in the popular music. The "protest" lyrics that Jimmy so admired in Dylan and tried on for size with Curtis Knight were now in vogue. "Like a Rolling Stone" was followed at the top of the record charts by Barry McGuire's "Eve of Destruction," which warned of nuclear doom. Other hit songs in the final months of 1965 and in early 1966—including "Laugh at Me," a song about long hair and unorthodox clothing sung by Sonny Bono, and "I Fought the Law (and the Law Won)" by a West Coast band called the Bobby Fuller Four—echoed the same point of view.

Jimmy fit this world even more comfortably than he fit the world of flash and flesh uptown. He did not join protest marches and he sometimes still wore a suit onstage, with his hair slicked back in a "conk." But more and more often he was casually dressed, adopting some of the style of his friend Mike Quashie, wearing tight-fitting pants and his first pieces of gaudy jewelry. His dialogue was becoming freer too, ranging from talk about the Watts riots of the previous summer (1965) to dreams of space travel. Most important was Jimmy's accelerating drug experimentation. By the middle of 1966 he was following Timothy Leary's advice, "Turn on, tune in, drop out!" eating a small piece of blotter soaked with LSD two or three times a week and smoking grass almost daily. Sometimes he was seen in clubs sucking from a small plastic baby bottle filled with a Methedrine-and-water solution.

Occasionally Jimmy was asked to record demonstration tapes with friends. In June 1966 he went into New York's Abtone Recording Studios with a black tenor saxophone player named Lonnie Youngblood, two other guitarists, Lee Moses and Herman Hitson, and a producer, John Brantley. These tapes were made available after Jimmy died. Much of the material was repetitious and recorded poorly—typical for such sessions—and on some of the albums several takes of a single instrumental were labeled "Part I," "Part II" and

"Sequel" to fill out the discs. Many of the songs took their lyrics and titles from the jargon of the period—"Go Go Shoes," "Get Down" and "Groovemaker."

Nonetheless the Hendrix guitar shines through. It is clear that given the freedom to experiment and play without the restraint imposed by someone else's familiar hit or the dictates of a bandleader like Little Richard, Jimmy was able to break new ground, creating new effects.

Some said his "bent notes" were ugly. One friend even said Jimmy produced sounds on the guitar "like he was strangling a chicken." But all those notes in a row a quarter tone sharp created an extra tension. Jimmy also used one of the rings on his fingers as a bottleneck player uses a metal cylinder, or grabbed the microphone stand and ran it up and down the fretboard for bold, searing slide effects.

Sometimes Jimmy played the back of his guitar's neck nearly as much as the front, tapping it with his knuckles to bring out harmonics, and other times he merely grabbed the neck and shook it to get a wild vibrato that couldn't be produced either by hand or with the tremolo bar.

The over-all effect on the sessions with Youngblood and the others was startling. Yes, the quality of the recording was questionable and so was the musicianship of the other sidemen. But Jimmy's guitar work was shimmering. On one song, an original of Jimmy's called "Red House," even his voice sounded practiced, confident.

The Cafe Wha? was an extremely dark basement club in the middle of the busiest block of MacDougal Street where unknown performers were welcome to "audition" in the afternoons. There was no payment for these performances, but depending on the reaction of the daytime crowd and the opinion of the club manager, there was a possibility of employment at night. When Jimmy heard about this policy, he assembled a small combo of friends and went in as Jimmy James and the Blue Flames.

Jimmy performed every trick in his repertoire that afternoon, and the band was given a job, playing five nights a week for five to twenty-five dollars a man per night, depending on the size of the audience and the mood of the man who ran the place. Jimmy continued to deal drugs to make ends meet.

Jimmy named his band the Blue Flames, the name used by the great gospel-tinged blues singer Junior Parker. Parker recorded a number of rhythm-and-blues hits during the same period. Jimmy included several of these in his show, including "Driving Wheel," "In the Dark" and "Annie, Get Your Yo-Yo," and it was this kind of material, rather than the theatrical gimmickry, that began to attract other performers to the club.

One of these was the young white blues guitarist John Hammond, Jr., whose father, John Hammond, Sr., was the legendary Columbia Records producer who discovered and signed a wide range of artists from Billie Holiday to Bob Dylan. The young Hammond was playing the Gaslight nearby, and he told *Guitar Player* magazine:

"One night between shows—it was a warm evening out—I went upstairs and my friend who was working at the Players Theatre on MacDougal right next to the Cafe Wha? came over and said, 'John, there's this band playing downstairs that you've got to hear. This guy is doing songs off your old album and he sounds better than you.'

"So I thought I'd check this out. I went down there and he was playing all these tunes off this album I'd done called *So Many Roads* [Vanguard 79178], and he was playing the guitar parts better than Robbie Robertson had.

"He was a really handsome black kid, playing with these guys who could barely keep the beat. They were terrible. Anyway, I went down there and introduced myself to him. He knew me and had my albums and he was just knocked out that I was there. See, I had all these Muddy Waters and Howlin' Wolf tunes on the *So Many Roads* album and he had gotten them from my record. At least, this is what he told me."

This may not have been true. There is reason to believe that Jimmy got the songs elsewhere; after all, he was exposed to the blues for years all over the country with some of the all-time blues greats. It's also possible that Jimmy was flattering the young guitarist because of his father's association with Bob Dylan. In any case, a casual friendship was struck and Jimmy and John began jamming together.

"When my job was through at the Gaslight," John says, "Jimmy and I got together and worked out with a little group that he had. There was a guy in his band named Randy Wolfe, who later moved to the West Coast and called himself Randy California and formed this group called Spirit, and he was fantastic then, playing slide guitar. I was just playing harmonica and singing, because those guys were heavyweight electric guitar players. Jimmy did one solo number, a Bo Diddley tune—'I'm a Man,' I think—and he did it real good. And he did it the way I did it—off that album."

Hammond says he and Jimmy rehearsed for about two weeks, then he hired Jimmy to join him in the Cafe a Go Go, another basement club, around the corner on Bleecker Street. What the Cafe Wha? lacked in class this one offered, attracting an audience of the socially hip, including many pop stars. Jimmy decided to go for it, to pull out all the stops. He may have been a sideman once more, playing guitar to John's harp and voice, but as Hammond himself recalled years later, "No way was he going to be my guitar player. He was his own star."

The word went out about this "new" guitar in town. Along with folk music, the blues were enjoying a spirited revival in 1966, thanks in large part to the success, ironically, of British groups, such as the Animals and the Rolling Stones. Leading the pack in the U.S. was Mike Bloomfield, who was performing with the Paul Butterfield Blues Band, a Chicago-based combo then playing in another Village club. A few years later Mike talked with *Guitar Player* magazine.

"I was the hot shot guitarist on the block," Mike said. "I thought I was it. I'd never heard of Hendrix. Then someone said 'You got to see the guitar player with John Hammond.' I went right across the street and saw him. Hendrix knew who I was and that day, in front of my eyes, he burned me to death. I didn't even get my guitar out. H-bombs were going off, guided missiles were flying—the surf—waves. I can't tell you the sounds he was getting out of his instrument. He was getting every sound I was ever to hear him get right there in that room with a Stratocaster, a Twin [amplifier], a Maestro fuzztone and that was all; he was doing it mainly through extreme volume. How he did this, I wish I understood. He just got right up in my face with that axe and I didn't even want to pick up a guitar for the next year.

"I was awed. I'd never heard anything like it. I didn't even know where he was coming from musically, because he wasn't playing any of his own tunes. He was doing things like 'Like a Rolling Stone,' but in the most unusual way. He wasn't a singer, he wasn't even particularly a player. That day, Jimi Hendrix was laying things on me that were more sounds than they were licks. But I found, after hearing him two or three times that he was into pure melodic playing and lyricism as much as he was into sounds. In fact, he had melded them into a perfect blend."

Bloomfield introduced himself: "Man, where you been?"

"I been playing the chitlin' circuit and I got bored shitless," Jimi said. "I didn't hear any guitar players doing anything new and I was bored out of my mind."

"He told me he knew he could do more on the guitar than anybody he ever heard," Bloomfield said. "There was a cult thing happening at the time. Guitar players were into

[81]

freak sounds that were hand-derived, rather than coming from devices. Robbie Robertson could do it. Roy Buchanan. Out on the [West] Coast, Jerry McGee. And in Chicago, me and Harvey Mandel. Hendrix was on the same road. Except that with Hendrix, as many times as I watched him play, I couldn't figure out what he was doing. I stared and stared and stared and I couldn't understand his hand positions. His thumb was so big, his hands were so outsized, nothing looked orthodox. Even when he played songs like 'Rolling Stone,' where I really knew the chords, I could never connect what he was doing with his hands with what I was hearing.

"And there was no great electric guitarist in rock and roll that Jimi didn't know of," Mike added. "I could ask him about records that I knew had real fancy parts, where the performer was ahead of his time or playing funky on a record that wasn't particularly funky. For example, Jimi knew all about a very early Righteous Brothers record on which there's a guitarist who plays very advanced rock and roll guitar for that time. There's another record by Robert Parker, who made 'Barefootin',' called 'You Better Watch Yourself' that has a real hot guitar player with a style more like Hendrix than most session players. Jimi said it wasn't him, but that he knew the guy—somebody named Big Tom Collins. He knew *every* hot guitarist on record!"

It was inevitable that others would hear of Jimmy and also be impressed. One of these was Linda Keith, then the girl friend of Keith Richard, the guitarist in the Rolling Stones, who were then touring the U.S. She had seen Jimmy in the Cheetah when he was backing up Curtis Knight and had gone home with him once to listen to his Bob Dylan records. At that time he told her he wanted to record, so after she rediscovered him at the Cafe a Go Go, she began taking her friends to see him. The first, a record producer she doesn't identify today, failed to see anything in Jimmy that he liked. And then she took Chas Chandler.

[82]

By now Jimmy was back at the Cafe Wha? with a drummer and a bassist, his two-week job with Hammond at an end. The way Chas remembers it, he took one look and decided he wanted Jimmy to go home with him to England, where he promised that he and his business partner, Mike Jefferey, would record him.

Brian "Chas" Chandler was twenty-eight, only five years older than Jimmy, but he knew his way in the music business. Since 1964 he had been the bass player for a British group called the Animals, fronted by the singer Eric Burdon. They were all from Newcastle, a rough, sooty mill town in northern England. The Animals were hugely popular by the summer of 1966, with more than a dozen hits, including their first, the old blues song about a whorehouse in New Orleans, "The House of the Rising Sun"; "We Gotta Get Out of This Place"; "It's My Life"; and "See See Rider," which went onto the best-seller charts the week Chas walked into the Cafe Wha? Chas said he was quitting the Animals to go into production. Jimmy was impressed by Chas's attention, but he was not immediately convinced.

"The Animals had just started our last American tour," Chas told British journalist Chris Welch, author of *Hendrix: A Biography*. "Jimmy didn't just say, 'Yeah, man, I'll come over to England.' He was worried about the equipment we had in England and what the musicians were like. One of the first things he asked me was if I knew Eric Clapton. I said I knew Eric very well, and that I saw a lot of him socially at that time. He said, 'Well, if you take me to England, will you take me to meet Eric?' I told him that when Eric heard him play, he would be falling over to meet Jimi, and that clinched it."

Of course, it wasn't quite so simple. It was true that Jimmy had little to keep him in America. The pay at the Cafe Wha? was miniscule, and there were no offers anywhere else. In fact, if it hadn't been for Linda Keith—who stayed on in New York when the Rolling Stones resumed their tour—Jimmy wouldn't have had a place to stay. Linda moved him into her hotel room, gave him money and a coat, bought him a new Stratocaster.

Still, *deciding* to go to England was one thing and *doing* it was another, because doing it required a passport and getting a passport demanded a birth certificate. Weeks passed before this document was obtained by mail from Seattle, and while waiting, there seemed to be other hurdles.

The first was Jimmy's voice. However willing he may have seemed in his letter home to his father to sing in a "sloppy" voice, and however confident he may have sounded in some of his early demo tapes, he still expressed insecurity, and he sometimes showed it too. Mike Bloomfield remembered him as "mumbling" the lyrics to songs onstage at the Cafe Wha? and said Jimmy told Chas he was "afraid" to sing.

"That's when Chas said, 'Fuck it,' " Bloomfield said. " 'Your voice is okay and you've got enough going on the guitar, so don't worry about your voice.' "

There were other problems too.

"D'you have a record?" Chas asked one day.

Jimmy looked puzzled. Did Chas mean recordings? Or did he mean a police record? Jimmy began to stammer, not knowing what to say. Chas saw that Jimmy was embarrassed.

"It's a'right, mate," he said. "We all get into trouble. What'd you get nicked [arrested] for?"

Jimmy told Chas about the joyriding he did in Seattle as a teenager, said he went into the army to avoid prosecution, and so the charges were dropped. And then Jimmy laughed and said, "You know, I, uh, wondered if you meant do I have a recording. Like, a record album."

Chas looked surprised. "Do you?" he asked.

"Well, not really, but I been in a studio."

[84]

Now Chas looked concerned. "You under contract to anybody?" he asked.

Jimmy shook his head and laughed. "No, no. Just sideman stuff. Member of Little Richard's band. Jams. Stuff like that. Nothing serious."

Chas looked at Jimmy. "You certain? This is important, mate."

"Well . . . ," Jimmy began, "there might have been a coupla pieces of paper and a coupla people . . ."

Years later Chas was able to laugh at the trouble he had trying to get Jimmy to remember *what* pieces of paper he had signed and *who* the people were. One he told the story to was Michael Goldstein.

"Chas kept him in a hotel room, I think, for three days, trying to remember everybody that he had ever signed a piece of paper with," Michael says. "They were running around and they bought a lot of contracts back. I mean, Jimmy signed anything in those early days. I think Chas told me once that they bought up about ten contracts that were on him for different things."

Finally, when Chas thought he had Jimmy free and clear, he called Pan American Airways.

" 'ello,"he said. "I'd like two first-class tickets to London. One way."

CHAPTER

5

The British capital in 1966 was what *Time* magazine called "Swinging London," a city where "ancient elegance and new opulence are all tangled up in a dazzling blur of op and pop." The journalist Philip Norman put it the same way in his biography of the Beatles, *Shout!* What made it so exciting, he said, was that the pop explosion was "happening against a tolerant background of non-swinging London—of black taxis, red buses, Grenadier Guardsmen, the sacred monuments and statues past which the young, outrageously dandified, zoomed laughingly in open-top Mini Modes; the Union Jack itself translated to a novelty kitchen apron or carrier bag. The essence was audacity, like the Beatles'; it was a certainty that, because *they* had got away with it, everyone could."

Got away with what?

With everything.

With short skirts (on women—or "birds," as they were called) and long hair (on men). With Sergeant Pepper uniforms and pants so tight you couldn't sit down in them.

With rock-and-roll around the clock and smoking hashish in the streets.

According to those in London, the phenomenon had declined almost to extinction by the time American journalists noticed it. Nonetheless, once *Time* and then *Life* and *The Saturday Evening Post* published their stories, the city was awash with American visitors looking for action. London began to swing again.

In the pop world of the sixties the musician was king, and to be both a musician and British in the Beatles era was to approach sainthood. For this reason Chas thought London was the perfect launching pad for Jimmy's new career. If Chas could put Jimmy together with some English sidemen and make a recording deal in England, then get Jimmy booked into some of the right London clubs, Jimmy could *then* return to America almost as if he were British himself.

With this and his partner Mike's success with the Animals, and the continuing support of those who had seen Jimmy in New York—including Linda Keith and the Rolling Stones—Chas believed there would be no trouble doing any of this. Before he could make a move, however, he had to audition sidemen and get Jimmy a government permit to work in England.

(Terry McVay, who was a road manager for the Animals' final U.S. tour, accompanied Chas and Jimmy to London and says that as they passed through customs, he carried Jimmy's guitar, "because we didn't want anyone to know he was going to work.")

Chas also had to keep reassuring a very nervous Jimmy Hendrix about how comfortable he would be in Swinging London.

"On the plane he had been worrying how his American style of playing would fit with English guys," Chas told Chris Welch, "so I decided when we got to London Airport to drive to Zoot Money's, which was on the way into town. I thought if he met Zoot, it would dispel his fears about English musicians. We arrived at Zoot's house at 11 A.M. and Jimmy started jamming for two or three hours. The house was full of musicians and it made him feel he could settle in England. He took to Zoot like a fish to water."

Zoot was a keyboard player steeped in rock, jazz and the blues, and was one of the half dozen musicians in London whose influence far outdistanced his affluence. Much admired by every other musician in town, Zoot never had any hit records, in England or in the U.S., but he was recognized as one of the primary musical tastemakers of the London scene. Chas could not have picked a better place to introduce Jimmy into the "right group," and his doing this so soon after arriving showed his eagerness to get things happening.

That evening, following a long jam session, Chas checked Jimmy into the Hyde Park Towers Hotel, and over the next couple of days he took the guitarist on a round of the hippest London clubs. That first week Jimmy saw Paul McCartney, Ringo Starr, Pete Townshend, Eric Clapton and John Mayall. Jimmy was bug-eyed.

Chas also introduced Jimmy to his partner, a thirty-three-year-old no-nonsense former British commando and onetime Olympic skier who had gotten into music management when he was operating a dance hall in Newcastle. One of the early groups he booked there was Eric Burdon's band, the Animals. Mike was slender, with longish blond hair, wore glasses and had a spooky air about him—what one friend believed was the result of military training, the ability to "enter a room, completely blocking his physical sounds and his inner presence." Still, he seemed genuinely excited about Jimmy's potential and set about convincing government authorities that the guitarist had a talent that couldn't be duplicated by any unemployed English musician.

While waiting for the work permit, Jimmy continued to

make the rounds. Eric Clapton remembers the night that Jimmy came to him: "I think he did a Howlin' Wolf number or something, but he did his whole routine. He did all the things with his teeth, playing the guitar with his teeth, and layin' it on the floor, and playin' it behind his head, and, you know, doin' the splits, the whole thing. It was incredible."

Another night, jamming with Brian Auger's Oblivion Express, he did the same thing, this time with France's "Elvis Presley," Johnny Halliday, in the audience. Halliday fell all over himself getting to Jimmy after the set and insisted that he come to Paris to open for him in a concert at the Olympia Theatre on October 15.

"From that moment we were in a whirlwind finding him a backing group," says Chas. "In two weeks—just in time for the show—we had Mitch and Noel."

Noel Redding arrived first. He walked through the doors of Chas's offices on Gerrard Street saying he wanted to audition for lead guitar with the New Animals. He was told the spot was filled, but Chas asked him if he could play bass.

"O'course," he said, although he'd never played bass in his life.

"Well, there's this new guitarist in town . . ."

Noel borrowed Chas's bass and jammed a bit with Jimmy in his hotel room. Jimmy told him what chords to play and he played them well. Jimmy quickly called Chas. "I think we've found a bass player," he said. Later Noel would say, "I'll switch to bass. I don't see anybody else playing lead guitar with this bloke."

Noel was twenty-one, a former art student from the seaside resort of Folkestone, near the famous white cliffs of Dover. His experience was limited, and when he arrived in London he was "skint"—dead broke; he remembers fondly that Jimmy gave him "ten quid [$25] and a bar of chocolate." He says it was his good memory for chord sequences that got him the job. Jimmy taught him how to back up "Hey Joe," and Noel remembered the chords exactly the following day when they played together again.

Another reason Noel was picked was his appearance. He was rail-thin, weighing only one-hundred-twenty-nine pounds, wore big round glasses and had a full head of frizzy reddish hair. Image was important in the sixties—as always—and the youthful firm of Jeffrey and Chandler was aware of it.

John "Mitch" Mitchell, the drummer selected a day or so later, came with greater personal confidence and more talent. He was only nineteen but had been performing publicly from the time he was three. At thirteen, he was in *Macbeth* on BBC Radio, hosted his own television series three years later, and was the original Artful Dodger in *Oliver* on the London stage. Mitch also cut a record with another actor, Chris Sandford, and then went on to join a band called the Riot Squad. It was after leaving Georgie Fame's Blue Flames that he happened into Chas in a club, said he was available, and that was it.

The final decision was what to call the trio. At Chas's suggestion, Jimmy's name was changed to "Jimi," a spelling he believed would help the audience and the media remember the group. He and Jeffrey also believed that Jimi's name should be included in the band's name. After much discussion they settled on the "Jimi Hendrix Experience," and after only three days of rehearsal they left for Paris to perform in the French capital's most prestigious hall. They'd learned only three songs, so they "faded" the rest of the set, playing long-established hits like Otis Redding's "Respect" and Wilson Pickett's "Land of a Thousand Dances." Halliday was so pleased, he took the trio on tour to play concerts in Munich and Hamburg, West Germany.

Jimi sent a postcard home to his father, his first communication in months: "We're in Munich, Germany, now. We

An early publicity photo of the Jimi Hendrix Experience: (left to right) Jimi, Noel Redding, and Mitch Mitchell. Jimi's manager persuaded him to drop the second "m" from his name to give it more punch

just left Paris and Nancy, France. We're playing around London now. That's where I'm staying these days. I have my own group and will have a record out in about two months called 'Hey Joe' by the Jimi Hendrix Experience. I hope you get this card. I'll write a decent letter. I think things are getting a little better. Your loving son, Jimi."

It was true. Chas believed that if all went well, a single could be in the stores within a month. Once they were back in London, Jimi and Mitch and Noel were rushed into a studio to record a few songs that Chas could take around to the record companies, among them the song that Chas first heard Jimi play in New York, "Hey Joe." This had been recorded by a Los Angeles band called the Leaves and had been a Top 40 hit in the U.S. the previous summer, but it never was released in Britain, and Chas thought it an appropriate introductory tune.

By now Chas and Mike were beginning to worry about expenses. They claimed they had spent nearly £10,000 on the Experience—about $25,000—with no income so far; payment for the brief Halliday tour didn't even cover the costs. Only a small sum was expected from a record company as an advance against future royalties, but every shilling was needed and needed badly, so Chas started making the rounds with great enthusiasm.

First he went to an old, established company, British Decca, which had released many of the early American rockers, including Buddy Holly, Duane Eddy, the Everly Brothers and Little Richard, and also had some of the top contemporary English stars, Tommy Steele and the Rolling Stones among them. An executive at Decca turned Chas down cold, saying about Jimi: "I don't think he's got anything."

Other companies disagreed, and the following week Chas received two offers. The first was from another long-established label, Polydor, not known for its interest in or success with pop and rock music, although some young musicians from Australia calling themselves the Bee Gees were signed at about the same time. Polydor, with great reserve, agreed to release "Hey Joe" in December.

At the same time, Chas ran into some old friends, Kit Lambert and Chris Stamp, and members of the band they managed, the Who. The Who's guitarist, Pete Townshend, was regarded as one of the best in his field, one of the pioneers in "feedback guitar." When he heard Jimi play at one of his early London jams, he said he actually felt "threatened." Besides being an excellent musician, Pete was a superb businessman and he knew that the sensible thing to do in such a situation was to offer the "threat" a contract and at least make a profit from it.

Kit Lambert also heard Jimi play, and over a drink the same night at a club called the Scotch at St. James, he promised to have a record out by Christmas "if I have to take it round the shops myself." This would be on a new label he and the others owned, Track Records.

Chas and Mike could not get out of their commitment to Polydor, but decided to let their friends at Track have all future products after the first single, "Hey Joe."

By now Jimi and Noel and Mitch had signed agreements with Chas and Mike for music publishing and recording as well as for management. As managers, the firm of Jeffrey and Chandler Ltd. took a hefty 30 percent. (Most personal managers of the time accepted 15 percent as their commission, although the Beatles' manager, Brian Epstein, was taking 25 percent.) Chas and Mike also laid claim to a 3 percent producers' royalty on all recordings and 50 percent of all earnings from a jointly owned music publishing company.

What remained was split between the three members of the Experience 50-25-25, with Jimi taking the largest part.

All of which meant little or nothing with no work and no money coming in. "When we got back from France,"

Chas recalls, "things were very quiet. It was very hard to get work and no one would touch him. I was fast running out of money. I had six guitars and I sold five of them to pay for a reception at the Bag O'Nails."

The Bag O'Nails was one of the most fashionable discothèques in London, and Chas invited all the local talent agents, concert promoters and club managers to the reception. It was a fabulous party, from all accounts, but otherwise it was a failure. Jimi may have been the darling of the British pop cognoscenti, known to such luminaries as Eric Clapton, Pete Townshend, Zoot Money, the Rolling Stones and the Animals, and he already had a following on the European continent, but the club owners in London and elsewhere in England apparently could not have cared less. Only one promoter came forward at that reception and he offered the Experience a meager £25 ($65) to open some shows for the New Animals.

"At Croydon, on the first gig, I think the audience were shocked," Chas says. "Their reaction wasn't excitement, I think they were numb! They weren't sure what it was about. Next we got a gig at the Roundhouse in Chalk Farm. Jimi got his guitar nicked [stolen] and I was flat broke, so I had to sell my last guitar. I swapped my last bass for a new guitar for Jimi. Two days later 'Hey Joe' hit the chart. It was all done by the skin of my teeth. The deejays hadn't been playing it on the radio, but the word had spread through the ballrooms and it started to sell. I think we had about thirty shillings left between us."

"Hey Joe" entered the *Melody Maker* chart at Number 48 on January 7, 1967, and after that Jimi and Noel and Mitch were invited to play in the most exclusive London discothèques, including a return engagement to the scene of their disappointing press party, the Bag O'Nails, and to the Speakeasy, the 7½ Club and the Marquee. The Experience also made its first television appearances, performing on

Jimi, Noel and Mitch in an early publicity photo

COURTESY WARNER BROS. / REPRISE RECORDS

[96]

Ready Steady Go, and then on *Top of the Pops,* closing out the month co-billed with the Who at the prestigious Saville Theatre, then being operated by Brian Epstein.

With success at hand, Jimi was in heaven, or the next best place to it by contemporary standards, in Soho. This was the noisy district of narrow London streets famous for its foreign restaurants, Carnaby Street boutiques and trendy discothèques, where Jimi found a small apartment, which he immediately painted all black. Blackout curtains were hung over the windows. Even the satin sheets were black.

"Jimi was *the* new guitar in town," says an observer of the London scene, "and he was a threat to people like Clapton and Townshend. All the birds were falling all over him. Even Mick Jagger felt threatened. Today Jagger says only the nicest things about Jimi, but back then it was different. A lot of that had to do with Marianne Faithfull. There were a lot of birds in and out of Jimi's life at the time. Kathy Etchingham was one who stuck. But it was Marianne who made the biggest talk."

She was Mick Jagger's live-in girl friend when she and Jimi met. She was a vocalist who had risen to fame about the same time the Stones had, recording one of their early songs, "As Tears Go By." More hits followed. Marianne married, had a child, was divorced and drifted into relationships with Brian Jones and Keith Richard before starting to go with Mick soon after his previous girl friend, the model Chrissie Shrimpton, attempted suicide.

"Mick was the king and Marianne was the queen," says the London source, "and Jimi was the jack of spades. It made for some of the best gossip available."

Marianne went to hear Jimi at the 7½ Club. Her knowledge of American blues, gained from listening to some of the records in the Stones' collection, and her recognition of Jimi's ability to play the blues commanded her attention, and she sat alone on the floor for the entire show, enthralled.

The party that followed the performance was a classic for the time, with Brian Jones, Linda Keith, Paul McCartney, Kathy Etchingham and Chas, Noel and Mitch all in attendance, besides Jimi and Marianne.

"It was electric," says one of those present, "and Jimi could do no wrong. It wasn't just that Brian and Paul were there. He had three women all fawning over him—Linda because she felt some claim from New York, Kathy because she was his 'old lady,' or at least most people thought she was, and Marianne, who had been living with Mick for only a few weeks and was happy with Mick but still felt this incredible attraction. Jimi just sat there in the middle of it, smoking hashish cigarettes and grinning uncontrollably."

Jimi was not at all hesitant to express how he felt about his women. They were to be enjoyed, he said, and enjoyed in large numbers.

"It's so good to indulge the beauty of a girl you've never seen before," he said one day while drinking with London friends. "But it's not the last girl. You don't have to let something like that hang you up. You see a green coat and purple suede shoes prancing on the corner . . . so you fall in love right there in a *second!* I'd go down on her. I'd do *anything!* But after fifteen minutes you're down in another part of the street. You yourself have the privilege to get unhung up over somebody. As soon as possible, if you want it to be as soon as possible. At any time, man. It's your own life. Freedom is the key word . . ."

This cavalier philosophy also seemed to govern Jimi's feelings about money. In the same rambling conversation—it started as an interview with *Beat International* and turned into a party when he was joined by friends—he first expressed a fairly typical attitude about saving for when he was older: "I want to make the money as where I can live when I get bald, you know, when all these little curls fall out and the teasing and the hair spray and what they call all those things I do with my hair, when all this shit falls out, I want to get that money, get that money to hold me together to do what I want to do in *life*."

But, he added, he wasn't going to dedicate his life to money. In fact, he said, "Money to me is like if you're lost in the woods and you have to go use the rest room, right? There's no rest room for a hundred miles but there are leaves, so what you do is just bend over and, you know, make sure you don't fall on your, you know, and then you just use the leaves. You have to use the leaves if you don't have no tissue or whatever it is. And that's exactly what money is for me—something I might have to use."

At the time Jimi said this he still was not earning much. At one point in the conversation he spoke directly to the tape recorder that was running nearby, commenting on the music in the background: "Just in case anybody can hear the guitar in the background, that's me playing. Starving." And then he laughed.

Hungry or not, the music flowed and, most important, the trio worked. It may have been created quickly, its members strangers rather than the old friends that made up most rock bands, but Jimi, Mitch and Noel played as if they had been together for years.

Much of Jimi's repertoire at the time comprised startling arrangements of songs made successful by other singers. "Hey Joe," for instance, was a song identified with several Los Angeles bands—besides being a hit for the Leaves, it was a standout part of the repertoire of Love and of the Byrds— yet from the opening crash of guitar feedback on Jimi's version, the song was entirely his. (And the lyric message of a man going out to shoot a woman who had cheated on him fit perfectly Jimi's developing image as a macho stud-about-town.) Jimi also paid tribute to Dylan with a carefully crafted "Like a Rolling Stone" that was masterful in its originality, yet seemingly offhand, and to the great blues guitarist B. B. King with a race through his "Rock Me Baby" that strung a curtain of bluesy notes across the sound of a buzz saw gone amok. And in "Wild Thing," a hit for a group called the Troggs, Jimi assaulted his guitar with his hips and mouth and sang, "C'mere, let me sssssssssssssssock it to you!"

He stretched even further in his original songs. By now he had dropped the vocal on his funky blues "Red House" and used it as his most traditional piece, establishing himself as an absolute master of the blues form. In the more melodic "Purple Haze," written one night at the Upper Cut Club in London and recorded the following day, Jimi introduced deliberate guitar distortion and some of his early voodoo-cum-psychedelic lyrics:

> Purple haze all around
> Don't know if I'm comin' up or down.
>
> Am I happy or in misery?
> Whatever it is, that girl put a spell on me.
>
> Purple haze all in my brain
> Lately things don't seem the same.
>
> Acting funny, but I don't know why
> 'Scuse me while I kiss the sky.

In another original, "Laughing Sam's Dice," the initial letters stood for Jimi's favorite psychedelic, and the lyric formed a travelogue through outer space. In still other songs Jimi was sexually direct, as in "Fire," when he shouted, "I have only one burning desire/Let me stand next to your fire!" and in the classic "Foxy Lady" he growled an overt threat: "Here I come, baby/Comin' to GITCHA!"

Using only a small bank of amplifiers, a fuzztone and a wah-wah pedal, Jimi was creating with these songs a musical

[100]

density approached by only a few other trios, most of them, coincidentally, British. The Who, the Cream (with Eric Clapton on lead guitar) and the new Yardbirds were a part of this same "power trio" movement. But it was the Jimi Hendrix Experience that first captured the broad-based public imagination.

As is usually the case, the media played a significant role in creating this acceptance, and the acceptance came, typically, by way of rejection. When "Hey Joe" appeared on the record charts and Jimi and Noel and Mitch performed that song on the popular *Top of the Pops* television show, Fleet Street's sensation-hungry newsmongers came charging in with prose purpler than Jimi's haze. The mildest of the characterizations was "The Wild Man of Pop," while other images were "Wild Man from Borneo" and "Mau-Mau."

There was no surer way to make Jimi and his band a hit

The Jimi Hendrix Experience at the time "Hey Joe" appeared on the charts

with young people. It worked in 1963 when Fleet Street reported that the youthful Beatles had been ejected from a dance hall for wearing leather jackets. And it worked again in 1965 when London's establishment press asked its readers in big headlines: WOULD YOU LET YOUR DAUGHTER MARRY A ROLLING STONE? And now it was working for the Experience. The rule was: If the adults didn't like a band, surely the youngsters would.

As "Hey Joe" quickly ascended the record charts—going to the Number Six position—the jobs came more frequently, until Jimi and his new friends found themselves running all over the rainy winter English countryside, working six and seven days almost every week, sometimes two and three shows each day.

Then, on March 4, the trio returned to the Continent. "Britain had been our first target and Europe was our second," Chas told the *New Musical Express*. "It was there in those first few experimental appearances that I realized his enormous visual attraction and there that the 'smashing routine' really began by accident.

"Jimi was pulled offstage by a few over-enthusiastic fans and as he jumped back on the stage, he threw his guitar on before him. When he picked it up, he saw that it had cracked and several of the strings were broken. He went barmy and smashed everything in sight. The German audience loved it and we decided to keep it in as part of the act when there was a good press about or the occasion demanded it."

What happened next topped this. On March 31, on the first date of a tour with Engelbert Humperdinck and the Walker Brothers, Jimi set his guitar aflame. This too was most deliberate—a gimmick planned to excite both press and audience.

"We were sitting around in the dressing room trying to think of something new to put in the act," Chas told Chris

Welch. "I think it was [pop writer] Keith Altham's idea to set fire to the guitar. Jimi had been doing a number called 'Fire,' and Keith said wouldn't it be great if he could start one. So we sent the roadie out to buy a tin of lighter fuel."

Jimi played the song at the end of his set, which opened the show, and then he put his guitar on the stage near the amplifiers and wandered toward the audience to distract their attention. He talked to them in that familiar spacey style and told them he had a special treat for them while Noel and Mitch kept up a pounding beat.

In the darkness Chas was on his hands and knees spraying the guitar with a thick coat of lighter fluid. Finally he shouted an "All right, mate!" to Jimi, who then dropped to his knees by the guitar and picked up a box of wooden matches.

The first match went out.

So did the second.

And a third.

And a fourth and a fifth and a sixth.

Noel and Mitch kept up their thundering as, backstage, Chas tried to distract the promoter of the tour, Tito Burns.

At last there was a *whoooooooooosh!* of sound and the darkened stage burst into fiery light as flames leaped four feet above the guitar. The audience screamed. Jimi picked up another guitar and joined his sidemen in the finale.

The promoter and the manager of the hall—the Astoria Theatre, in London's Finsbury Park section—converged on Chas immediately as the compere—master of ceremonies—for the show rushed out to extinguish the flames, burning himself in the process. After the smoke had cleared, there was an investigation, but while clearing away the microphones in the area in front of the stage, Noel casually picked up the empty fuel can and packed it away.

"I demand the guitar as evidence!" the theater manager cried afterward. "I demand it!"

[103]

Jimi was holding the blackened guitar in one hand, staring at the man. "You going to buy me a new one?" he asked, smiling. "I have another gig t'morrow, y'know."

"For the rest of the tour they didn't take too kindly to us," Chas says. "John Walker was a bit of a big head and he would waltz into our dressing room and say, 'I don't want any upstaging tonight. Who do you think you are?'

"There was a lot of ill feeling backstage and they would screw up the lights or put the house lights up on the audience during the act. It was quite a tour."

The dates came more quickly after that. Suddenly the Jimi Hendrix Experience was one of the half dozen most in-demand groups in Britain. Night after night Jimi and Noel and Mitch were on the road, traveling from city to city with their road manager, Gerry Stickells, driving a van full of equipment, the three musicians following along in a car that constantly threatened to quit.

They played the Odeon, A.B.C. and Gaumont theater chains, and the prestigious Saville again. Often there were two shows a day. In the entire month they had only three days off. Twice they performed in concert in the hinterlands, then rushed back to London for a television show, appearing on three programs that month, once on *The Simon Dee Show* and twice on *Top of the Pops*.

By now "Hey Joe" had been replaced on the British record charts by Jimi's second single, "Purple Haze" (which went to Number Three). Then in mid-May a third single, another original, "And the Wind Cries Mary," was released, at the same time the first album appeared.

This was an eleven-song package provocatively titled *Are You Experienced?* with the names of the group and album emblazoned in purple letters across a yellow cover. In the center was a round photograph of Jimi and his British sidemen, distorted by the camera and, probably, a lot of LSD. The over-all impression was that of a square, flat Easter egg.

The album did not include "Hey Joe," which was owned by the first label, Polydor, nor did it offer "Purple Haze" and "The Wind Cries Mary," all three of which would go into the American album. But it did include Jimi's extended original blues, "Red House," "Foxy Lady" and another of Jimi's early forays into science-fantasy, "Third Stone from the Sun," a long instrumental.

This last song represented Jimi's fast-developing interest in space travel and the occult. It took its name from the earth's position in the universe and featured a number of sounds like those in a science fiction movie soundtrack: echoing guitar slides, feedback, windlike phasing, and a recording of a rocking subway train (sounding very much like a space shuttle?).

In terms of impact, probably the most important tune was the title song, "Are You Experienced?" This was one of the most explicit in Jimi's repertoire of musical innuendo, a direct call to his audience:

If you can just get your mind together
Then come across to me
We'll hold hands and then we'll watch the sun rise
From the bottom of the sea
But first,
Are you experienced?
Have you ever been experienced?
Well, I have.
I know, I know, you'll probably scream and cry
That your little world won't let you go.
But what in your measly little world are you trying to
    prove
You're made out of gold and can't be sold?
So, uh, are you experienced?
Have you ever been experienced?
Well, I have.
Ohhh, let me prove it to ya!

The over-all impact was tremendous. Here was every threat in rock-and-roll, all wrapped up in the latest peacock finery. A black man with scarves tied around his neck, Edwardian jacket fashioned from upholstery material, hair frizzed out to here! And on either side of this dark man stood two frail white Englishmen, their wardrobe also from Carnaby Street, their hair grown out and curly. It wasn't unprecedented for whites and blacks to play together—the history of jazz was filled with such groups—but until the advent of Hendrix, in recent popular music such mixing was rare, and success was always limited severely by it.

If that weren't enough, the songs and the onstage performance were both overtly sexual. Jimi not only sang about the sexual act, he performed it with his guitar—humping and grinding his skinny hips, waggling his tongue, sticking his guitar neck between his legs, then moving it to and fro vigorously.

The vision was as violent as the sound. As Don Menn in *Guitar Player* magazine noted several years later, "The sounds of a neck shredding or an amp flying apart, of a string popping, writhing, and melting away; of a dismembered pickup amplifying its own unravelling through a shattered speaker were sounds that Jimi did not invent, but nevertheless used to a particular 'musical' degree. They fit in well with his more aggressive, raw finales. Peter Townshend of the Who was doing this before Jimi, and he picked it up in art school. 'Auto-destruction' was an offshoot of 'happenings' staged in the early sixties. They were created by painters who used the everyday world not *for* a canvas, but *as* a canvas when they concocted events such as dropping a piano from a crane, filling the splintered wreck with hay, and then incinerating the whole mess. In the early part of his career, Jimi smashed many guitars, burned a few, and harpooned his speaker cabinets sometimes for show, sometimes out of frustration, and occasionally to create a raucous acoustical effect. It was all part of his trying to get the most from his equipment, and when he could wring no more from it, he'd pound it out."

By May, Jimi was the leading male sex symbol and rock-and-roll threat in all Europe. This did not go unnoticed in America.

News of Jimi's recording success, his Mau-Mau image and his smoking guitars reached the U.S. through the British music press. Every week copies of such publications as *Melody Maker,* the *New Musical Express, Music Week* and *Record Retailer* were air-mailed to hundreds of record company executives, who believed this would keep them in touch with the font of English pop success.

Mainly these were "gee-whiz" tabloids, with lots of photographs and exclamation marks, whose editors and writers were supported by record company advertising in exchange for being allowed to exploit the subjects of those ads in any way they wished so long as the stories weren't overly damaging. Thus these journalists were, in effect, an integral part of the record company promotion effort, just as the writers and editors of movie fan publications served the film industry. The odd thing was that the music (and film) company executives—who should have known better—usually believed what they read in these publications, living out their own hyperbole.

Jimi Hendrix was offered £50,000 ($120,000) for signing over North American record distribution rights to Reprise Records of Burbank, California. Chas Chandler accepted the offer, and on May 20, 1967, the Jimi Hendrix Experience was added to the growing Reprise roster—sight unseen, sound unheard. The move represented a simple but expedient roll of the dice in a business in which making a $120,000 mistake was better than passing up an act that could attract millions later on. Pop music was one of Western culture's most exciting crap shoots in the 1960s, and the man who ran Reprise wanted a piece of the action.

Jimi Hendrix in concert

His name was Mo Ostin and he had come to his position after serving the founder of the company, Frank Sinatra, as a bodyguard. He was also trained as an accountant. And he was, like everyone else at Reprise, so very, very "straight." At the time, no other individual and no other record company could have seemed less suitable—or ready—to experience the Hendrix Experience.

Reprise had just been sold by Sinatra to Warner Brothers Records in a deal that also involved the distribution rights to several Sinatra films. "Reprise was pretty much a failure from its beginning," says Stan Cornyn, today a senior vice-president, then a young writer just out of college who had won a Grammy writing liner notes for a Sinatra album. "And so Warner Brothers Records, which had just gotten into the black ink, was saddled with another turkey named Reprise."

Sinatra's records weren't selling, although he had had a couple of hits in "Strangers in the Night" and "That's Life" the year before. Nancy Sinatra shared her dad's success the same year with "These Boots Are Made for Walkin'," and Frank and Nancy had a Number One song that spring (1967) with "Somethin' Stupid." That made the company sound very successful, but it wasn't. Frank and Nancy were not selling many albums, which was where the big money was. (Singles were beginning to be regarded as a way to sell albums. One hit single could sell many more albums than the single originally did.) Nor were the other artists on the label faring well. Dean Martin had a hit television show, but he wasn't selling singles *or* albums. And Trini Lopez was such a meager success, he went to England to record an album called *Trini in London* in an attempt to revive his sagging career. And—most important—Trini Lopez was about as "far out" as Reprise got.

"In a way," Stan Cornyn says, "it seemed ridiculous to sign Hendrix. Absolutely ridiculous! We didn't know *any-*

thing about the Jimi Hendrix Experience. We didn't know anything about *rock-and-roll!* But Mo was out to change the label's image because he believed that that could save the company. The alternative was to let it become a tax write-off for the parent company, Warner Brothers, which really only wanted distribution rights to Frank's movies. And that would've been the end of Reprise."

Quickly, then, a single was released, the explosive version of "Hey Joe," backed with "51st Anniversary."

CHAPTER

6

June 1967 was not a month, it was a celebration.

May ended with a visit to Sweden, and on June 1 there was a coveted engagement at the enormous Palais des Sports in Paris. Two days later, back in London, Jimi's next single, "The Wind Cries Mary," appeared in the Number Six position in *Melody Maker*'s weekly chart of hits and his album went to Number Three. The day after that the Experience again played the prestigious Saville Theatre, and then they were packing for America.

The reason for Jimi's return to his homeland after eight months of exile was something called the Monterey International Pop Festival. Initially this was conceived by an independently wealthy scene-maker named Alan Pariser. Pariser went to Ben Shapiro, who was at that time established in the hip business ethic of Los Angeles as an agent for Bob Dylan, Peter, Paul and Mary, and Ravi Shankar, among others. The idea was to create in pop music in California what Italy had in its San Remo Festival—a nonprofit "music mart" for the serious and perhaps unappreciated creators and experimenters in the popular music mainstream.

Shapiro liked the idea but thought it should be a profit-making venture. Since he promised he would raise $50,000, and then did so, Pariser went along, hiring Derek Taylor to handle publicity. He had been the Beatles' press officer, and following one of the Beatles' American tours, he had remained in the U.S. to help launch the Byrds and "psychedelicize" the Beach Boys' image. Taylor was known as the Western Hemisphere's only honest publicist—an image he had created for himself—and it was believed his presence would be good for the organization.

Pariser and Taylor visited John and Michelle Phillips, who formed one half of the Mamas and the Papas, and once they, in turn, had met with Paul Simon, they decided to make it a free concert after all. Said Derek Taylor afterward, "What John said he thought, and Simon said 'right' to, was that no one would get any money at all for doing the festival and all the profits would go to charity and wouldn't that be great because all the best respected performers in America would want to do something groovy like that without contaminating themselves with money or lies or deceptions or ego collisions. Just a flower-strewn festival for love."

And so Shapiro was given his $50,000 back, and Simon and his partner, Art Garfunkel, Pariser, and Lou Adler, who was the Mamas and the Papas' manager, each tossed in $5,000 to cover immediate costs. John Phillips and Lou Adler were made co-directors, and an impressive board of governors was named, including Donovan, Mick Jagger, Paul McCartney, Jim McGuinn, Johnny Rivers, Smokey Robinson, Paul Simon and Brian Wilson.

"Entertainers who have starved and become rich are forever haunted by guilt," said Derek Taylor, who was retained as publicist. "Phillips and Adler, Simon, Garfunkel, Andrew Oldham of the Stones, McCartney of the Beatles and all the rest were delighted to have found a way of giving something back to the industry. Their motives were unquestionable; they wanted to be generous, to make a gesture. The spirit around them became unbelievably cheerful and the phones began to ring. Every major pop artist in the world was called. Will you work for the festival? No one said no."

In more cynical times such idealism would have seemed laughable. But this was June 1967, the start of what came to be called "The Summer of Love." That same month the Beatles released their greatest recorded work, *Sergeant Pepper's Lonely Hearts Club Band,* an album of such dazzling brilliance that an entire generation would—at least in part—be defined by it.

At the same time, another city, San Francisco, was exploding with color and new ideas and the sounds of a thousand guitars. A run-down neighborhood that took its name from two of its streets, Haight and Ashbury, was now mecca for a new life style, a new morality. There was real revolution in that air. The discothèque was OUT and the cavernous dance hall was IN. Indirect lighting was replaced with "psychedelic" blends of stroboscopic flashers, liquid color blobs, black light, moires, films and slides. Victorian poster art was reincarnated to advertise dances held by homegrown groups with such names as the Grateful Dead, Quicksilver Messenger Service, the Jefferson Airplane, and Big Brother and the Holding Company. Two former Harvard professors, Timothy Leary and Richard Alpert, announced a new religion, the League for Spiritual Discovery, using LSD as its sacrament. "Turn on, tune in, drop out!" became the catchwords of the time. Even staid old journalism was being altered as the "underground" newspaper blossomed, along with "underground" radio, a maturation in broadcast sound that seemed to come when Top 40 radio didn't grow up with its audience.

Everything was changing. The puddles of projected

light; the smell of sandalwood incense mixing with that of marijuana; body painting; Robert A. Heinlein's *Stranger in a Strange Land* (and grokking); paisley; Winnie the Pooh buttons; a vigorous antiwar movement; guitar amplifiers turned up to ten—it all began to run and flow, becoming an amorphous mass of sight and sound that stretched to the horizon and beyond. And in June there stood at the apogee a proposed gathering of singers and musicians near the California coast, in Monterey.

It was McCartney who suggested the Jimi Hendrix Experience. "The Experience and the Who," he said. "You can't do the festival without them."

So Phillips put a call in to Chas Chandler in London, offering no money for performing but a willingness to pay for airfare and accommodations. With the Mamas and the Papas, the Beach Boys, Simon and Garfunkel, the Byrds, Dionne Warwick and the Who already committed, Chas could not say no.

From all over America more bands came. From Memphis: Otis Redding and Booker T and the M.G.s, including Jimi's old friend from Nashville, Steve Cropper; from Chicago; another old friend, Mike Bloomfield, with his new band, the Electric Flag (and Buddy Miles on drums) and the group he left to form it, the Paul Butterfield Blues Band; from Los Angeles: Canned Heat, the Mamas and the Papas and the Buffalo Springfield; from New York: Laura Nyro and the Blues Project; and from San Francisco: Janis Joplin. Giving the three-day program an international flavor were the world-famous sitarist Ravi Shankar, from India, and the bands from Britain: the Who, Eric Burdon's New Animals and, last, the Jimi Hendrix Experience.

And the audience was, as one writer put it, "totally benevolent." Wearing antique clothing or costumes—cowboys and Indians were numerous—they came "on their best behavior, just to prove love could work, and they succeeded."

There were between 60,000 and 90,000 present, and there wasn't a single unpleasant experience.

However much goodwill there was in the audience, and among the musicians too, competition was lively backstage. This three-day concert (June 16–18) may have been the kickoff party for the Summer of Love, but that didn't mean the performers abandoned their egos. This pull-out-all-the-stops, battle-of-the-bands attitude was especially remarkable on the second day, when, according to Pat Hartley, there was a noisy disagreement in the dressing rooms between representatives of Jimi and the Who. Pat was a friend of both Jimi and Roger Daltrey, the Who's vocalist.

"The argument was that now that we've got the whole fucking world out here to this concert, who's going on first?" Pat recalls. "If the Who go on first, Jimi's going to blow them away, right? And if Jimi goes on first, nobody can follow him. A real show biz argument about excellence. Forget about the rest of it. So they yelled and screamed and carried on for a while, and it was decided that the Who go on first, to the group's eternal regret."

The Who topped all previous performances, closing their set with "My Generation," a hard-rocking, hostile anthem that cried, "People try to put us d-d-down/Just because we g-g-get around/Things they do look awful c-c-cold/Hope I die before I get old!" At the song's conclusion Pete Townshend crunched his guitar to bits, Daltrey was pounding his microphone on the cymbals and smoke bombs were exploding all over the stage.

To a group from San Francisco fell the clean-up chores. The Grateful Dead had agreed to serve as a sort of buffer between the two explosive acts from London, and their set was, in contrast, quite mild. The Dead were the perfect choice, giving the audience a breather while keeping spirits high.

"You know what foldin' chairs are for, don't you?" the

Dead's guitarist asked, referring to the seats in the open amphitheater. "They're for foldin' up and dancin' on!"

For the rest of the Dead's set the audience danced.

Then came Hendrix, introduced by his friend Brian Jones. The first couple of songs failed to do very much, but then Jimi told the audience he was going to play one of Bob Dylan's songs. At the same time, he played the opening chords to "Wild Thing," to keep the audience guessing. Continuing the playful suspense, he jokingly referred to Mitch Mitchell looking like Dylan's grandmother. And then he crashed into "Like a Rolling Stone," and the people were on their feet. For a finale he went right into "Wild Thing."

He was wearing a ruffled orange shirt and red velour pants so tight, as one critic noted, they "outlined his crotch to the thirtieth row." He played his guitar with his teeth and behind his back and between his legs, waggled his "anteater tongue" during the instrumental break, then went over and outrageously humped one of the amplifiers. Finally he turned again to face the audience, dropping to his knees, sitting astride his instrument so that the neck extended like a third leg. For a few moments he caressed the strings. Then he retrieved a can of lighter fluid from behind an amplifier and squirted it over the guitar and set the thing aflame.

The *Los Angeles Times* critic, Pete Johnson, said, "Jimi Hendrix, Mitch Mitchell and Noel Redding were the rage of England in that summer of love and psychedelia, but they had yet to play the United States and thus were no more than a rumor to most of the Monterey crowd. Their appearance at the festival was magical: the way they looked, the way they performed and the way they sounded were light years away from anything anyone had seen before. The Jimi Hendrix Experience owned the future and the audience knew it in an instant. When Jimi left the stage, he had graduated from rumor to legend."

Not everyone was so accepting. Other critics, including

At the Monterey International Pop Festival, June 18, 1967

the quirky but influential Bob Christgau of New York's weekly *Village Voice,* called Jimi an Uncle Tom, a caricature, a modern incarnation of long-dead Negro minstrelsy. And in a review of the film, which was released later, keyboardist Al Kooper cynically observed that Jimi was "well received, leading me to believe that vaudeville is indeed *not* dead . . ."

Still others were embarrassed for other reasons.

"We had never seen Jimi Hendrix before Monterey," says Stan Cornyn, one of the two executives who were representing Jimi's American record label at the festival. "So we went up there with our wives, and me with my thirty-five-millimeter camera, spectating but certainly not indulging in anything. Mo and his wife, Evelyn, and I and my wife, Gail, would walk those marvelous green acres and feel a little bit like Dorothy in the Land of Oz, having a marvelous time

[119]

spectating warmly in a new culture. We did, in fact, see Jimi Hendrix come out and squirt lighter fluid on his guitar. He had a pink boa which he threw about, and I do remember Mo saying how embarrassed he was by the spectacle of it. Because it was not yet what the sincere record company executive would want to bring home to his peers.

"Also, I had the strange feeling of *déjà vu*, because we'd already seen Pete Townshend smash his guitar an hour before. So it was not the hottest, most original thing I'd ever seen. None of us was into the aesthetics of chainsaw psychedelic guitar, either, so it was funny to look at and excruciating to hear. Clearly, Jimi Hendrix was for all of us an acquired taste, and I'm not sure that many ever finally acquired it."

However unimpressed the men from Reprise and the snobbish critics from New York were, backstage all was pandemonium. As Jimi exited the stage, he fell into Brian Jones's arms, then was swallowed up by other performers, groupies and businessmen, all of whom wanted a piece of him.

Hugh Masekela, the jazz trumpeter from Africa, worked his way through the throng. "You killed 'em!" he shouted at Jimi. "You killed 'em!" Nico, who was one of Andy Warhol's actresses, came wafting right behind Masekela to deliver a tonguing kiss.

Mike Jeffery, oddly, was focusing his attention on a broken microphone stand rather than the celebration going on around him.

"This cost sixty quid, you sods!" Finally he was dragged away by the young, portly publicist Michael Goldstein, who said he represented the Cheetah in New York and Frank Zappa's Mothers of Invention. Quickly Goldstein elicited from Mike a promise that he could represent Jimi's group for three months.

At the same time, San Francisco promoter Bill Graham

asked to have Jimi play at his prestigious Fillmore Auditorium.

The next day Jimi was in Los Angeles, staying with Peter Tork, the guitarist for the Monkees, who had cohosted one of the concerts at Monterey. Jimi was staying in Laurel Canyon in the Hollywood Hills, at the center of "new Los Angeles society." Near Peter's house were the homes of old friends Eric Burdon and Buddy Miles and Arthur Lee, along with several new friends from Monterey, including David Crosby, Mama Cass Elliot and the Chambers Brothers.

For the first few days he relaxed, snorting cocaine and smoking grass and drinking wine with friends. Once he visited the odd little offices Reprise Records had on the second floor of what had been the Warner Brothers Pictures machine shop, but no business was conducted.

"He came up and had an extraordinary, weak handshake," Stan Cornyn recalls, "and that shifting kind of voice, and he was always answering questions a little more cosmically than you were prepared for. It was extremely dangerous to ask him, 'How are you?' I don't remember his answer, but it was not something I was prepared to hear. And then he drifted on. Probably wearing something purple and magenta."

"That night," says Buddy Miles, picking up the narrative, "Jimi and myself and Neil Young and David Crosby went to Stephen Stills's place on the [Malibu] beach and jammed for three days."

There was only a single depression in nearly a week of skyrocketing highs. That came when a car in which he was riding—Peter Tork's GTO—was in an accident near Malibu Beach. The ankle Jimi broke in his Screaming Eagle days was injured, but not seriously. Others in the car, including Mike Bloomfield, David Crosby, and Steve Stills, who was driving, were not hurt.

Meanwhile the job offers were stacking up. Peter Tork called Dick Clark, who was promoting an upcoming Monkees tour, and insisted that Jimi go along with them. Elmer Valentine asked Jimi to play at the Whisky a Go Go on the Sunset Strip and Steve Paul called from New York to see if Jimi would work at his new club, the Scene. And the local "underground" newspaper, the Los Angeles *Free Press*, implored him to join an all-star lineup of groups at a free concert and "love-in" in aptly named Elysian Park. Jimi's managers said yes to everyone.

"After his set in the park," says Elmer Valentine, "they announced that Jimi would be in my club that night. I had Sam and Dave playing in the Whiskey and they were stiffing. I asked them if I could put Jimi on with them. The people started lining up. Mario [the club's manager] raised the price from three dollars to five dollars—it didn't matter. The kids came right from the park. Sam and Dave arrived that night, saw the crowd and thought it was for them. When Jimi finished his set, the place cleared out. He burned his guitar, he did the whole thing, and when he left, so did everyone else. *Nobody* stayed for Sam and Dave."

The tour with the Monkees began a few days later, in Jacksonville, Florida, on June 24, and it proved to be a turning point for Jimi in the United States. And to understand why, it is necessary to know who, and what, the Monkees were.

The Monkees story began only a year before, in the summer of 1966, when more than four hundred young men answered an advertisement in one of the Hollywood trade papers announcing tryouts for a new television series that was to resemble the recently popular Beatles film *A Hard Day's Night*. The series became an instant hit, and the Monkees' first two singles, produced by anonymous studio musicians, both went to the Number One spot on *Billboard*'s record charts. By the summer of 1967 their first three albums had done just as well, the group was earning $50,000 a concert and its four members were dominating the "Fab Fax" and "Kissable Klose-Up" pages in all of the fan magazines in the Western world.

On the face of it, the booking seemed a great coup, an opportunity to introduce Jimi to a national audience in the best arenas and stadiums. But there was a catch. The Monkees' audience was prepubescent; Jimi's was far more adult.

It was, then, a classic bit of miscasting. Still, everyone went along—either in innocence, ignorance or hope. Stan Cornyn says somewhat apologetically today that at Reprise Records "in those days anything beyond Dean Martin fell into one category. And the Monkees and Jimi Hendrix were beyond Dean Martin. So nobody at the time in Burbank had any feelings of absurdity in pairing them. After all, they both played loud."

In New York just before it began, Mike Jeffery also gave the tour his most enthusiastic blessing, telling his new publicists, Michael Goldstein and his associates—who had also been hired to represent Eric Burdon's New Animals—and Chas Chandler that it was a "great deal." When Goldstein ventured the opinion that the Monkees had a different audience from Jimi's, Mike said he thought the exposure was important.

"I said it would be a fucking disaster," Chas said later. "But Mike had signed the deal and it was too late. I told the boys I wouldn't go with them on the tour. They went and died the death."

They were given only twenty minutes to open the show, hardly enough time to create their kind of "experience." Worse, that experience wasn't suited for the audience, composed largely of ten- to twelve-year-olds, who were there only to see the made-up Hollywood group rather than the made-up English one. At the first two concerts Jimi was actually booed.

Gloria Stavers was the tall, attractive former model

then editing *16 Magazine*, which had more than a million readers, nearly all of them prepubescent. "*16 Magazine* was 'Monkee City'," Gloria says, "and the Monkees fell in love with Jimi when they met him at Monterey, said if he didn't go on tour with them, there was no tour. There was a girl singer, a blonde from Australia, who was on the tour too, and she was doing a diary of the tour for me. They were in New York, staying at the Warwick Hotel, and she called me and said Jimi was depressed. I went over to the hotel with her, and Jimi was crestfallen. He was smoking joint after joint after joint and he was a heartbroken man. They'd kicked him off the tour."

The aborted tour contract *was* a disappointment for Jimi, but his managers made the best of it, telling the press that Jimi was dropped from the Monkees tour because the Daughters of the American Revolution objected to his erotic performance style. It wasn't true, but it was exactly the sort of story that newspapers liked, so they published it, whether or not they believed it. Even as late as 1967, more than ten years after Elvis shook his hips, the-rock-star-as-bogeyman remained a popular media theme.

"We decided to fan the flames," says Pat Costello, one of the publicists working with Michael Goldstein, "so we wrote irate letters to the Forest Hills Stadium, where Jimi had appeared with the Monkees. We wrote Warner Brothers Records. We wrote the daily newspapers. We tried to think who the general public would write to and we pretended to be parents. You know, 'My daughter attended a Monkees concert last night and something really obscene played first. How dare you!' It was Michael's idea. He went to Jeffery with it and Jeffery made no objection, so we ran with it."

Meanwhile, in New York, Jimi shyly gave his first interviews from his room at the Warwick and in the evenings went from club to club to sit in with old friends. John Hammond remembers that Jimi played with him at the Gaslight in the Village on two nights, bringing Eric Clapton along. Another night Chas held a press party at the Cafe Wha?, where he had "discovered" Jimi exactly one year earlier, and on still another, Jimi and Noel and Mitch went into Steve Paul's Scene and blew a Los Angeles band called the Seeds off the stage.

Jimi also called his old girl friend, Fayne Prigon.

Fayne recalled: "He says, 'Um, I got this really nice album. I got two cats that play with me and everything.' And he, ah, said, 'And I brought you something too.' I said, 'Yeah, well you bring it when you bring the album.' I'm thinkin' he's brought me some fabulous present back from London."

"Jimi," Fayne begged over the telephone, "please tell me what it is."

Jimi laughed and said, "Acid . . . some acid."

Fayne was mystified. "Acid?" she said.

"You know," she stated in the Warner's documentary, "I had no idea what he was talkin' about. I thought maybe he had a cauldron of acid or somethin' he was gonna drop on me. And I looked over to Arthur [Allen, who was also present] and Arthur said, 'LSD.' You know, and I said, 'Oh, LSD.' You know, I was tryin' not to sound too disappointed."

Later that day, when Jimi arrived, he swallowed two of the little tabs and Arthur and Fayne each took a half. As Arthur recalled it, he and Fayne got "tore up," and in Fayne's words, Jimi returned to "normal."

"I knew Jimi could take more of anything than we could, you know what I mean?" Fayne said. "Because he was already abnormal, so whatever he took just brought him back around to normal, then he gotta start from there, you understand? So, like, we knew if he could take, you know, a gallon, we'd better take a pint."

Jimi then visited his former employer, Curtis Knight,

A publicity still that helped to set the Jimi Hendrix image

MICHAEL OCHS

and joined him and some other musicians in a recording studio.

The tape was rolling and the musicians were wailing in the small dark room.

Jimi called out, "You're not gonna release this?"

"No, no, no," Curtis Knight called back over the music. "Just jammin'. Old times. Old times."

There was one scheduled paying show while he was in New York, when he was co-billed with the Young Rascals at the Rheingold Festival in Central Park, an important concert sponsored each summer by a local beer company.

"Jimi didn't blow the Rascals off the stage," Chas conceded later to Chris Welch, "but he was given a tremendous reception. We got seven more dates as a result."

At the same time, Jimi's second American single, "Purple Haze," was selling well, after the first, "Hey Joe," had stiffed. (It was generally agreed that it had been thrown into the marketplace too soon after the Leaves' hit version of the same song.)

Most important, Jimi was the talk of the rock and drug "underground," just as he had been in London. Several of the top clubs in New York had closed their doors for the Monterey Pop Festival so the owners could attend, and when they returned they brought with them reports of Jimi's outrageous sound and style.

Jimi really wasn't doing anything much different from what he was doing a year before in the Village. The size and makeup of his band had changed, but the powerful guitar playing was the same, and so were the visual tricks. Nonetheless *he* was far different now. A year before in New York he was hungry and searching for a break. Now great success was upon him and stardom was imminent.

Jimi also *looked* far different from the way he had appeared a year before. His old friend Mike Quashie was still doing the limbo and singing calypso songs at midtown

Manhattan's African Room. He remembers when Jimi came in for a visit.

"I hadn't thought about Jimmy James at all," he says, "and then one night I spotted this dude at the bar with a big basketball-sized Afro. Last time I saw him he was wearing his Vaseline conk. Well, I didn't recognize him at first, but when I left the stage I did and said, 'Jimmy?' "

Jimi flashed Mike his familiar big-toothed grin and said, "Yes?"

"Wooooooooeeeee!" Mike cried. "What you do to yousef? You a rill nigger now!"

CHAPTER

7

For Jimi it was a time of great excitement but also great tension, and he was drinking heavily and consuming more and more drugs. Chas Chandler noticed it. "At first," he said, "he never drank much—three whiskies and he was happy." But now there were signs of strain, and Chas watched the alcohol intake accelerate.

One reason, of course, was the sudden success. With increased acceptance and acclaim came celebration and the pressures of stardom—both good excuses to drink or take drugs. Also important was the confusion Jimi felt about the immediate turn his career was taking. He had been away from the United States for a year, had been back only two months, and now he was told he was to leave again, to return to London for a tour of Europe. On the eve of his album's release in the U.S., it didn't make much sense. If he returned to London, how could he promote *Are You Experienced?* How could he do interviews and tour the U.S., steps that in the 1960s were thought necessary to sell records?

It was true that Jimi had been introduced properly—at Monterey—and despite the aborted Monkees tour, he had played some of the country's first-line clubs, from the Whisky a Go Go in Los Angeles and the Fillmore in San Francisco to the Scene and Central Park in New York. With a minimum of dates, Jimi's stardom in the U.S. had taken off like a rocket. But there was a significant catch: the album wasn't in the stores. And by the time it was, in late August, Jimi wasn't in the U.S.

Jimi's second single, "Purple Haze," and his album, *Are You Experienced?*, both appeared for the first time on *Billboard* magazine's record charts on August 26. Ideally, that would have been the date to start a national tour. But on August 27 the Jimi Hendrix Experience was thousands of miles away, moving its equipment into London's Saville Theatre. In America success would have to take care of itself—with only the assistance of a publicist who didn't have a group to be photographed or interviewed, and a record company that still was more than a little embarrassed about the whole thing.

It is easy to say this happened through bad management. In fact, Chas Chandler talks today of fighting with his partner Mike Jeffery over the decision to blame the disastrous Monkees tour on the archconservative DAR. "He said I was a stupid idiot and shot off to Majorca for seven months," Chas says. And although the American agent Frank Barsalona held an option for a national tour, Chas says Mike had signed with another agency. "I went through a four-month period trying to undo all the fuck-ups."

Even so, returning to England did make *some* sense. After all, in many ways the Jimi Hendrix Experience was a British act. Although its dynamic guitarist was an American, few thought of him as such. He was a relative unknown in the U.S. when he arrived for the Monterey concert, but a star in Europe. Dressed in the latest Carnaby Street clothing, introduced at Monterey by a Rolling Stone, flanked on both sides of the stage by British musicians and surrounded by managers with British accents, how could anyone have thought of Jimi as anything *but* British?

Consequently only *Jimi* was "home" in the U.S., and the others around him were homesick. So back to Blighty they flew—Chas to "undo all the fuck-ups," the others to a series of well-scattered performances and to demands from their English record company to produce another album.

It started badly. Jimi and Noel and Mitch had just left the Saville Theatre stage, on August 27, to thunderous welcome-home applause, when they were told in their dressing room that Brian Epstein, who had promoted the show but was better known as the Beatles' manager, was dead of an overdose of barbiturates. The second show was canceled.

A week later, on September 3 and 4, Jimi performed in Gothenburg and Stockholm, Sweden, and the audience seemed unmoved. A tape recording of the show in Gothenburg reveals unemotional applause, a couple of whistles and one cheer.

And then it turned around.

Returning once more to London, Chas took the three musicians into a studio to begin work on what was to become, according to Jim Miller in *Rolling Stone,* rock-and-roll's "finest voodoo album." This was *Axis: Bold as Love,* a dozen spacey song poems accompanied by high-volume "psychedelic guitar" and wrapped in an album cover that closely resembled one of those illustrations in a book by the Swami Bakdavedanta: Indian women in saris bearing scimitars, elephants wearing jeweled crowns, hissing cobras, transcendental wise men with long tongues, and in the middle of it all a twenty-armed Jimi Hendrix Experience looking exactly like a piece of Indian statuary.

It was self-indulgent, just as the Beatles album earlier that year, *Sgt. Pepper,* had been. It opened with the voice of Chas Chandler, increased electronically to double speed. Chandler portrayed an announcer on Radio Station EXP. "Tonight," he said, "we are featuring an interview with a very peculiar-looking gentleman who goes by the name of Mr. Paul Corusoe, on the dodgy subject of are there or are there not flying saucers or . . . ahem . . . UFO's. Please Mr. Corusoe, please could you give your regarded opinion on this nonsense about spaceships and even space people?"

To which Jimi, playing Mr. Corusoe, replied, "Thank you. As you all know, you just can't believe everything you see and hear, can you? Now, if you will excuse me, I must be on my way."

At this point the announcer began spluttering and finally got out the words, "I don't believe it!," just as Jimi flew into his electric guitar. There followed nearly two minutes of raucous feedback, electronic whining and unidentifiable noise effects, serving as an introduction to the first song, which casts Jimi in the role of an extraterrestrial space traveler who is astounded by and unable to comprehend the stench of a planet that seems to be burning.

The songs themselves were a varied lot. "Little Wing" was a love song, written for Devon Wilson. ("When I'm sad, she comes to me/With a thousand smiles she gives to me free/It's alright, she says it's alright/Take anything you want from me.") Another, "Spanish Castle Magic," was updated 1950s rhythm-and-blues. "If 6 Was 9" was a topical hippie song. ("White-collared conservative flashing down the street/Pointing their plastic finger at me/They're hoping soon my kind will drop and die/But I'm gonna wave my freak flag high, high.") "Castles Made of Sand" was a fatalistic lament about broken relationships.

The most complicated composition was the title song, "Axis: Bold as Love." Jimi knew that the earth revolved on an axis and had come to think that a recording spins on a turntable in much the same way. Thus he could make the jump from planetary balance to a tranquillity born of music, which was his eternal, burning love. "I'm as bold as love," Jimi sang. "Just ask the Axis, he knows everything."

When he was asked about the title, *Axis: Bold as Love*, he concisely explained the images that attracted him and the image he wished to project:

"I just thought about the title. There might be a meaning behind the whole thing. The axis on the earth turns around and changes the face of the world and completely different civilizations come about or another age comes about. In other words, it changes the face of the earth and it only takes about one-fourth of a day. Well, the same with love. If a cat falls in love or a girl falls in love, it might change his whole complete scene: *Axis: Bold as Love*. One-two-three, rock around the clock."

What Jimi had done was significant musically. The principal stylistic features of black soul music—the characteristic vocal and instrumental phrases, typical rhythms and so on—remained, but Jimi's lyrics were basically "white." And with a decreased emphasis on the vocals—Jimi was still insecure about his voice—came reliance on amplification, distortion and what Jim Miller described as "the refinement of white noise into psychedelia."

"The result," wrote Richard Middleton in *Pop Music and the Blues*, "is that the balance of the Soul synthesis is destroyed. Mind is dulled, thought paralyzed, individual consciousness all but demolished. One does not listen to details, feeling that to let one's consciousness go is more important."

The actual studio creation of this mind trip was not easy. From the way the participants describe the recording of *Axis: Bold as Love*, the construction of the pyramids in Egypt was simpler.

Noel Redding remembers the sessions at the Olympic Studios as exercises in great frustration. "We didn't rehearse," he told Chris Welch. "We'd go in and learn a song. Jimi would tell us what he needed. We'd do about four bass tracks, then drums and vocals and rhythm guitar, and when it got to the thirty-sixth guitar overdub, I would lay down in the studio and go to sleep."

What Chas recalls is worse. "Eric Burdon was on his big acid scene then," he says, "but Jimi would just say, 'Oh, he's an acid freak' and put that whole scene down. It wasn't until the time of the second album that I realized he had in fact been taking it. He'd split for a couple of days, and I realized he was on acid. At that time everybody thought it would sort out their problems. I took it eight times and was spaced out for eighteen months. Halfway through *Axis: Bold as Love* he was dropping it every day. I told him he'd have to be straight some of the time. At first I thought it would give him a new slant to his lyrics, but he'd lose his temper.

"There were so many people hanging around him, he couldn't be himself. We had an argument about it and he said, 'Okay, no more.' Then someone would turn up at the studio with a bag of goodies and pour some more down his throat."

Between recording dates Jimi and Noel and Mitch performed in some of the best places in Britain, including the Royal Albert and Festival halls, the Saville again (with Arthur Brown), and the Marquee Club; also in the Olympia Theatre in Paris and in a dozen clubs and ballrooms in outlying English towns. At first they performed only on weekends, then when the album was ready for shipment, in November, the concerts came at the rate of four to six a week, moving the group all over the British map—from Sussex University in Brighton, in the south of England, to the Empire Theatre in the Beatles' hometown, Liverpool; from the Guildhall in Portsmouth to Sophia Gardens in Cardiff, Wales. On November 27, Jimi's twenty-fifth birthday, the week the album was released, they were in Belfast, Ireland.

[134]

Jimi celebrated by getting drunk and swallowing a cap of LSD.

At the same time that Jimi was touring Britain and the Continent, some of his money was beginning to flow into a mysterious bank account in the Bahamas, the West Indian British colony known for its warm climate and beautiful beaches. Officially, tourism was claimed as the major modern industry, but the dozens of banks in the capital city of Nassau serving as tax havens for foreign investors probably attracted much more cash.

One of these havens was the Yameta Company Ltd., a fictitious company formed by Mike Jeffery through his London attorney for the purpose of finding and developing and recording musical talent. The idea was that although Jeffery would actually work with the talent, Yameta would be paid for the same services. In this way Jeffery could pay Yameta huge sums for these services and declare those sums as deductible business expenses, and then, because he also—secretly—owned the company he paid, he could fly to Nassau, withdraw the money from the Bank of Nova Scotia, where he kept the account, and put it in his pocket, tax-free.

Many other bands tried the same dodge, including the Beatles, who diverted the proceeds from their film *Help!* into a Bahamian company. Unfortunately that money was banked entirely in sterling, and when the pound was devalued in 1967, the Beatles and their tax-haven partner lost $200,000.

It started in 1965 with a $50,000 check from the Animals' American record label, MGM, and was designed to sidestep the exorbitant British income tax Jeffery would have had to pay on his American earnings. Jeffery told his clients, first Eric Burdon and the Animals and then Jimi, Noel and Mitch, that their money would be safe in the Yameta account, where it would gather interest until they were old, retired or needed it. Jimi took Jeffery at his word, although it was never made clear how the guitarist, as an American citizen, could benefit from a British tax haven.

Years after Jimi was dead, lawyers trying to unravel the mystery said "at least a million dollars" went into the account, but the musicians never saw a penny. In fact, the Yameta account was said to be empty at the time of Jimi's death. If this was true, where did the money go? American attorneys representing Jimi's estate decided not to investigate. Realizing that the legal battle would have to be fought in Britain, they believed that even if any blame could be placed, there would not be any money to collect, and the estate would be out the cost of the fight.

But a personable, fast-talking attorney in Beverly Hills, Mickey Shapiro, did ask those questions. In 1974 he went to call on Sir Guy Henderson, the tall, thin, aristocratic former chief justice of the Bahamian Supreme Court who was Yameta's lawyer in the Bahamas and who was a member of Yameta's board of directors. When the meeting was over, Shapiro had a carton of documents that speak for themselves. Fifty-three were statements from the Bank of Nova Scotia, showing a wildly fluctuating and rather suspicious balance. In addition, there were canceled checks, minutes of Yameta board meetings, memos and correspondence. One of these letters, dated in January 1968, was from the New York accounting firm of Price Waterhouse, esteemed for its participation in counting ballots for the Academy Awards. Even Price Waterhouse seemed confused, concluding its examination with a barrage of questions. Whenever Mickey Shapiro pressed Sir Guy to explain any of these transactions, the former chief justice replied that he was merely following instructions.

In January 1968 Jimi was unaware of all this, focusing his attention on and apparently feeling the effects of his rapidly accelerating success. This was made quite clear the first week of the year, when, on January 2, he was named the

Number One musician in *Melody Maker* and *Disc and Music Echo* polls and two days later was arrested in Gothenburg, Sweden.

Later Jimi wrote about the ordeal in a song called "My Friend." In it he sounded hurt and bitter. "Y'all pass me that bottle and I'll sing you all a real song," he said, to the background of a bluesy harmonica. And then: "Well, I just got out of a Scandinavian jail/And I'm on my way straight home to you . . ." But, Jimi cried, the one he was on his way home to was just like those growing numbers around him who were looking for a handout and giving him no support. "You know good and well I don't drink coffee," he sang, "so you fill my cup full of sand . . . I'm findin' out its not so easy . . . it gets very lonely out this road . . ."

Jimi began drinking early in the day. Friends say it was deliberate, say he was drinking to get drunk. Reports of what happened vary greatly. Some say Jimi began arguing with Noel. "I asked him what happened," Chas says, "but he didn't know himself and I never really got the full story. But I think Noel hit Jimi and Jimi laid out two cops and tried to jump out of the window."

Others said Jimi got drunk and began playing the drums in his room at the Opelan Hotel. This apparently was followed by screaming and the sound of smashing mirrors and breaking furniture. A newspaper report quoted Gothenburg police as saying they arrested Jimi "after three of his colleagues sat on him to calm him down."

Whatever happened, Jimi was taken to jail, where he spent the night, charged with drunkenness. Photographs of Jimi, wearing a black hat and a thigh-length sheepskin coat draped over his shoulders and flanked by two uniformed policemen, appeared in newspapers around the world the next day. And on January 12, following uneventful concerts in Copenhagen and Stockholm, Jimi appeared in Gothenburg court, where he agreed to pay for damages to the hotel

Jimi in Stockholm after being arrested for drunkenness

room and was fined an amount equal to all his Swedish earnings.

Back in the United States, in his absence, Jimi was becoming a superstar.

Although the most recent singles released in America, "Purple Haze" and "Foxy Lady," had gone only to Nos. 65 and 67, respectively, on the best-seller charts—compared to England, where Jimi's first three singles all went into the Top 10—the first album in the U.S. was a solid smash. The American record market was changing. A maturing audience, increased affluence and the growth of album-oriented radio—stations that played album tracks rather than singles—had caused long-play records to sell in much greater number. By 1968, for example, only a few San Francisco bands, such as the Jefferson Airplane, with "White Rabbit" and "Somebody to Love," had hit singles, but dozens were approaching superstardom on the basis of concert appearances and album sales alone. The Jimi Hendrix Experience was enjoying the same success.

What made this more remarkable was the fact that Jimi was in Europe all during the crucial period when the album *Are You Experienced?* achieved its greatest acceptance, going to the Number Five position in *Billboard* and attracting important critical attention.

Jon Landau, *Rolling Stone*'s top-ranked critic, who would later produce and manage Bruce Springsteen, referred to the "poor quality of the songs" and the "inanity of the lyrics" and said the album was "unrelentingly violent, and lyrically, inartistically violent at that. Dig it if you can, but as for me, I'd rather hear Jimi play the blues."

On the surface it seemed a devastating review. But it was not. Landau also called Jimi a "great guitarist and a brilliant arranger" and said of the album that it "made a tremendous technical advance in the use of three instruments. The superfluous has been eliminated, the tightness of the arrangements is total, the ornament and the background-foreground concept have been limited, if not eliminated, and the level of individual virtuosity is extraordinarily high."

Other influential publications chimed in. Tom Phillips wrote in *The New York Times* that Jimi's stage act would "make a sailor blush." He said the album cover reinforced "the degeneracy theme," and he described the trio as looking like "surrealistic hermaphrodites." Therefore, he said, "it comes as a real surprise to find that the disk is a serious nightmare show, with genuine lust and misery and also a highly successful blending of simple folk-blues forms with advanced electronic sound effects.

"There are plenty of good cuts on this disk, ranging from the straight hard rock of 'Fire' to the eerie futurism of 'Third Stone from the Sun.' The sound is robust and hellish and tightly controlled; and Hendrix, who writes the lyrics, knows what he is writing about."

There were other signs of Jimi's success besides reviews and royalties. One was the increasing number of opportunists now circling the Experience. The most notable of these were Curtis Knight and Ed Chalpin, who had signed Jimi to a recording contract when he was a sideman for Knight in 1965. Soon after Jimi's first album began selling for Reprise, Chalpin sold thirty tracks to Capitol Records, which rushed an album of its own to the marketplace, releasing it in November.

However much legal right Chalpin, Knight and Capitol had to market this early Hendrix product, the manner in which it was done was offensive. The record was not representative of what Jimi was doing in 1967 and was an embarrassment to him as a musician. Moreover, while it did show the early elements of the style he later developed, it was so badly recorded as to be of little historical value. Just

[140]

how badly was borne out by the fact that the album's Capitol producer, Nick Venet, publicly admitted he found only eight of the thirty tracks salvageable, and even those had to be remixed.

Most offensive of all was the packaging. Although the material was for the most part more than two years old, the picture used on the cover was taken at Monterey and the album was called *Get That Feeling: Jimi Hendrix Plays, Curtis Knight Sings,* indicating strongly that Jimi played a much grander musical role than he actually did.

Warner-Reprise threatened legal action, arguing that the album would hurt sales of their own record and Jimi's growing reputation. Capitol was unmoved. "We need not discuss our business with anyone," said one top executive.

Clearly it was time for Jimi to return to America.

CHAPTER

8

Now Jimi's career was being planned more carefully, efficiently, wisely. It remained a provable fact that record sales rose following personal appearances, and Chas and Mike were determined not to repeat the mistake of the previous year, when Jimi left the country on the eve of an album's release.

Chas and Mike also planned a total media blitz, with interviews everywhere that Jimi went and a concentrated effort from his London and New York publicists to get him into every magazine and newspaper on the European and North American continents.

In Britain, Chas and Mike were using the dapper, middle-aged Leslie Perrin, who kept his offices on tony Oxford Street. His prose was out of step for the time, but his client list was impressive, including many other top British rock bands, among them the Rolling Stones.

"Jimi Hendrix has put the fizz back into show biz with his way-out brand of explosive showmanship," Perrin wrote. "No one sleeps when the Jimi Hendrix Experience is on and no one wants to."

Jimi, with Mitch and Noel in the background

[144]

Attached to the release was the typical personality "fact sheet," revealing Jimi's hobbies ("reading science fiction, painting landscapes, daydreaming, music"), favorite foods ("strawberry shortcake, spaghetti"), his dislikes ("marmalade, cold sheets") and professional ambition ("to be a movie star and caress the screen with my shining light"). Jimi was also misidentified as "James Maurice Hendrix," and it was noted that his birthdate was in 1945, which made him three years younger than he really was.

A copy of this release was sent to his American publicist, Michael Goldstein, and to his record company in California, where it was reproduced with somewhat out-of-focus photographs of the trio and sent to everyone on a dozen mailing lists, from radio disc jockeys to the editors of *Life* and *Vogue*.

The conservative executives at Reprise Records had changed their tune. Sales figures were available for his early records, and although the first single had bombed and the second, "Purple Haze," hadn't gone high on the charts, it still sold over 100,000 units, as did the follow-up single, "Foxy Lady."

At the same time, the first album, *Are You Experienced?*, was still a top seller a year after its release. It remained on the charts for two years, eventually selling more than 2.2 million copies. And with advance orders for the second LP, *Axis: Bold as Love,* climbing in advance of the upcoming tour, it seemed that record would sell equally well.

Said Mo Ostin, then head of Reprise and currently chairman of the board of Warner Brothers Records, "When we saw the numbers those records could sell, we said, 'There's something going on here.' We could struggle with a middle-of-the-road artist to sell maybe three hundred thousand albums. We could sell *two million* Jimi Hendrix albums! Frank Sinatra and Dean Martin never sold two million albums!"

When Mo had seen Jimi at Monterey, Mo's face had been ashen. Now his cheeks were flushed again as profits soared.

Thirty English musicians and one black American guitarist trooped through London's Heathrow International Airport with an entourage of almost one hundred managers, girl friends and equipment handlers, looking much like an army of gypsies—all hair and silk and velvet, hung with fringe, feathers and beads. Eric Burdon took an aisle seat, surrounded by the other New Animals. Elsewhere in the big BOAC jetliner were musicians in groups called the Nova Express and Soft Machine. Peering out a window was one of the original Animals, Alan Price, a highly respected keyboardist who now had a group of his own.

Jimi sat next to another window, resplendent in black bell-bottom pants and black boots and a full-length black cape lined with sky-blue silk and embroidered on the back with two doves in flight. On his head he wore a favored black bolero hat adorned with a purple plume. Jimi had dropped some acid before boarding, and once in the air, he aimed an 8-mm movie camera out of the window, filming the fluffy clouds below.

Jimi had no notion how big he was. It was true that in Europe he was a superstar, but in America? When he had left New York nearly six months before, in August, his career there had just begun to accelerate. He had no way of knowing how fast. Nor had he any way of knowing how anxiously he was awaited until he walked onto the Fillmore Auditorium stage in San Francisco on February 1.

Two great guitar bands preceded him—first the blues of Albert King, whose quiet, unhurried style of bending notes had done so much to influence hundreds of guitarists, including Jimi. He was followed by John Mayall, a British musician whose band, the Bluesbreakers, over the years included such sidemen as Eric Clapton, Mick Taylor (who

[146]

would replace Brian Jones in the Rolling Stones), and Peter Green, Mick Fleetwood and John McVie, founders of Fleetwood Mac. Both bands were received with respectful but subdued applause because this was a Hendrix audience and this was his first night in America performing as the headline act.

There was a hush in the big old ballroom as the equipment was moved into place. Hundreds of young faces—many of them painted—were pushed up near the tall stage, peering into the darkness, psychedelics exploding in their brains, creating individual light shows to rival the one that filled the giant screen behind the 12 stacks of Marshall amps with 48 speaker cabinets.

The room went dark as two thousand modern-day Indians and gypsies shuffled and murmured expectantly, bloodshot and dilated eyes held open in wondrous love. The crowd pressed forward as Jimi, Noel and Mitch took their places in silence.

A low hum was heard.

And then a subtle whine.

Building slowly. A single note from the cosmos, stretched and getting louder. Climbing, scaling, screaming now. Then falling into a rumbling, ear-popping crash: the sound of football-field-sized sheets of steel falling from the tops of cliffs.

The lights came on, revealing Jimi in his black and sky-blue cape, his white Stratocaster guitar held like a machine gun or, perhaps, a penis.

"Comin' to *gitcha,* baby!"

And then the crowd began to dance.

The next day Jimi met with the young editor of *Rolling Stone*, Jann Wenner, and the photographer Baron Wolman, giving them enough material for a flattering two-page spread in what was becoming the only national "underground" newspaper.

In the interview Jimi tried to explain what he felt when

A 1968 Bill Graham advertisement for Jimi's concerts at the Fillmore and Winterland theaters in San Francisco

he played, always difficult even for the most articulate musicians. It was, he said, "not depression, but that loneliness and that frustration and the yearning for something. Like something is reaching out." It was as close as Jimi would ever come to describing the blues.

And then it was back on the road again—to Arizona State University, where he performed for 20,000, and into the Anaheim Convention Hall, near Disneyland, where a critic for one of the Hollywood show business trade papers panned him for not playing the guitar with his teeth or setting the guitar afire.

If it bothered the critic for the Hollywood *Reporter*, it bothered Jimi more. Not that he minded the bad review. Not at all. He minded being expected to perform tricks instead of music.

"They want me to be a monkey on the stage," he told his friends.

It was an old conflict, one that is experienced commonly in the entertainment industry. It was the conflict between image and reality. For example, Raquel Welch is expected to be a sexpot offscreen as well as on, when in reality she is quite modest. Because of John Wayne's, Clint Eastwood's and Humphrey Bogart's images as movie tough guys, they were often plagued by men who picked fights to prove something to their girl friends.

Changing the public image to more closely match the private one is always a risky thing. When Marilyn Monroe announced she wanted to play Grushenka in *The Brothers Karamazov*, the media scoffed and the public tittered.

It was happening in rock-and-roll too. By the time Jimi began his first big American tour he wished he'd never heard about pouring lighter fluid on electric guitars, Elvis Presley was insisting he could make movies without any songs in them, and the Doors' lead singer, Jim Morrison, who was known widely as "The Lizard King," was declaring himself a poet. The audience got nervous.

There is an old show business maxim that says the performer should give the audience what it wants. There is another that says the performer should leave that audience wanting more.

Almost a full year earlier, one of Jimi's fellow musicians, guitarist Jeff Beck of the Yardbirds, warned of this problem. In the British music weekly *New Musical Express*, on May 26, 1967, Beck said: "Jimi's only trouble will come about when he wants to get off the nail he has hung himself on. The public will want something different, and Jimi has so established himself in one bag that he'll find it difficult to get anyone to accept him in another."

On February 11, two days after his concert in Anaheim, Jimi was in Seattle, his first visit there since leaving for the paratroopers five years before. He was greeted at the Seattle airport by his brother Leon, his father and Al's new wife, a Japanese woman named Ayako, and her young daughter, Janie, then was taken to his father's small home for a quiet press reception. Jimi retired to a corner of the living room with Leon and a couple of Leon's friends while Al drank beer and answered questions from Seattle reporters.

The next night Jimi and Noel and Mitch performed at the Seattle Center Arena. "There were maybe eight thousand or nine thousand there," Leon says. "Most of them looked like businessmen, and they didn't seem to get it. There were a lot of black people, and they weren't into that kind of show, that kind of music."

Jimi was not pleased. His father says Jimi was excited to be home again, but if that was true initially, the excitement quickly died. It was at that concert that Jimi told Seattle what he thought of it: "I hate you, Seattle! I hate you, Seattle! I hate you, Seattle!"

While playing the guitar with his teeth.

Jimi's mood got blacker the following day when he was driven to Garfield High School to receive an honorary diploma. The principal made a speech. Then the most popular radio personality of the Pacific Northwest, Pat O'Day, offered some flattering remarks about Seattle's prodigal son. Finally Jimi stepped to the microphone.

He seemed embarrassed. "I'm, uh, uh, glad to be here," he said. "It's, uh, really, uh, good to be here. Really."

For a moment he stared blankly at the auditorium full of students, remembering how painful his own days there had been. He felt no different now.

The students stared back at him.

"Uh . . . uh . . . are there . . . ," Jimi asked, "are there any questions?"

There was a long silence.

"Uh, there must be somebody," Jimi said.

A student called out, "How long have you been away from Seattle?"

Jimi thought for a while and finally answered, "Oh, for about five thousand years!"

And then he turned and walked offstage. The assembly was quickly dismissed.

Jimi never did collect his diploma.

Elsewhere in America Jimi was embraced.

On February 10 *Axis: Bold as Love* entered the *Billboard* album chart and within two weeks it was in the Top 20. There were sold-out concerts at the Whisky a Go Go and Shrine Auditorium in Los Angeles and at the coliseum in Dallas, where Chas and Mike expected to make about $7,000 and walked away with almost four times that much.

However rewarding and reassuring the record sales, applause and gate receipts, in rock-and-roll there is another barometer of success more accurate and immediately enjoyable—to most male performers, anyway—and this is the number of female fans who offer their bodies in tribute. In the 1960s these individuals were called "groupies," for the musical groups they followed. It is safe to say that in the late winter and early spring of 1968 Jimi was the Number One groupie catch.

"The groupie scene developed around Jimi so quickly," says Pat Costello, who was still helping Michael Goldstein with the U.S. publicity, "because he satisfied so many fantasies."

Never was this more evident than when on a cold and windy night in Chicago, February 27, two young groupies waited for Jimi outside the Chicago Opera House, then followed him to his hotel between shows and enthusiastically introduced themselves.

"Hi, we're the Plaster Casters," the older one said, "and we're here to make a plaster cast of your rig."

"Rig" was British slang for penis, and the girls knew that Jimi knew that. He stopped near the hotel elevators and smiled down at the girls.

"My *rig?*" Jimi laughed.

"Well, yes, if you don't mind."

The older girl, Cynthia, twenty-one, nodded to her companion, Diane, who was seventeen and the daughter of a policeman. Diane was carrying a black attaché case with PLASTER CASTERS OF CHICAGO lettered in tape on the outside.

"We have all the equipment here. It won't hurt and it'll only take a few minutes of your time."

"You want to make a plaster cast of my cock?" Jimi asked. "Like a statue? A plaster statue?"

The girls bobbed their heads.

Jimi laughed again. "How you gone do that, darlin'?"

The older girl actually blushed when she said, "Well, the first thing we have to do is get your rig hard."

Jimi roared with laughter now and said, "Right on! Come on up to the room."

Upstairs in his suite Jimi quickly peeled off his skin-tight bolero pants as the two young girls began setting up their equipment. The first step was to mix warm tap water

The Plaster Casters with their handiwork

with a powdered alginate, the material used to make molds for dental work. This gummy substance was then put into a large flower vase and Jimi was told to get ready.

One of the girls now covered Jimi's erect "rig" with Vaseline so he wouldn't get stuck in the alginate, and he was told to plunge into the vase. A few minutes later the vase was removed, leaving a perfect mold. The next day plaster was poured into this mold, creating an exact replica of the outsized Hendrix "rig."

The girls wrote in their diary: "We need a ratio of 28:28 [a much larger than normal amount of mix] and found this just barely sufficient. He has got just about the biggest rig I've ever seen! We had to plunge him through the entire deptn of the vase. In view of these dodgy precedents, we got a BEAUTIFUL mold. He even kept his hard for the entire minute. He got stuck, however, for about 15 minutes (his hair did), but he was an excellent sport—didn't panic ... he actually enjoyed it and balled the impression after it had set. In fact, I believe the reason we couldn't get his rig out was that it wouldn't GET SOFT! We rubbed a little warm water around the top of his balls and eventually it slipped out."

This was not a trivial event.

In that room in the Conrad Hilton Hotel rock history was made.

At precisely the time when Jimi met Diane and Cynthia, two "underground" publications assigned writers to the "groupie" phenomenon. Soon afterward *Rolling Stone* devoted an entire issue to the subject, giving two pages to the Plaster Casters, while the *Realist* (whose editor, Paul Krassner, had ghostwritten Lenny Bruce's autobiography, *How to Talk Dirty and Influence People*) devoted its cover story to the girls exclusively. Both stories were illustrated with photographs of the girls and of their handiwork.

These publications had a limited but influential national readership, and quickly the word went out. Soon "aboveground" publications, including *Newsweek*, were assigning reporters to the groupie story, and the Plaster Casters were always mentioned. In this fashion the story of the creation of Jimi's plaster "rig" was making the media rounds.

Larry Dietz, then the editor of *Cheetah* magazine, recalls that he was invited to a small gathering of music and publishing people. The hostess of the party was Ellen Sander, who wrote about rock music for the *Saturday Review* and who had the Plaster Casters' casts on display for the occasion.

"The men all looked at the casts when they came in," Larry says, "then they retreated as far from them as they could get. There were six or eight of the casts, most of them

[154]

rather small and shrunken. That is, they seemed so because of Hendrix's, which was eight or nine inches long and really big around. I went over at one point and actually touched it. There was absolute silence in the room. I mean, it was impressive—although I wouldn't have wanted it visited upon my teenaged sister. One man at the party actually bolted from the room in embarrassment—and he was the president of a record company. What could have been a great two-hour cocktail party turned out to be fifty minutes of awkwardness."

There was no escaping it now. With such documentary evidence gaining such widespread exposure, it was as if a century or more of Caucasian fear about the size of Negro genitalia was being irrefutably confirmed. From this time forward in editorial offices from coast to coast Jimi Hendrix was superstud.

The media never let go of Jimi. Writers began to fall all over themselves trying to describe what they thought they saw at his concerts. On February 22 a writer in Dallas called Jimi a "wild man," and three days later in *The New York Times* Mike Jahn called him "the black Elvis Presley." When Jimi reached New York for a concert at Hunter College on the twenty-ninth, a reporter from *Life* was researching a story (for a March issue) in which he would describe Jimi as the "most spectacular electric guitarist in the world," and another, from *Time* magazine, was preparing a piece that would be headlined (in April) WILD, WOOLEY & WICKED. In *Eye* magazine, a new *Life*-sized slick color publication aimed at the growing pop audience, Jimi's performance was called "pyschedelic vaudeville."

Describing a concert in Cleveland, *Time*'s reporter wrote: "Shouting, 'Stoned! Stoned!' his listeners surged forward, clawing at the kicking feet of the policemen who ringed the footlights. After the performance, they shredded curtains, ripped doors off their hinges and generally wreaked the worst havoc on the Music Hall since it was battered three years ago by the Beatles."

Meantime, in London, the High Court ordered Decca Records in England not to release the controversial Jimi Hendrix/Curtis Knight *Get That Feeling* album. A lawsuit brought by Jimi's American label pointed out that Jimi was merely a member of the group backing Curtis at the session when the album was cut, but that the record jacket gave the impression that Jimi was the leader.

In the U.S., Jimi's managers were not so successful when the same month a New York district court judge refused to grant an injunction that would have restrained Capitol Records from selling or distributing the same album. The judge did order Capitol to change the jacket design, but that was small compensation. Because of Jimi's popularity, *Get That Feeling* sold nearly 100,000 copies, and Jimi didn't get a penny of the earnings.

And that wasn't the end of it. Knight and his friend Ed Chalpin still had a piece of paper claiming Jimi was Chalpin's until 1970. So they took the New York court decision as a green light to produce and distribute as many *more* records as they wanted to produce, all drawn from the early tapes. Eventually they released twenty albums with titles like *Jimi Hendrix 'Live'* and *The Great Jimi Hendrix in New York*. A number of the individual tracks were excellent. The albums as a whole were not. Jimi hated them, hated being ripped off.

The albums were from "bits of tape they used from a jam session," Jimi told *Rolling Stone*. "Bits of tape. Tiny little confetti bits of tape. Capitol [Records] never told us that they were going to release that crap!"

New York City was splendid in the spring.

Artist Peter Max was spreading his pop art stars and rainbows everywhere you looked. Poet Allen Ginsberg was thumping the drum—or, more accurately, clinking finger cymbals—for two transplanted-to-Manhattan-from-India gurus. And a new "political" group, the Yippies—who took their name from Youth International party—were snake-dancing through Grand Central Station, humming "Om" and urging onlookers to "Rise up and abandon the creeping meatball." If in 1967 San Francisco appeared to be at the center of the Aquarian universe, by 1968 New York was catching up fast.

Out of town on the weekends for concerts in Rochester, Newark and Toronto, Jimi settled into a suite of rooms at the Warwick Hotel, made them his headquarters, even threw a big party there, attended by Truman Capote, Bob Dylan's record producer, Tom Wilson, and Mike Bloom-field. That got him invited by the management to leave, so Jimi moved into a seventeenth-floor suite in the Drake, an-other midtown hotel that put him a five-minute taxi ride from his favorite haunts.

One of these was Steve Paul's Scene, on Forty-sixth Street between Eighth and Ninth avenues, near Times Square. The club, though small, was appropriately named, because Steve, who became a close friend of Jimi's, was one of the city's most popular scene-makers. If Jimi wasn't at the Record Plant, a recording studio nearby on Forty-fourth Street, he was at the Scene. Quickly a hard core of friends formed around him.

One of these was Pat Hartley, a part Jewish, part Mo-roccan black who sometimes worked as an actress for Andy Warhol and who talked at a hundred miles an hour.

"Places like the Scene we liked to hang out basically because we could dance all night," she says. "The extra added attraction was having live people performing. Also, being a chick and not having to be taken out was another reason for going there. You didn't have to have a date. I mean, Devon Wilson, who had known Jimi forever, she and I gave each other dirty looks in bathrooms all over town for a long time! It was a steady progression from this club, that club. We were all young actresses, professional extras really. Heather married Roger Daltrey [of the Who] and she was living with Devon at this time and so Heather and I used to do this film, that film. So it was an amorphous group of people all together."

The club was dark and crowded each night, and when Jimi sidled in about midnight, usually Pat was there with Devon or Heather or Jenni Dean, who was another no-nonsense supergroupie of mixed Jewish and Negro background. These were the ones Jimi respected, saw regularly through the years. There were others who meant less to him.

"I remember times in clubs where chicks would come and obviously they've been preparing themselves in the bathroom for half an hour for this big number, you know, they've got the lipstick on, the courage up . . ." Pat Hartley viewed these groupies with amusement and petulance. "And out they come and over to the table, boom, boom, boom. And the moment anybody would get up, I mean, all, all, all places at the table were continually full. I mean you couldn't get up for a second without eight people charging for your chair. And they'd sit down and by the time they got there, they were so fucking uptight, you know, about having to go through this massive preparation. What were they gonna say, and how were they gonna say it, and how were they gonna make the best impression possible? That they came on like a bunch of snots. I mean, Jimi would turn around and say, 'Hi, my name is Jimi, who are you?' "

These were the ones Jimi took back to his hotel room for one-nighters. "Jimi seemed to be screwing as a way of venting his anger," said Curtis Knight. "Everywhere he turned, he was getting 'young tender ones,' as he used to call them. He was getting so much pussy, he told me, that he was living on it: 'Pussy for breakfast, dinner and supper.' "

According to Knight, Jimi told him that many times he

would be "falling asleep from some all-night orgy and I would hear a gentle knock on my door. I'd stagger to the door naked and peep out, and there would be some sexy, cute little thing standing there, and she would ask if she could come in, and most of the time I'd say yes. But sometimes they would be waiting in bed for me when I didn't feel like being bothered, and I'd just get the roadies to throw them out."

Jimi wrote, and sang, about these "young tender ones" in "Crosstown Traffic," a song he recorded for his next album:

All you do is slow me down
I'm trying to get on the other side of town
I'm not the only soul who's been accused of hit and
    run
Tire tracks all across your back
I can see you had your fun
But, uh, darlin', can't you see
My signal turn from green to red
And with you I can see
A traffic jam straight up ahead

The recording sessions, at Jimi's beloved Record Plant, were going on and on. This was to be Jimi's first double album and the first to give him the room to stretch musically, to break away from the two- to three-minute single format. But there was friction. Jimi was growing increasingly unhappy about Noel's bass playing and began insisting that *he* play all the bass parts as well as lead guitar. Today Noel says Jimi made the sessions impossible.

Noel told Chris Welch, "It got to the point once in New York when I told him he was a stupid cunt. He depended too much on himself as writer, producer and musician. He was always trying to do it his way. There were times when I

Jimi in the recording studio

used to go to a club between sessions, pull a chick, come back, and he was still tuning his guitar. Oh, hours it took! We should have worked as a team, but it didn't work."

Chas Chandler was growing disillusioned too.

"There was a dreadful atmosphere in the studio, which was full of hangers-on. We did six tracks . . . and nobody was ready to compromise anymore. All I was doing was sitting there collecting a percentage [as producer]. So I said, 'Let's call it a day.' "

In May, Jimi went to Miami to headline a two-day pop festival held at Gulfstream Race Track, near Miami. Noel and Mitch went two weeks early, with Mitch taking a hotel room and Noel—ever looking to save money—moving into the promoter's house. This was Marshall Brevitz, a round, balding nightclub owner with no previous experience in staging outdoor shows.

Marshall brought in three flat-bed trucks for stages, so there would be no wait between acts; while one band was performing on one stage, another would be setting up. Huge scaffolds were erected along the front of the grandstand for the lights and speakers. Helicopters brought in the performers, landing in the infield near where fireworks were being set up for the first night's finale.

Taking his lead from what was done at Monterey, Marshall brought in a variety of acts from all over—Frank Zappa's Mothers of Invention, representing Southern California "freak," the power trio Blue Cheer from San Francisco, Arthur Brown from England, the Blues Image from New York, and from Detroit the great bluesman John Lee Hooker. Several local bands filled out the bill.

The first day was a success, attracting an audience of 25,000 and ending with a forty-foot-high peace symbol blazing in fireworks. The second day was a disaster, when the clouds over eastern Florida were seeded in an effort to end a long drought. Even before the first act went on, it was raining. John Lee Hooker played acoustic guitar for two hours as Marshall paced back and forth in the dressing rooms. It rained harder. With all the musicians fearing electrocution if they plugged in their guitars in the downpour, the festival was canceled, and as a result, Jimi was "shorted" between $4,000 and $5,000.

Back in New York, he was spending his money as fast as it poured in. Bills from the Record Plant frequently came to as much as $5,000 a week. His hotel rooms, chauffeurs and generosity cost even more.

"Money was no object to him," says Buddy Miles, who spent time with Jimi when he was in New York, even began recording with him. "He had wads of money and he just gave it away to strangers. I saw him do it many times."

"Hendrix spent money like a sieve," says Michael Goldstein, who was still his U.S. publicist. "It ran through his fingers. You know that gold tooth in Buddy Miles's mouth? Jimi paid for that. He bought a tremendous amount of clothes, and then left them all over New York in various girls' apartments. He bought a house for his parents. And on the road it was even worse. I remember once we were in Los Angeles and Jimi and Noel and Mitch were staying at the Beverly Hills Hotel in one of the expensive bungalows. I'm looking around. I'm looking at Noel and Mitch and I said, 'What is this? We're spending a hundred dollars a day for this!' "

Mitch looked up from his magazine at the short, fat publicist. He was annoyed. "Well," he said, "we're making it."

Now Michael was annoyed. He didn't like to be contradicted. "That isn't the way to make it," he said. "Think about it."

Mitch backed down somewhat. "Well," he said, "it's . . . see, we're all staying in the bungalow, so it's not really a hundred dollars a day. It's about thirty dollars a day for each of us."

"Yeah?" said Michael back. "What about room service?"

Mitch and Noel said nothing in response.

"I mean," Michael says, "you got to remember that those guys knew how to use room service! I told them, 'Did anybody ever think about going out and buying a case of liquor and leaving it here?' Michael sighed heavily, remembering the money spent. 'It was *not*," he said, "a Jewish group."

CHAPTER

9

Michael Jeffery was becoming increasingly worried.

The Experience was now one of the highest-paid performing acts in the history of entertainment, commanding as much as $50,000 a night. The trouble was that there hadn't been that many nights lately—only five since February. So on May 15, after headlining at the Fillmore East in New York, for which the trio was paid $10,000, completing an old contract, Jimi, Noel and Mitch flew to Europe for a series of five high-paying concerts in Italy and Switzerland. Stopping in London en route, Jimi visited with old friends. His longtime road manager, Gerry Stickells, hired a new assistant, Eric Barrett, a slim, long-haired Englishman who had been a friend of Noel's and who was then working for a band called the Nice.

Eric remembers the concerts with mixed feelings. The problem, he says, was the equipment. Jimi always played with everything turned up to ten on the volume knobs, causing the amplifiers always burned out by the end of the show.

"You goddamn faggot limey!" Jimi cursed. "Fix the fuckin' amps! Now!"

Afterward Jimi apologized, but it was apparent he was still upset, until June first, when he left the others and flew to Majorca for a brief vacation. There he jammed with the house band at the club Mike Jeffery owned, Sergeant Pepper's, and seemed to relax.

Finally, there was a big outdoor festival back in Britain at Woburn Abbey, the three-thousand-acre estate owned by the Duke and Duchess of Bedford. And then it was back to New York.

In his managers' offices, there were important papers waiting for Jimi. Negotiations had just been concluded between his attorneys and the bothersome Ed Chalpin and his PPX Enterprises. By now Chalpin had released four albums from tapes Jimi had made with Curtis Knight. Besides *Get That Feeling* on Capitol, issued in 1967, there was another, titled *Flashing,* on the same label, and two bearing the London imprint, *Get That Feeling* (with different tracks) and *Strange Things,* all rushed into the record stores in 1968. On two of these—the second *Get That Feeling* and *Flashing*—Jimi heard his own voice off-mike, talking to Knight, "You're not gonna release this?" And Knight answering, "No, no, no. Just jammin'. Old times. Old times."

Jimi remembered when that had happened—in 1967, after he returned from England. With good reason, he felt betrayed.

It didn't matter. Jimi's lawyers had lost their fight. What had happened was unfair but not illegal.

Leo Harman was the counsel in charge of negotiations at Warner-Reprise. He says Chalpin was given a 2 percent "override" on Jimi's first three albums—the third as yet unfinished—and complete rights to Jimi's fourth, with a guarantee of $200,000. Chalpin also kept the right to market the tapes he had from Jimi's recorded jams with Curtis Knight.

In exchange Chalpin gave very little, merely turning over his 1965 agreement with Jimi, which had only four months to go. He also agreed to drop all further claims against Jimi in the U.S.

For Chalpin it was a resounding victory. His gamble had paid off and would continue to pay off, handsomely, for many years. Eventually he would receive more than a million dollars.

For Jimi it was a crushing defeat. When he was told that the awful tapes from his past would continue to haunt him, he was angry. And when he was told that on top of that he actually *owed* Chalpin another album, he was furious.

It was then that he decided to include a song in his next album for Reprise that he had recorded in England the previous year, taking it into the Record Plant to remix it. This was Bob Dylan's "All Along the Watchtower," a song in which Dylan castigates businessmen who don't understand him but gleefully run off with all the profits they can make.

Besides the "settlement agreement," the lawyers also negotiated a new recording contract, one that eliminated the Bahamian trust company, Yameta, as a recipient of Jimi's record royalties, while increasing the royalty rate from 3 to 5 percent. In return, Jimi promised to deliver two albums and four singles each year for four years—fairly standard demands made of musicians at that time.

Yameta was paid well for this. Upon execution of the new contract—it was signed by Jimi on June 24—Reprise had to pay Yameta $250,000 in cash, with additional payments of $50,000 to follow on the first, second, third and fourth anniversaries of the signing.

"It's hard to understand how we came out on this," the Warner-Reprise lawyer says, "but I guess we did."

"When you talk about Jimi Hendrix and Reprise," says Stan Cornyn, who was by now in charge of "creative services" at Reprise, "it is an amazing and convoluted story of

deals and re-deals and un-deals. I think that was terribly annoying to Mo [Ostin, the president], but Mo is a pragmatist
who can say, 'Value is value, even if you're getting
screwed.' "

How did Jimi feel about his new contract? He signed it
just as he signed most papers put in front of him by his managers. He turned the pages, pretending to read them. But it
never made much sense, the convoluted language that lawyers used. He turned the pages, but he did not see the words.
And then he affixed his hasty, sprawling signature.

The July issue of *Eye* magazine was on the stands, and
in it Jimi was praised adoringly. The writer, a young novelist named Michael Thomas, called Jimi "the Cassius Clay
of Pop," saying, "Muhammed Ali, when he was Cassius
Clay, did not have very good manners either, and that was
why he became the first champion of the world in a long
while to have as much charisma as courage. He was a
good fighter because he could hit hard and step lightly. He
was an outasight champion because he was a ham. He
went boogalooing down Broadway with Marianne Moore,
he made up all those outasight poems, and he was sexy.
Jimi Hendrix, though, might make him blush. Jimi's got
muscle, he's just as mean and a lot more provocative. The
reason I could've asked twenty-five dollars for my five-dollar
seats at one of his recent New York concerts, and gotten it
(as one enterprising young man in the queue behind me
did), is not because he plays the guitar so well, but because
he plays it so absurdly. And, Mamma, you know, he looks
so fine.

"Hendrix is a master of ceremonies. He saunters onstage, looking like a buccaneer Othello come to Camelot, in
velvet and lace and boots of Spanish leather, a Mexican
bandit's hat on his head with a feather in the gold chain-
band, his silk blouse open to the navel, a shiny gold medal-

lion sparkling on his chest, his crotch grimly outlined. He's the black sheep all wrapped up in the golden fleece."

Jimi sauntered from scene to scene. He was cruising now. Success was in his pocket, and because concerts were infrequent, he could pretty much do whatever he wished, whenever and however he wanted to.

No one could predict his daily routine, because no one knew where he slept. He still had a suite of rooms in an East Side hotel, and he occasionally moved his guitars and clothes into a motor lodge nearer the Record Plant, but more often he was with one of his ladies, who sewed for him and cooked for him and took drugs with him and slept with him.

Usually he awakened in early afternoon. After breakfast he did some drugs, usually grass, which was a constant companion for him. Then he would go shopping or drift somewhere in a limousine or cab to visit friends. Maybe he would eat again, about 10 P.M.; maybe not. Jimi didn't eat often, keeping a flat, muscled stomach that always made him look as if he needed a meal.

At night he liked to visit the twenty-four hour record store on Broadway, Colony Records. Day or night he liked to browse at Manny's Forty-eighth Street Musical Instruments Store, where the owner, Henry Goldrich, catered especially to him.

"Any new kind of toy or sound effect he bought immediately," Goldrich says. "Whenever he walked in, he was good for fifteen hundred to two thousand dollars."

Most of his evenings were spent at the Scene or in other clubs, or at the Record Plant, where he was still slogging away on his third album. He invited some of his friends to sit in with him. Buddy Miles played drums on a couple of songs and Stevie Winwood played organ on a couple more. Jefferson Airplane's bassist, Jack Casady, took Noel's place in one late-night session. Another visitor was Al Kooper, who had played organ for Dylan's *Blonde on Blonde* album, and who later was a member of the Blues Project and Blood, Sweat and Tears.

Track after track after track he laid down, creating his songs the way an artist applies layers of paint to canvas to create an effect that requires all the hidden levels below. Jimi always worked with Eddie Kramer now, the engineer who was with him in London when he made his first records. Kramer was infinitely patient with Jimi and seemed to understand what he wanted.

For the most part, Kramer scoffs at attempts to explain the recording process. "I think the mystique should remain," he told *Guitar Player* magazine. "Analyzing it to the point that you want in your magazine is not a good idea. Part of the mystique is what I created with him in the studio, and I'd like to leave it at that."

Was this true? Or was Kramer ducking the question because he too was mystified by Jimi's playing and its capture on three-quarter inch tape?

The truth is, it wasn't easy for him to explain. Like so many musicians, Jimi was extremely articulate on his instrument, but not when it came to talking. Even so, Jimi was always ready to try, and occasionally he was *very* articulate. It was while recording this album that he invented a phrase that soon became almost a cliché, or catchphrase, in his frequent, rambling dialogues: "electric, or sky, church music."

"We're making our music in electric church music—a new kind of bible, not like in a hotel, but a bible you carry in your hearts, one that will give you a physical feeling," he told a writer for New York's *East Village Other*, a weekly "underground" paper. "We try to make our music so loose and hard-hitting, so that it hits your soul hard enough to make it open. It's like shock therapy or a can opener . . .

"Lots of young people now feel they're not getting a fair deal, so they revert to something loud or harsh, almost verging on violence. If they didn't go to a concert, they might be going to a riot. They are young. The establishment hasn't put them in a cage yet. Their music hasn't been put in a cage yet. It's more than music. It's like church, like a foundation for the lost or potentially lost . . .

"We're in our little cement beehives in this society. People let a lot of old-time laws rule them. The establishment has set up the Ten Commandments for us saying 'don't, don't, don't.' Once you say 'don't,' you've made two points against yourself. Then all of a sudden kids come along with a different set of brain cells and the establishment doesn't know what to do. The walls are crumbling and the establishment doesn't want to let go. We're trying to save the kids, to create a buffer between young and old. Our music is shock therapy to help them realize a little more of what their goals should be."

Obviously Jimi was talking about some of his "protest" songs, but just as clearly it was his sound and not just his lyrics that he used to make his point.

"Verging on violence," he said. "Shock therapy."

Slowly the album came together, becoming a musical collage of old-style finger-picking and space-age sound effects; cruel and gritty words spat out at the establishment—and at an old rock-and-roll target, the female sex—and escape from this world into another. The sessions may have been chaotic, as everyone agrees, but Jimi remained in control, creating a unifying energy that held sixteen tracks spread over four sides together in much the same way bits and pieces of magazine clippings are held together in a collage by the artist's well-defined vision. Jimi called himself the "producer and director" of the album, which meant that, in the end, Chas was out and it was Jimi's album and his alone.

Confident that the album was nearly done, Jimi flew to Los Angeles to be with friends, roaring through the Hollywood Hills with Buddy Miles, haunting the clubs on the Sunset Strip. Once a wide avenue of fine restaurants and boutiques supported by nearby Beverly Hills, in the middle 1960s Sunset Boulevard was occupied by young people who'd stormed it and taken over like an invading army. The *Los Angeles Times* was claiming a three-million-dollar loss to Sunset Strip property owners and businessmen, due entirely to the hippies. Retail sales and real estate values were reported down 30 percent, and another one million dollars was called a loss to the taxpayers in increased law enforcement as arrests there averaged between 150 and 200 a week, most of them for curfew violations and drug possession.

Whisky Menu

1. **GIANT "ANIMALS" BURGER (The way Eric likes It)** ..1.00
   Big enough to fill up a hungry "ANIMAL" with Grilled Onions,
   Lettuce and Tomato and French Fried Potatoes
   With Cheese Melted on the Meat 1.10

2. **"JIMI HENDRIX" TREAT (Super Sausage)** 1.00
   Of course on a Wah-Wah Bun, Choice of Sauerkraut or
   Cole Slaw, topped with Lettuce, Tomato, Relish and
   Onions, as you like them (Raw or Grilled)

3. **STEAK "BILL COSBY" (New York Steak)** 3.95
   Broiled to your liking and topped with juicy "FAT ALBERT"
   Mushrooms, Grilled Onions, French Fried Potatoes and
   "OLD WEIRD HAROLD'S" favorite Salad

4. **GRILLED CHEESE GOODIE** 1.00
   Made Special For "DOORS" Fans
   Tasty American Cheese Grilled on Dark Pumpernickel Bread
   (if you so desire) with Sliced Tomato, Pickle and French Fried
   Potatoes. This Sandwich Will Light Anyone's Fire

5. **PIZZA (the way the "JEFFERSON AIRPLANE" dig it)** .1.35
   Two Pieces at a Time
   Your Taste Buds Will Take Off When You Bite Into the Ten Inches
   of Crisp Dough, Multitudes of Cheese and Superb Tomato Sauce

6. **"BYRDS" NEST SALAD BOWL** 1.00
   Many Unexpected Surprises in this Crispy Offering, with Special
   Freaky "MUTHERS" Dressing. (Watch out for high-flying Byrds)

7. **THE "MASEKELA" (Basket of French Fried Potatoes)** . .50
   For Munching with Special Savory "C.T.A." Sauce, if you like.
   Try it and take a ride on the "C.T.A."

8. **"JOHNNY RIVERS" DELIGHT (Le Dog Hot)** .... .75
   What can we say? Except it's as great as it's namesake
   and you can have all the trimmings as well as French Fried Potatoes

Jimi is immortalized on a menu at the Whisky a Go Go in Hollywood

Jimi loved it. It was like being in the middle of a new age and a battle zone, all wrapped up together.

One night Jimi told his limousine driver to take him to the Whisky a Go Go, and as he got out of the car, the doorman greeted him warmly, asking him if he remembered the promoter in Miami who'd "burned" him back in May.

Jimi looked at the man quizzically. He didn't think he'd been ripped off. It rained; the promoter couldn't help that. Jimi said nothing, waiting for the man to go on.

Well, the doorman said, that man, Marshall Brevitz, was now operating in Los Angeles out of a hole-in-the-wall club about a mile away. The doorman said he was warning all musicians to stay away from the place because Brevitz was a burn artist . . . and if they *did* play there, they would never work at the Whisky.

Jimi got back into the limousine and told the driver, "Take me to Marshall's."

Jimi smiled as the big car pulled up in front. The club was called The Experience, and Marshall had had an artist paint a huge face of Jimi on the front of the building; you entered by walking through his mouth. Jimi greeted Marshall noisily and asked if he could play.

"What it was," Marshall says, "was a blacklist. The people at the Whisky didn't want me to succeed. By his performing at the club Jimi was telling other musicians the Whisky blacklist sucked. So for the next week, ten days, Jimi came in every night. He even told me to call the radio stations to say he was there. Then at the end of the week, minus a thousand dollars to cover the beer and wine Jimi and his friends drank, Jimi told Gerry Stickells to be sure that the club got to keep every dollar that came in, which Gerry had been holding. Gerry counted out the cash. I'm telling you now, Jimi Hendrix kept The Experience alive."

Jimi also helped produce an album, *Expressway to Your Skull*, for the Buddy Miles Express, a group that Buddy

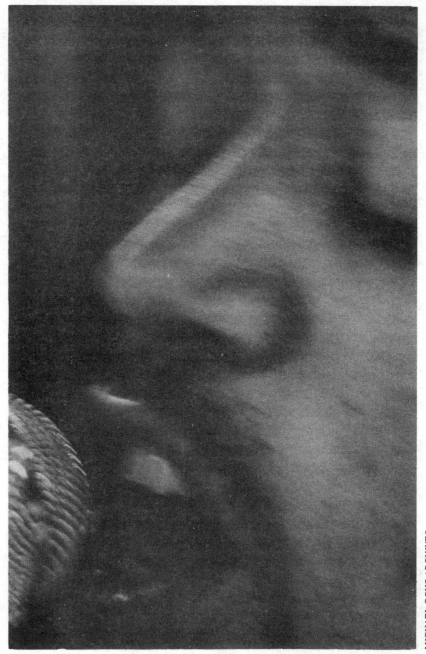

started that month from the wreckage of Mike Bloomfield's Electric Flag, and went into TTG Studios to lay down some final guitar tracks for one of the songs on his own album.

Other events of the visit were not so positive. Driving like a maniac around the twisting canyon streets, stoned on psychedelics and drinking heavily, Jimi wrecked his new Stingray Corvette. Next day he bought another, and that night he wrecked that one too. Fortunately no one was hurt.

The same thing cannot be said for what happened next. Versions of the story differ. But one thing is clear: a young girl was hurt. Some say Jimi was drunk and he threw a brick at her or that he beat the girl's head against the fender of his car.

However, the most reliable story comes from Steve Gold, who was soon to begin managing Eric Burdon. He said Jimi threw the girl down a flight of stairs, breaking her leg. Gold says he and his wife took the young fan to the hospital.

"Jimi hardly said thank you," Gold says. "He had no feeling for groupies. They were to be *used.*"

Nor was that the end of that. Eventually Jimi paid the injured fan $10,000 in cash to keep her quiet.

Back in New York in mid-August, Jimi's business affairs were equally complicated.

On August 22, soon after the Experience had played to sold-out audiences at the Auditorium Theater in Chicago, Jimi, Noel and Mitch were called into their managers' office to sign some more papers. The first set were letters to their booking agents at the General Artists Corporation, their music publishers at Sea-Lark Enterprises, and their record company, Warner Brothers-Seven Arts, advising them that all future money owed them should be sent directly to Jeffery and Chandler, and not to Yameta "or any of its representatives unless we should so advise you in writing in the future." This was merely the paperwork required to solidify the group's new recording agreement.

The other papers signed that day involved new agreements with "Messrs. Abrahams, Gold & Hecht, C.P.A.'s." They first authorized their accountants to pay their attorneys, "Messrs. Steingarten, Wadeen & Weiss," $75,000 for services regarding the Chalpin lawsuit and two other actions. Of this sum Jimi was to pay $30,000, the remainder to be divided equally between Noel and Mitch and their managers.

Worse was the news that Chalpin had filed suits in Europe against Jimi and his two London-based record companies, Track and Polydor. Instantly both companies put a hold on all future royalties due Jimi and the others. Track and Polydor also sued Jimi for getting them into the mess. It was for this reason that the accountants then had the three musicians sign an agreement protecting the accountancy firm from any future legal damages.

"We hereby jointly and severally agree to indemnify your firm from any and all claims which may be asserted against you or any of you in respect of the receipt and disbursement by you of any monies paid in respect of the Jimi Hendrix Experience, its personal appearances, and royalties of every kind and description."

The next day, on August 23, Jimi's road crew began moving his big Marshall amplifiers and boxes of sound-warping gadgetry to New York's Singer Bowl, where he was to appear that night with his old friends the Chambers Brothers and Janis Joplin. This kind of double-headliner booking was becoming common by 1968. On the West Coast, the Doors often were paired with Jefferson Airplane. Earlier in the year Jimi had shared the Fillmore East stage with Sly and the Family Stone. The only question was—as always—who was going to go on first. At least that was a conflict for some. Not for Jimi. By now there wasn't anyone anywhere who wanted to follow him.

Jimi and Janis talked and drank backstage together

Jimi on stage

MICHAEL OCHS ARCHIVES

[177]

while the Chambers Brothers rocked through a set that included an extended version of their hit "Time." Then Janis, who would split from Big Brother and the Holding Company the following month, went out and tore the place apart for an hour and a half. The audience was exhausted when Jimi appeared. And Jimi seemed annoyed.

"Jimi was a changed man," says his friend Rae Warner, who played in the Chambers Brothers band. "At this time he wanted everyone's attention in the whole world."

"That's right," says Willie Chambers. "He'd get highly upset on the stage if people wouldn't give him their attention."

"So at the Singer Bowl he walked off," Rae explains. "Between the first act of the evening and the last act before him—Janis—the energy of the audience was totally drained. There was no hope for him to express anything and he left the stage. Most shows run forty-five minutes and Jimi usually did sixty. But he left early. Real early. Dragging his guitar behind him."

All around Jimi there was conflict. It seemed that none of the old relationships were working. Chas and Jeffery were at each other's throats. Chas said he wanted out and was returning to London. His wife was pregnant and they wanted the baby born at home. Besides, Chas told friends, he and Jimi were quarreling, not only in the studio but on the road. While traveling, he said, Jimi was "becoming unmanageable."

There were other conflicts brewing. Chas told Jimi he thought he should get a different lawyer. Having the same attorney that Jeffery had—Henry Steingarten—when Jeffery managed Jimi was a clear conflict of interest, or at least opened the door for it. Worse, Jimi was fighting with Noel and Mitch. Especially Noel, who kept riding Jimi about the cars he wrecked in Los Angeles, telling him he needed glasses. Noel also didn't appreciate Jimi's using Jack Casady on the new album. Nor did Mitch like Buddy Miles playing drums on the record. Both musicians felt threatened—so threatened, in fact, that Noel formed a new band, called Fat Mattress, and asked Jeffery to manage it.

Finally Chas said, "That's it! I'm leaving."

This time he meant it, so Jeffery became Jimi's sole manager, buying Chas's interest for $300,000 in cash and a small percentage of future earnings.

As all this was going on, Jimi and Noel and Mitch—accompanied by Cat Mother and the All-Night Newsboys and Fat Mattress, both managed by Jeffery—flew off to Denver, where Jimi wrote some spacey liner notes for the new album, to be called *Electric Ladyland.* He then flew on to Seattle.

Jimi was in Seattle for three or four days before appearing at the Center Coliseum. This time the 18,000-seat arena was sold out.

"We talked about the world," his brother Leon recalls. "I could talk to him. I'd dropped acid by then. He said acid was the beginning of the end of the world. He said he couldn't talk to nobody. Nobody understood him. We'd get together with Dad and the family and they didn't understand. Jimi would talk about other worlds and Dad would say, 'Hey, you been drinking?' I turned him on to all my old girl friends and we had some fun."

The following day Jimi was in Vancouver, and then it was back to Los Angeles for a concert the next weekend, on September 14, at the Hollywood Bowl.

A week later, on September 21, "All Along the Watchtower" was released as a single, and on October 12—as Jimi was midway through a three-day series of shows at the Winterland in San Francisco (and staying with his friend Buddy Miles in Mill Valley)—500,000 copies of *Electric Ladyland* were shipped to eager record stores. Both went onto the charts immediately.

This was not surprising. A slick package, with lots of photographs (most by Linda Eastman, then a young photographer, eventually Mrs. Paul McCartney) and more than an hour and forty minutes of music, it was much more than just another new album among the hundreds to arrive in the stores each week.

No, *Electric Ladyland* was in a separate, heady class because of Jimi's status. Like new albums from the Beatles, the Rolling Stones, Bob Dylan and a very few others, it's release was what *The New York Times* writer Bob Palmer later called a "genuine cultural event." Such albums "seemed to fuse the rock audience into a palpable, coherent community," Palmer said. "They were messages from the community's seers, to be savored and probed for hidden meanings and listened to again and again, with joy and reverence, until the group's next album came along."

For example, what happened in Bob Krasnow's office at Blue Thumb Records wasn't all that unusual. Whenever a new Jimi Hendrix album was received, the office was closed to the public, telephones were taken off the hook and a select group of friends was invited over to drop acid and listen to the album until everyone was "straight" again. Picture twenty-five to thirty young adults, most of them in the record business, sitting in a suite of offices in Beverly Hills, eyes dilated, hearts beating furiously, images rushing and mixing wildly, walls and desks and typewriters warping and changing shape, going on Jimi's trips with him.

The album opened with a track called ". . . And the Gods Made Love": the sounds of winds, or wings, in space. Followed by the gentle and soulful title track, with its invitation, "Have you ever been to Electric Ladyland . . . it's time we took a ride." The third track was his angry vision of many of the girls of rock, "Crosstown Traffic," and the fourth track was his seemingly endless—on acid—"Voodoo Chile." For this one he alternated singing with the guitar in the ageless blues tradition and playing fast, wailing blues

[180]

riffs, riding the tremolo bar, "verging on violence" (as Jimi said).

"The night I was born, Lord, I swear the moon turned a fire red," he cried. "Lord knows, I'm a voodoo chile!"

There was something for everyone on this two-record set. There were soul-type vocals on "Long Hot Summer Night," reminiscent of Jimi's days with the Isleys and Solomon Burke. In the very next song, "Come On," Jimi demonstrated his stunning guitar virtuosity, playing in a half dozen different styles. Another song, "Rainy Day, Dream Away," makes the dope connection very clear, with inhaling, coughing and sniffing sounds punctuating a lyric whose message was simply "Lay back and groove on a rainy day." And for Jimi's many fellow (space) travelers there was "1983 . . . (A Merman I Should Turn to Be)," a tale of Jimi's escape from the apocalypse by returning to the sea.

"Neptune champion games to an aqua world is so very dear," Jimi cried. " 'Right this way,' smiles a mermaid. I can hear Atlantis, full of cheer."

The album was released in Britain a month after its distribution in the United States, and controversy raged. This was because in England there was a different cover, a double album sleeve covered with naked female flesh: twenty-one enigmatically smiling young women, three of them holding photographs of Jimi or his albums.

STORM OVER JIMI'S ALBUM—STORES REJECT SLEEVE AS PORNOGRAPHIC was the way the headline read in one British weekly, *Top Pops*. "Certain W. H. Smith and Boots stores are selling the album in brown paper bags. Track Records, who issue the album, have expressed surprise at the trouble it has aroused. The picture was taken by David Montgomery, who has also photographed the Queen. Track says it should be looked upon for its artistic merit."

TITS 'N' ASS LP BROWN-BAGGED IN ENGLAND, headlined *Rolling Stone*. "The fight for decency moves on."

It didn't matter. The critics and fans loved it.

"Jimi Hendrix's new album, *Electric Ladyland*, is a musical freeway," said Richard Goldstein, the important arbiter in *The Village Voice.* "You come away feeling that it's overlong, indiscriminate, and needlessly jammed. But beyond these first impressions—which are an inescapable part of the Jimi Hendrix Experience—it is clearly a major artery. Hendrix's phrasing is as powerful, his musical presence as persistent as ever . . .

"For sheer texture, this is an uncanny piece of sound-collage. It comes at you whining, sighing, or curling its lip in arrogant dismay . . .

"I suspect the reason why his all-star lineup [the use of Buddy Miles, Stevie Winwood, Al Kooper and others on several songs] works is the firmly established subservience his back-up musicians must inevitably accept. No one short of Joseph Stalin could upstage Jimi Hendrix, and backed by even the most distinctive rock stylists, it is his guitar we hear first—loud and together.

"Dig how this works in 'Voodoo Chile,' the album's strongest cut and probably the finest rock appreciation of blues you'll ever hear. Hendrix is always out there, like an electric minotaur, flaying away at the business of being absurdly black with the kind of groovy contempt the English call Flash. And, Jumpin' Jack, that word was made for the Jimi Hendrix Experience."

Others were no less accepting. In the *Observer* in London, the reviewer called "All Along the Watchtower" "orgasmic, spluttering, aching, as if the entire fabric of the world is being torn apart. It is an assault savage and sexual, masturbatory and cruel." It and the album were called "pop genius," and Track Records was hailed for its having a "major triumph on their hands not only commercially but, more important, artistically."

"Hendrix is the Robert Johnson of the sixties," said Tony Glover, himself a musician, in *Rolling Stone,* "and really the first cat to ever totally play *electric* guitar . . .

"Hendrix, psychedelic superspade??? Or just a damn good musician/producer? Depends on whether you want to believe the image or your ears."

As these and other similar reviews came in, Jimi was in movement still, settling into a suite of rooms in the Beverly Rodeo Hotel in Beverly Hills for a few days, then moving east again for a concert November 23 at the Philharmonic Hall. Four days later he celebrated his twenty-sixth birthday, and two days after that, on the twenty-ninth, Jimi and Noel and Mitch played the Westchester County Center in White Plains, New York, a rich suburb of New York City.

There was another fast trip to London, where Jimi ran into Chas. Jimi knew that Chas and Mike had dissolved their partnership, although neither one had provided much information about the split to Jimi or the others.

This was odd, because Jimi's original two-year contract with Jeffery and Chandler was about to expire. It would have been wise, it seems, to have been open about the split. That they weren't may explain what happened next. When Chas saw Jimi, he told him that *he* wanted to manage him—without Jeffery. Jimi liked Chas, despite the troubles they had had in the studio while recording *Electric Ladyland*. Jimi felt that Chas, as a fellow musician, understood him better than Mike did. So he said yes.

Word quickly reached Mike in New York, and he sent one of his assistants to London to stop Jimi.

"Kathy slept on the floor outside Jimi's hotel room that night so she could catch him before he left in the morning," says another of Jeffery's co-workers. "Jimi liked Kathy, trusted her. They had talked about writing some songs and poems together. She talked him out of signing with Chas and took him back to New York with her."

What happened after that was so ironic and in some ways so typical.

On the surface everything seemed perfection itself. To the outsider, to the public and even to the media the Jimi

Hendrix Experience was solidly entrenched—perhaps the most popular and prosperous band in America. Security was a certainty.

Producers were approaching Mike Jeffery every week asking to make a feature film for release in the theaters.

Dozens of concerts lay ahead, with fees now pushing past the $75,000 mark.

Singles were on the record charts on both sides of the Atlantic—"Crosstown Traffic" in the U.S. and "All Along the Watchtower" in Britain.

Electric Ladyland was, according to the trades, the Number One best seller in both England and the U.S.

Despite Jimi's profligate spending, there was even some money in the bank.

And that is when the band broke up.

Insiders were not surprised at all. Noel and Mitch had been complaining openly and steadily for months. So Noel did what he had always wanted to do—play lead guitar and sing—and in December, in Los Angeles, he recorded fourteen songs with Fat Mattress, with Mitch helping out on drums. Together and individually, they told friends that Jimi was impossible to work with.

"Screw 'im!" Noel said. "I'm goin' home to me 'umble estate in County Cork."

Mitch said he was going to do the same. His estate was outside London.

And so they did, leaving Jimi partying it up in New York.

CHAPTER

10

All through the Christmas-New Year's holidays Michael Jeffery talked to Jimi and to Noel and to Mitch, crossing the Atlantic three times in two weeks.

They had Michael over the proverbial barrel. The band's agents had committed them to dozens of appearances, starting January 4 in London, when the Experience was expected to play three songs on the *Lulu Show,* and ending with Madison Square Garden in May and a flurry of huge pop festivals in June. Of course the three musicians were contracted to their managers and agents to perform, but if they *wouldn't* perform, what then? It was quite common for entertainers to walk away from their contracts.

How serious were they about their open refusal to play together? Some wondered if they, like so many other acts, merely were being difficult as a maneuver to improve their contract? Or were they really another of 1968's rock-and-roll breakups? There had been quite a few. Al Kooper had left

Blood, Sweat and Tears soon after introducing it. The Byrds had split for the third or fourth time, reformed as a country band, and then broken up again. Janis left Big Brother. Steve Miller lost three of his four sidemen. John Sebastian departed the Lovin' Spoonful for a solo career. Dave Mason walked away from Traffic, and then Traffic disintegrated. The Spencer Davis Group went in several directions. The Yardbirds became Led Zeppelin. Graham Nash left the Hollies. Eric Clapton dropped out of Cream, effectively killing the group. And Eric Burdon left the New Animals. All in 1968.

Mike Jeffery cajoled and begged and finally resorted to yelled threats.

"You sonsabitches won't ever work again," Michael screamed. "You have contracts and it won't just be me suing you. Everybody in the business will be suing you. Every fuckin' farthing you bleeding shits make will disappear into some solicitor's pocket, I swear it! Don't be fuckin' stupid!"

However angry Mike was, however motivated the anger was by the threat of diminished income for himself, he was correct in his appraisal. Finally he prevailed, and Jimi, Noel and Mitch agreed to go on—at least until they had done the concerts.

Jimi and Mitch agreed to continue entirely for economic reasons. They were both very close to broke. Of the three, Noel was the only one who had his money, but even that was diminished when he produced his album with Fat Mattress. Still, he agreed to return only after Michael agreed to use Fat Mattress as the opening act in all of the upcoming Experience dates, regardless of whether other bands had already been booked. For Noel it was a coup, an unbeatable opportunity for introducing his group. For Michael and the concert promoters it offered nearly as much—first Noel playing lead guitar with Fat Mattress, and then bass with the Experience: a nice gimmick. In fact, for a while there was

[186]

talk of Mitch forming *his* own group as well. But it didn't happen.

Jimi was welcomed on his arrival in January in London as royalty returning from a tour of the Commonwealth. Appropriately, but unknowingly, Jimi moved into a flat in the building that was once the home of George Frederick Handel, one of the musical geniuses of the eighteenth century and composer of *The Messiah*. When Jimi was told that he was sleeping where Handel slept, and then was told who Handel was, he laughed and said he wouldn't ignore tradition—he intended to compose while in the Brook Street flat but was going to produce "twenty-first-century music, that sort of scene."

The apartment was typical. Small: only three rooms. But the ceilings were high, accommodating the hanging fringed Morrocan tapestries that Jimi fancied. And the ever-present black satin sheets were covered with a colorful Persian spread. Instead of the customary couch and chairs, there were big overstuffed pillows of brightly patterned Indian cloth with small embedded mirrors. Incense seemed to be burning constantly, along with the small lumps of hashish rolled up in strong Turkish tobacco.

The television appearance with the *Lulu Show* went smoothly, except that Jimi ran overtime playing Cream's biggest hit, "Sunshine of Your Love," as a tribute to the broken group. That was followed by two days of interviews, and then the trio was off to the European mainland for a grueling tour of nineteen shows in sixteen days.

First stop was Gothenburg, Sweden, where two shows were scheduled on the eighth. At the first, Noel was so drunk he fell off the stage during the first Fat Mattress song, stuck his head back up just long enough to cry, "Carry on, mates!" and then passed out. Two more shows followed in Stockholm the next day, then there were two in Copenhagen, followed by two more in Hamburg, Germany. Düsseldorf, Cologne, Münster, Munich, Nuremberg, Frankfurt, Stuttgart, Vienna and Berlin finished off the sprint. Everywhere the big smoky halls were sold out, and the concerts were recorded on film.

"Our idea," says Steve Gold, who was producer of the film, contracted the previous month by Jeffery in Los Angeles, "was to keep shooting concerts until I got a great one. We had four-track quadraphonic sound. English cameramen. A German crew in Germany. We got what we wanted at the Royal Albert Hall in London, but that wasn't until February. It was great, absolutely the greatest. Jimi was at his peak."

Most others who were there disagree. They say Jimi may have looked well and played well, but around him there was chaos and an impending sense of disaster.

Just because Jimi and Noel and Mitch were on the stage together didn't mean they were together musically. Chas Chandler, who saw one of the performances in Gothenburg and another in the Royal Albert Hall, says it was like three people soloing simultaneously. Tapes of the performances confirm this.

Chas and Gold, among others, also report that Jimi was still undecided about his management. Chas says that Jimi asked him in Gothenburg to take over his career and that in London, Mike even asked Chas for his assistance. Chas thought about it quickly and decided he wasn't interested— it would be too painful.

The Royal Albert shows were successful nonetheless. The hall is one of London's most opulent, all in red plush and dark wood. Built to honor Queen Victoria's prince consort and promote the arts and sciences, in the 1960s it was rather like New York's Carnegie Hall, only just now being made available to popular musicians.

Additional prestige accrued from the announcement that the two Albert Hall concerts were "farewell" performances—the last shows of the tour. So all of London's finest came, including many of the best musicians, some of whom joined the Experience onstage.

Jimi gave the audience what they wanted, a collection of his familiar songs; "Stone Free," "Foxy Lady," a thirteen-minute-long version of "Red House," "Fire," "Voodoo Child (Slight Return)," another long rendition of the Cream's "Sunshine of Your Love," and a new song written over the holidays, "Room Full of Mirrors." If there were any doubts about how Jimi was feeling, this song put an end to them.

Jimi had some of his friends with him when he started playing it: Dave Mason on rhythm guitar; the flutist from his *Electric Ladyland* album, Chris Wood; and a conga player from Africa who had recorded with the Rolling Stones. The rhythm was frenetic, dominated by the pounding drums and Jimi's piercing guitar, and the lyrics showed Jimi's pain:

> I used to live in a room full of mirrors
> All I could see was me
> Then I take my spirit and I smash my mirrors
> And now the whole world is here for me to see
> I said the whole world is here for me to see!
>
> A broken glass was solvin' my brain
> Cut and screamin', crowdin' in my head
> A broken glass was loud in my brain.
> It used to fall on my dreams and cut me in my bed
> It used to fall on my dreams and cut me in my bed.
> I say makin' love was strange in my bed.

After that Jimi went into a song he had been playing around with in the studio off and on for several months and would record when he returned to the U.S. This was the American national anthem, "The Star-Spangled Banner."

Distortion "verging on violence" filled the rich, red hall, followed by the wailing distinctive notes to accompany "Ooooh sayyyy, cannnn youuuuu seeeeee?" When this was played in America the audience would gasp. In London no one seemed to care.

However, it seemed an appropriate final song. On the way back to his nearby flat with his friend Kathy Etchingham he was stopped by several men.

"Yeah? Uh, what?" Jimi said.

The men in black suits asked Jimi what he had in his guitar case.

"A machine gun," Jimi said.

Just as one of the men began pulling a pistol from his shoulder holster, one of the others recognized Jimi. They identified themselves as members of the U.S. Secret Service.

"Aren't you Jimi Hendrix?" they asked.

Amid much laughter it was explained that the new President of the United States, Richard Nixon, was staying in a nearby hotel and Jimi had been stopped merely as a precaution.

"Oh, yeah," said Jimi, "well, you give ol' Tricky Dick mah best. Tell him . . . Jimi's comin' to gitcha!"

Jimi and Kathy walked on into the London night.

Electric Ladyland was still high on the album charts when Jimi returned to America, in early March. FM disc jockeys loved it, playing several of the tracks regularly; rare was the station that didn't play something by Jimi every hour. The album also was still being praised consistently by the most respected critics and magazines.

Tom Phillips, writing in February in *Jazz & Pop,* made references to Brahms, Ravel, Berlioz and Beethoven and said Jimi's story about mermaids and mermen in "1983" was reminiscent of Jules Verne. He concluded: "Hendrix's genius lies in yoking the past and the future, and making them work together. He is all at once primitive, classical, and farther out then anybody else."

More exultant praise came from Jon Landau, music editor for *Rolling Stone*. In his 1968 year-end critique he praised Eric Clapton's band, Cream, but added: "For all their instrumental expertise, they never approached the excitement of Jimi Hendrix. Hendrix's *Electric Ladyland* was the only two-record set of the year that made it in my book. He is the authoritative lead guitarist, the coolest showman, an excellent songwriter, and a constantly improving vocalist. Of touring performers on the scene today, Hendrix is tops and 1968 was his year."

As if that weren't enough, *Rolling Stone* went one step further and in the same February issue declared that "For creativity, electricity and balls above and beyond the call of duty, he has won for himself the *Rolling Stone* Performer of the Year Award."

And if *that* weren't enough, two weeks later, in the next issue of *Rolling Stone*, featured prominently in a fourteen-page article on groupies, Jimi was described as the "Best Score." He never turned anyone away, said *Rolling Stone*. In fact, there was the time backstage when "He balled seven different chicks in the space of three hours. Each chick knew what was happening, but it didn't seem to matter. He was Jimi Hendrix."

An apocryphal story? Probably. So what? It was part of what *Rolling Stone* called "the legend of Jimi Hendrix as Satyr." Jimi's voracious sexuality was public knowledge, a part of American mid-century mythology.

A month later *Newsweek* ran its groupie story and the legend spread farther.

Soon after that the Whisky a Go Go in Los Angeles added a new sandwich to a late-night menu that already offered a Byrds Nest Soup Bowl and a Giant Animals Burger. It was called—without a trace of subtlety—"the Jimi Hendrix Treat, a super sausage on a wah-wah bun."

In the America Jimi returned to that March, the lines were clearly drawn. Everywhere he looked it was *Them* vs *Us.*

Them—from Jimi's view—included the new President, who took office in January, and Nixon's political partner, Spiro Agnew, both elected on a platform that promised what became a catchphrase for a decade, "Law and Order."

Us was everyone outside the establishment—the dancers and musicians and dope smokers and psychedelic gypsies in the movie *Monterey Pop*, released in January and still playing in selected theaters, and John Lennon and Yoko Ono, who made Jimi's English album nudes look tame by posing on their *Two Virgins* album cover with their genitalia exposed. Police confiscated the first 30,000 covers when the album arrived in the U.S. in January.

Them included those police. Also the television executives who maligned teenagers so brutally and continuously. From a story in *Time* magazine, published in March and reflecting shows of the previous month or two: "Kids on TV are pretty rotten. To Officer Pete Malloy of *Adam-12,* for example, a youth is the bearded hippie who shot Methedrine with his teen-age girlfriend and accidentally gave her hepatitis with a dirty needle. The *Hawaii Five-O* vice squad chased down a sinister guru who was freaking out vacuous young blondes on LSD. *The Name of the Game* recently had Gene Barry playing a magazine publisher kidnapped by a group of young radicals who planned to kill themselves at an Army chemical-warfare test site."

Us included Otis Redding because he was black (his "Sitting on the Dock of the Bay" was Number One in America for a solid month); Meher Baba, the Indian guru, because he hadn't spoken in forty-three years; and Timothy

Leary, who dared to write books called *Priest* (an autobiography!) and *The Politics of Ecstasy* (a blasphemy, according to *Them*).

Us vs *Them.*

It was Tuesday, March 18, when Jimi entered his favorite Manhattan recording studio, the Record Plant, to lay down the tracks for what would be his most controversial song, the one he had introduced inauspiciously in London's Royal Albert Hall, "The Star-Spangled Banner."

Eddie Kramer, Jimi's ever-present engineer, was waiting in the darkened control room as Jimi tuned his guitar in the adjacent studio. Both rooms smelled of marijuana smoke. Eddie's face was lighted from below by the hundreds of red, green and yellow-white lights on the sixteen-track control panel. Jimi sat hunched over his Stratocaster, tuning meticulously.

Eventually—at two hundred dollars an hour for the studio rental—Jimi began laying down tracks. Slowly a multilayered aural tapestry was created. Jimi began with apocalyptic crashing chords, then went right into the familiar "Oh-say-can-you-see" melody, with notes so high they hurt the ears.

There followed a little over four minutes of inspired musical noise, a triumphant electronic exercise that was simultaneously an assault on both hearing and patriotism. There were incredible highs and reverberating lows, layered one on top of the other, and what sounded like signals from outer space. It was every war weapon and every other machine in America—including computers, lawn mowers, blenders and sewing machines—all risen up together in song. The composer Francis Scott Key took as his inspiration for the song the bombs bursting in air at the start of the Revolutionary War. Jimi's all-guitar arrangement conveyed the same image of beautiful violence even more vividly than the original.

In concert.

RICHARD PETERS

[194]

RICHARD PETERS

It became the anthem for a new age in America. In 1969 the antiwar movement was peaking. Many performers had been recording protest songs for some time, notably Dylan's early "Masters of War," the Doors' "Unknown Soldier," Barry McGuire's "Eve of Destruction" and Country Joe's "I-Feel-Like-I'm-Fixin'-to-Die Rag," and Jimi had recorded several songs of the same genre. But not until now had anyone taken the national anthem itself, turned it inside out and made it the ultimate protest song.

When Jimi played "The Star-Spangled Banner" on April 19 in the Dallas Memorial Auditorium, the audience rioted, breaking chairs, rushing the stage and engaging in hand-to-hand combat with uniformed police.

In contrast, the Hendrix machine was running smoothly now. Mike Jeffery's office-apartment complex was humming. Usually Mike came into the office, from his upstairs bedroom, about 9 A.M., greeted his two employees, Bob and Kathy, with cool English cheer and gave the orders for the day.

At night Mike often haunted small clubs, looking for new talent. Besides Jimi, Fat Mattress and Cat Mother and the All-Night Newsboys, Mike had an Irish band called the Eire Apparent. Mike also backed some friends in producing a "psychedelic burlesque" in Billy Rose's old Diamond Horseshoe Theater. The show folded in less than a week, but for some time afterward Mike managed the musical arranger Ronnie Frangipani. It was an unlikely name, but so was that of another singer he signed, Tarot Delphi.

Mike was consistent in his contradictions. He was one of the entrepreneurs of the 1960s who tried to straddle the fence between *Them* and *Us*. As Noel Redding always said, you knew he had been a "leftenant" in the English army and not an enlisted man. He had the right accent, was a former spy for the queen, by blood a part of the establishment. Consequently he hated Jimi's desecration of "The Star-Spangled Banner," even though it wasn't *his* national anthem.

At the same time, Mike smoked dope and snorted coke and was drifting toward astrology. He was also dating a Canadian model named Lyn. She had known the musician Levon Helm in Toronto and had come south with him to the upstate New York village of Woodstock, where Helm and other members of a group known simply as The Band rehearsed with Bob Dylan and recorded an album, *Big Pink*.

Dylan's manager, Albert Grossman, had a home there too, and another of his clients, Janis Joplin, was in and out. Woodstock was like Greenwich Village, but with open fields and woods and cows, an aging rural bohemian colony whose individualism seemed almost mid-Victorian. It was the perfect mix for Mike, and he bought a big white clapboard house outside of town, surrounded with a white picket fence and called, in the English manner, White Gates. Mike and Lyn became lovers, and she gave up her modeling career.

In the office many of the chores were handled by telephone. Sometimes there were meetings with the accountants and lawyers and publicists. Papers were moved from desk to desk and business was conducted as in any other office, however unusual the "product" in this case.

By 1969 the popular music industry was just that, an industry. The only surprising thing about *Forbes* magazine putting the record business on its cover in 1968 was that it took the editors so long to realize the implications of annual sales in excess of a billion dollars and concert grosses adding another $500 million.

Of course Jimi was contributing his share to the success story. Already his first three albums had been certified "gold" by the Record Industry Association of America, meaning each had had retail sales of more than a million dollars. The Experience was also the highest paid act in the world, now getting $50,000 to $100,000 or more a night as a guarantee—half of it on signing the contract, the other half before going onstage. If all went well in the upcoming tour—and no one expected any less—Jimi and his musical partners could gross a minimum of $2,580,000. In addition would be the trio's share of poster sales, a burgeoning subsidiary industry.

Baltimore . . . New Haven . . . Philadelphia . . . Memphis . . . Dallas . . . Houston . . . Los Angeles . . . Oakland . . . Detroit—everywhere in the largest halls and all sold out.

And then the tour almost fell apart and Jimi's career teetered perilously.

On May 3, after flying into Canada from Detroit, Jimi was arrested by the Royal Canadian Mounted Police.

[197]

Jimi was used to customs checks from his trips to Europe. He accepted orders to open his luggage as routine. He wasn't stupid; he knew enough not to carry drugs from one country to another. What was the use? No matter where he went, his fans brought him a pharmacopoeia.

So Jimi was stunned when, at about 1:30 P.M., after stepping off a plane from Detroit, he was asked to open his flight bag, and when he did so, right there on top of his clean underwear Customs Officer Marvin Wilson saw a small glass jar containing four cellophane packets of white powder.

"What's that?" he asked abruptly.

Jimi looked at the jar and said he didn't know.

"It's not yours?"

Jimi looked genuinely shocked, "Uh . . . no. I don't know where it came from."

"This *is* your flight bag?"

"Uh . . . yeah. But I don't know where that jar came from."

Jimmy looked at Wilson and Wilson stared unbelievingly back.

"Honest," Jimi said.

CHAPTER

11

The tall, thin, black guitarist and the white Royal Mounted Policeman stood staring at each other. Then the officer picked up an aluminum tube, at the same time waving to a customs supervisor standing nearby.

"What's this?" Wilson asked, holding out the metal tube.

Jimi shrugged.

The metal tube—which contained what looked like resinous ash—and jar and four cellophane packets were all given to the customs supervisor. "I'd like to have all of this examined right away," the inspector said.

The supervisor nodded and invited Jimi into an office, where the Mounties had their field laboratory equipment. A chemist was put to work. Jimi sat, bored, in a folding chair, officially detained but not yet under arrest, while his road crew rushed off to the telephones to call New York.

Finally the chemist looked up from his work. He said only one word: "Heroin."

Jimi was rushed to police headquarters, charged with possession of narcotics and released on $10,000 bail, which was posted by a Toronto attorney.

A few hours later he was onstage before 12,000 fans in the Maple Leaf Gardens, many of whom had heard of the arrest on the radio or in conversation as they entered the auditorium.

Jimi walked onstage and said, "I want you to forget what happened yesterday and tomorrow and today. Tonight we're going to create a whole new world."

It was part of his usual rap. Jimi always talked like this to his audiences, but the arrest gave it special impact. Unfortunately the performance was mediocre.

At his arraignment two days later before Magistrate Fred Hayes, a preliminary hearing was set for June 19. The courtroom was packed with his fans. Jimi's lawyer, Steve Weiss, had flown in from New York. Jimi was wearing a pink shirt open to the waist, an Apache-style headband, a multicolored scarf around his neck, and beads. When the judge called Jimi's name—"James Marshall Hendrix of New York!"—he rose and delivered a lips-pursed sneer. There was no demand for a guilty/not guilty plea. Only a few words were exchanged and in just four or five minutes it was all over. For the time being, Jimi was free to go.

There had been other rock-and-roll arrests for drugs in the past dozen months. Eric Clapton, Neil Young, the entire Steve Miller Band, Barry McGuire, Brian Jones, John Lennon and Yoko Ono, Richie Furay and Jim Messina (then members of the Buffalo Springfield), Charles Lloyd, James Cotton and George Harrison all were jailed at least briefly during this period, but it was for possession of psychedelics, usually marijuana.

Jimi's arrest was different, and it was serious. A little pot was one thing. Heroin was something else.

One of the seven persons traveling with Jimi at the time

Jimi at Toronto City Hall in 1969 to face charges of illegal possession of narcotics

of the arrest was Sharon Lawrence. Later she would become one of Jimi's close friends, but on this day in Canada she put her job as a reporter for United Press International ahead of friendship and filed a story telling what happened.

At the same time, Gerry Stickells called New York to give Mike his report of the crisis. But Mike was vacationing in Hawaii, so he called Michael Goldstein, who was still on retainer as the group's publicist. Michael said he would take care of it and took a cab first to the offices of UPI and then to the Associated Press.

More than ten years later Michael still won't be totally open about what he did in those offices. However, he does take credit for "killing" the story, keeping it from going out to all the newspapers and radio stations that subscribed to the two wire services.

"See," he says, "I never minded stories like that being in *Rolling Stone* or in our own [underground] newspapers. Where it would hurt you was not there, it was in the daily papers across the country, which would make large concert hall promoters close down all your concert dates. I knew that a million dollars was riding on that story not getting on UPI and the AP wire.

"Sharon filed a story. It didn't get on the national wire. It got lost. That's what you pay a press agent for. He's there to get you out of trouble. People who work for wire services have needs, desires for information, or needs and desires for certain things. A press agent with an act like Jimi ought to have five hundred bucks in his pocket of the company's money to do whatever he has to do—to pay guards, to pay police, whatever. By his nature, a press agent is unscrupulous in defense of his act."

As Jimi resumed his tour—looking as if "there'd been a plane crash," according to Eric Barrett—Mike Jeffery returned to New York. Soon after, the only detailed press account of the arrest was on the stands in *Rolling Stone*. The story made it clear that some of those involved smelled a rat, suspected a setup.

First, *Rolling Stone* quoted Louis Goldblatt, Jimi's limousine driver, who said Jimi was genuinely stunned. Goldblatt and other observers also noted that the Royal Canadian Mounties—who wore blue uniforms and were the chief enforcers of Canadian narcotics laws—behaved "unusually throughout."

"For one thing, the Mounties . . . customarily do not wait at the airport to make dope busts, as they did in Hendrix's case. Another item is that all the inquiry and searching at the airport was done right out in the open at the customs gate. The more usual procedure is for officers and those being detained to retire from public view, in respect for the privacy of the accused. But Hendrix and company were forced to stand for hours under the gaze of scores of onlookers at the cake-shaped airport building—rent-a-car girls, cigar stand operators, porters, cab drivers and travelers—while the feds poked through their belongings."

The *Rolling Stone* reporter noted that someone might have been out to "get" Jimi by "laying a surprise stash on him," placing the drugs in his suitcase in Detroit just before he left for Canada, then telephoning ahead to tip off the police.

"Whatever the case," said *Rolling Stone*'s reporter, "the Mounties do not typically lie in wait at the airport, ready to pounce. Toronto authorities in recent months have been getting tough on the free-living hippie community of Yorkeville, more or less Toronto's version of the Haight-Ashbury, and there is the possibility that Hendrix may have been caught in the squeeze.

"The populace of Toronto are a very conservative lot and tend to look with suspicion upon anybody who looks and dresses a little different from themselves. Hendrix looks a lot different. Make an example of this freaky, frizzy-haired psychedelic spade (if you go by this reasoning) and maybe you can scare the freaks out of Yorkeville."

Jimi told Mike, by telephone, that he had been framed, that the bottle was a plant, and Mike more or less believed him. But he also had some doubt. He didn't know what to believe. So he turned to a worldly American friend for advice.

This was one of the most interesting characters in Mike's entourage, a fiftyish, sad-eyed jazz aficionado who had packed several lives into one. Born Gerald Herbert Breitman in Brooklyn, he now went by the name of Jerry Morrison, and sometimes listed his telephone under the name Lamont Cranston, who was radio's fabled Shadow. Before meeting Mike and Jimi, Jerry had been a song plugger, publicist and/or manager of a variety of performers, including Harry James, former Dead End Kid Gabe Dell, composer Lorenz Hart and Louis Armstrong. Then for five years, from 1955 to 1960, he was "public relations director" for the dictator of Haiti, Antoine "Papa Doc" Duvalier, becoming, by his own description, the third most powerful man in the Caribbean island. Apparently the relationship soured when Duvalier wanted Jerry to marry his oldest daughter and Jerry declined, soon after to flee for his life. Other adventures followed in Jamaica and in Central America, and sometime in 1968, back in New York and working again for Louis Armstrong, Jerry met Mike and began spending time with him.

Mike expressed his concern about Jimi's occasional use of heroin and the friends he saw who used it regularly, including Devon in New York.

"If it's around, it's dangerous," Mike said. "I want Jimi away from it. I want him *away* from those people!"

Jerry Morrison explains: "Mike believed that Jimi couldn't get his trip together in the city because of the leeches. He wanted me to find a house that was isolated and insulated."

The previous summer, in 1968, Jerry had introduced Mike to Woodstock, and now he suggested that Jimi get a house there too. Jerry was told to find a house, and he was assigned the task of making sure Jimi got everything he wanted in the house. Budget was not important, Mike said. Keeping Jimi out of trouble was.

On the road, Jimi flew from big city to big city, from the Coliseum in Charlotte to the Civic Center in Charleston to the State Fairgrounds in Indianapolis to the Civic Center in Baltimore, returning to New York on May 18, two weeks following the Toronto bust, for a single performance at Madison Square Garden with Cat Mother and the All-Night Newsboys and the Buddy Miles Express.

It was not a good time for Jimi.

Mike Jeffery told Jimi not to worry about the drug charges, saying he had everything well in hand, but someone else told Jimi that maybe it was Mike who had set him up, to keep him dependent and under control. After nearly losing Jimi to Chas in London, the friend said, Mike had gotten paranoid. Mike had never been able to develop a second truly successful act and was, himself, dependent economically on Jimi's continued management to keep his own many schemes and life style afloat. Jimi began to look at Mike suspiciously.

There was also the matter of the recording studio Mike suggested they build, a project that Jimi alternately loved and feared. Talk of constructing the studio started months before, after Mike totaled Jimi's recording costs for 1968 and was alarmed to find they'd spent nearly $200,000 at the Record Plant alone and another $20,000 to $30,000 at various studios in London and Los Angeles. When Jimi approved the idea of having his own studio and said he wanted to call it Electric Lady Studios, Mike began scouting locations and went to Reprise Records for a $250,000 advance against future royalties to get the project under way.

Months passed. Construction was begun. Problems ate up the record company money, and Mike began throwing in money of his own. The Minetta Stream ran underground where the studio was being built, under the old Village Barn on Eighth Street, requiring stronger foundations. A subway station fifty yards away made soundproofing far more expensive than was anticipated. And now Jimi said he wanted to dump the whole project.

Miked dropped his head into his hands, then looked up at Jimi and said, "You tell me you don't like the Record Plant because you can't just show up when you want to. You say you want total control. This will be your studio. You can go in there any time you want and stay all night . . ."

Jimi stood in front of Mike silently.

"Look," Mike finally said, "the damned place is almost ready. We'll be open in a month, two months at the most. You can't back out now! *I* can't back out! Goddammit, Jimi!"

Mike stopped, turning away to look out of the window near his desk. "Goddammit," he said quietly.

Jimi stood there for a minute, then turned and walked away without saying anything.

He went to his friend Sharon Lawrence and told her what was bothering him. He said nothing was going right—the bust, the studio, Noel and Mitch.

"I knew something was going to happen," Sharon said later, "and Jimi and I used to have a lot of talks about things, and Jimi liked Noel a lot, you know, loved him, really, and I said, 'Well, you are doing things that are making Noel and Mitch unhappy. You are not communicating with them. You are getting very messed up.'

"And so then more things came out and Jimi would say, 'I am worried that you are not paying my taxes.' Jimi was always saying, 'I don't want to end up like Joe Louis.' And he was very concerned his money was not being taken care of, and they kept telling him that his studio would be a great investment, and I said, 'Well, Jimi, you had better find out if your taxes are being paid before you go into such an expense. You have an investment with a man that you are not sure you trust.'

"So Jimi and I went to see Henry Steingarten [Jimi and Mike Jeffery's New York attorney] when he came to Los Angeles and we told him that Jimi wanted to withdraw from the studio and he also wanted to withdraw from Mike Jeffery as a manager."

Jimi was staying at the Beverly Rodeo Hotel in Beverly Hills, by now a favored refuge whenever he was in southern California. Steingarten was staying in another hotel some miles away, and for several days the two traveled back and forth to each other's rooms, generally with Sharon Lawrence present.

"Jimi found it very hard to say all this [voice his complaints] because he found it very emotional," Sharon reported later. "He was afraid the group was going to break up, and Jeffery and Stickells would tell him he would be nowhere if it broke up. And so Jimi started to tell Steingarten this, and he said, 'Sharon, you just tell him.' And Jimi would hover around my chair and say tell him this and tell him that. I had to keep initiating: 'Jimi would like to do this, Mr. Steingarten.' He told him he wanted to be bought out of the studio if Jeffery would reimburse him for his investment, and Steingarten, at that time, said he would take it up with Jeffery if Jimi felt that strongly, then, yes, they should do it, and Jimi then told him that to get out of the contract, if he didn't work again until it ran out, he was willing to do that to get away from Mike.

"Steingarten asked Jimi and me to gather as much evidence as we could in ways that Mike had been crooked, or had not Jimi's or the Experience's best interests at heart, and he asked us to find documents, to make notes, to tape anything and to talk to Gerry Stickells and see how helpful he would be."

It was during this time that I met Jimi Hendrix for the first time.

Jimi was still at the Beverly Rodeo, with Billy Cox, his bassist from his Screaming Eagles days, and Albert Allen, a friend from Greenwich Village, when I asked for an interview. Right away he talked about changing the structure of the band, said he wanted to have Billy on bass and the Buddy Miles group—renamed the Freedom Express—behind him, along with "three soul sisters, regardless of whether they're Italian or Irish or whatever." Jimi emphasized that Billy would not be replacing Noel necessarily, although he noted that Noel still had his band, Fat Mattress, while Mitch was in London "partying." Jimi also insisted that all the remaining concerts in the summer tour would feature the Experience as it was.

However, he said, any future group would not be called the Experience, or the Jimi Hendrix anything. Also, it would be larger in size, a "sky church sort of thing" that performed free or on a donation basis as often as possible.

Jimi's rap was as it always was, an amalgam of guru politics and hippie philosophy. He called security the "worst drug in American today," said "there's gonna have to be some people to get off their asses and try to get theirselves together, instead of sittin' around in smoke dens talkin' about 'Yeah, man, this is groovy' and then come up with no kind of solution."

"It'll take somebody like us to get it together," Jimi said. "Regardless of whether it's gonna be us, ourselves, as a band of gypsies, the feeling is there and that's what counts. If I die tomorrow, the feeling is there. Forget about the brand names. We put across the music. There's painters puttin' it across. There's actors. The idea is to do it as strong as possible, to work out a certain physical change.

"I know we can do it. That's not the problem. It's can you keep up? Don't worry about us. That's why we're suffering. That's why we party hard. That's why we suffer hard."

Jimi excused himself and joined Billy Cox, who had been tuning his bass incessantly, impatiently, and began a jam that lasted long into the soft California night.

The pressures continued. Reprise Records had been demanding a new album for more than six months and, when Jimi was in Los Angeles, resorted to what most record companies did when the artists failed to provide the contracted number of albums per year, producing a sort of "greatest hits" package. This one, called *Smash Hits,* included eight previously released songs—"Hey Joe," "Foxy Lady," "Purple Haze," "Fire" and "All Along the Watchtower" among them—and four never released in America—"Red House," "Can You See Me," "Remember" and "Stone Free."

It was nothing to be ashamed of, and the reviewers had kind things to say, but for Jimi it was a reminder of what he used to be musically, not what he thought he was.

The same week, on June 19, Jimi flew to Canada for his preliminary hearing.

Jimi stood mutely, flanked by his attorneys, as the state prosecutor read a list of the contents of the flight bag in which the drugs were found.

"Shampoo . . . hair spray . . . a large comb . . . vitamin pills . . . a pocketbook . . ."

Then finally: "Glass jar containing three packets of heroin . . . and a metal tube containing residue of hashish."

The judge, Robert Taylor, determined that the appropriate tests were conducted on the suspected drugs, then announced that Jimi would stand trial December 8 on the two possession charges. There were no other charges made, dispelling rumors that Jimi was trafficking or smuggling. Bail was held at $10,000, and Jimi flew back to Los Angeles.

The next day, June 20, he headlined the first night of a three-day festival at Devonshire Downs. As with so many other pop festivals, this was held in a huge, flat, open field, where a temporary stage had been constructed that rose ten feet, affording the performers security while offering the audience a semblance of visibility. It was hot and dry and dusty, without the trace of a breeze. Police helicopters hovered over the area, drowning out Buffy Sainte-Marie and some of the other, "softer" acts. There were so many jammed together—at least 50,000 in a space better suited to half the number—that it looked and felt like the railroad station scene as Scarlett O'Hara picked her way among the Confederate wounded in *Gone With the Wind*. Hundreds more, who didn't have the money for tickets or who chose to spend it on cheap wine and pills instead, charged the chain link fence erected by the concert promoters, clashing with police. Before the weekend was over, nearly 300 were injured, another 75 were jailed. It was not exactly a typical 1960s love-in.

Nor was it one of Jimi's best performances. Still upset by the hearing in Toronto the previous day, and frustrated by the lack of response he got because he didn't play his early hits, Jimi played a short, listless set and called the audience a "teenybopper crowd." Only once, when a well-known Los Angeles groupie, who called herself Sunshine after the LSD of the same name, climbed onto the stage and threw herself between Jimi's legs, did the audience, and Jimi, wake up. Sunshine dropped to her knees, then fell onto her back, keeping her heels beneath her rump. She began a humping motion as Jimi straddled her lithe and writhing form, holding the guitar between his legs, its neck held out before him like an erect phallus.

But Jimi tired quickly of this and stepped away, dropping back into a soulful blues.

He left the stage to a smattering of applause.

For this Jimi was paid $100,000, more than a third of the entire talent budget for the festival, which included thirty-three acts, among them the Byrds, Creedance Clearwater Revival, Joe Cocker, Johnny Winter, the Rascals, Steppenwolf, Spirit, Jethro Tull, Marvin Gaye, Eric Burdon and Three Dog Night. It wasn't a sum requested by his management, but offered by the promoters, causing many of the other performers to resent Jimi.

He returned to the festival grounds the next day, jamming for forty-five minutes with Buddy Miles, thus partially redeeming himself. But it wasn't enough. Jimi's audience wanted *more:* the old Jimi Hendrix, the Jimi they got a flash of when he had "jammed" so briefly with Sunshine.

Jimi couldn't have cared less. According to friends, he

hated himself for reverting to his old style of performance, said it wasn't his thing anymore.

A week later, on June 29, he and Noel and Mitch flew separately to Denver for another festival. This was the final show of the tour and, as it happened, the last for the Jimi Hendrix Experience.

Jimi took some friends with him to Denver, where a crowd of 40,000 waited.

The Mile High Stadium was named for the city's elevation. But Jimi laughed. On this day there was another reason. He had taken acid in the limousine on the way to the show.

One of his friends told Jimi that his favorite song was "Bold as Love," so Jimi started the set with it: "Anger/He smiles, telling him/Shiny metallic purple armor/Green jealousy . . ."

Jimi looked across the green football field into the blur of the distant stadium. Was the music reaching everyone? Did anyone care?

The acid was taking affect. Smooth flowing waves of color surrounded him as he sang: "Blue are the life-giving waters, taken for granted/They quietly understand . . ."

Jimi had been talking with friends in California about the healing properties of color and sound. Was he now healing his audience? Cleansing it? What was that movement? What was that noise he heard above the wail of his voice and guitar?

Suddenly the stage was engulfed. Fans came scrambling from everywhere. Police fired tear gas canisters point-blank into the throng. The wind blew the gas back over the stage. Noel and Mitch were in flight. Gerry Stickells grabbed Jimi roughly and hustled him backstage.

A van was waiting, doors open, engine roaring. Jimi was shoved inside. Noel and Mitch were there. Doors were slammed shut and locked just as the people reached it, faces pressed flat against windows, fists pounding on the sides and roof.

Tears poured down Jimi's cheeks. Everyone was coughing from the tear gas. Slowly the van moved through the crowd, its roof beaten flat by the time it reached the exit gate.

Jimi thought colors were healing. It didn't make any sense, what was happening. He was peaking on the acid now.

Before leaving Denver the next day Noel read in the local newspaper that Jimi was planning to expand the size of the band. Jimi had said no more to the Denver reporter than he'd said to others for several months, but Noel swore this was the first that he had heard of it. It seemed hard to believe. And it didn't matter. Noel was upset about many things. So he quit, flying back to England that day. "Jimi is a very good guitarist," he told *Rolling Stone*, "but he was very hard to work with. I think he suffers from a split personality. He's a genius guitarist and his writing is very good, but he whips himself. He gets everybody around him very uptight because he worries about everything. God knows why."

Why was Noel so surprised? Why was he upset? Had he forgotten all the pleading and cajoling of the previous Christmas holidays? Had he forgotten that Jimi finally had agreed to keep the band together only so long as it took to fulfill the summer concert commitments?

A friend close to the band says Noel—and the others—were not so forgetful as they were hopeful. After all, to Noel and Mitch and Jeffery and others dependent upon the Experience's earnings, it made no sense whatsoever to abandon a winning formula. It is human nature to want something that is good to go on and on. But for Jimi it was not good enough, and in the end Noel quit and flew off in a snit to save face.

"I could never understand why he worried so much,"

Noel said. "I mean, we were earning a fortune on the road. On three occasions we earned over $100,000 for a single performance. In the last twelve months I don't think we ever copped less than $25,000 for a night's work.

"The recording sessions were chaos, and onstage it was getting ridiculous. The audience wanted us to play the old Hendrix standards, but Jimi wanted to do his new stuff. The last straw came at the Denver Pop Festival when Jimi told a reporter that he was going to enlarge the band . . . without even consulting myself or our drummer, Mitch Mitchell.

"I went up to Jimi that night, said goodbye and caught the next plane to London. I don't think Jimi believed I'd do it. Later on he phoned and asked me to come back, but I said, 'Stuff it!' "

CHAPTER

12

Mitch followed Noel to London the next day, July 1, and a day after that both of them sat down with a reporter for the *Evening Standard* and said, yes, they had left the Experience and the split was irreversible. However many other reasons there were for the breakup, once again the only explanation given was that Jimi had not shared with Noel and Mitch his plans to change the makeup of the group.

The next day, July 3, was black. That was when news of Brian Jones's death reached Jimi in New York. Brian had been found the day before, the morning after a party, floating in the swimming pool of his English estate. Because Brian had been replaced in the Rolling Stones only a week before, at first there were stories of suicide. After all, wasn't Brian an excellent swimmer? An autopsy was held and death was called "accidental." Brian had merely jumped into the pool with too many drugs competing for control of his life. His bloated body was found saturated with barbiturates and alcohol, two central nervous system depressants, as well as some unidentified amphetamines.

Jimi was visibly depressed. Drug overdoses were commonplace in the music community, almost—horribly—a "tradition," especially in jazz and increasingly in recent years in rock. The Beatles' manager, Brian Epstein, had died from the same barbiturate-alcohol combination in 1967. Frankie Lymon, who had had a number of hits back in the 1950s, was a heroin casualty in 1968. Was Jimi merely upset at the loss of a friend? Or did it occur to him that there but for the grace of whatever gods there might be went James Marshall Hendrix too?

Typically, Jimi said nothing to friends. The only acknowledgment of Brian's death he made occurred during an appearance on Johnny Carson's *Tonight Show* with Billy Cox. Jimi introduced a new song called "Lover Man" and dedicated it to his dead friend.

The only other thing notable about the television appearance was that the black comic, Flip Wilson, who was substituting for Carson, had a watermelon on the desk and kept patting it during his talk with Jimi. Jimi looked embarrassed.

Mike had scheduled a long midsummer vacation for Jimi—he had the next six weeks off. The next firm date was for August 17, as the final act in a three-day festival to be held in an alfalfa field in upstate New York, about ten miles from where Jimi had his summer house. The young promoters of the festival were calling their event the "Woodstock Music and Art Fair . . . An Aquarian Exposition . . . 3 Days of Peace and Music." The roster of performers they had persuaded to appear was impressive, but the money promised was not. Jimi was to be the highest paid performer of the lot, yet he was getting far less than he was accustomed to—only $36,000. The promoters were saying the festival was going to be the world's largest, but no one was buying it. Two or three hundred thousand hippies in a cow pasture two hours' drive from New York? You've got to be kidding.

A later publicity shot showing the ravages of time

[217]

In the first week of July, Jimi put his life on "cruise."

His scene in New York remained well set and comfortable. Whenever he wished he booked time at the Record Plant and jammed with members of his "sky church," the close-knit core of musicians he was by now gathering around him. Of course there was Billy Cox, the quiet, stocky black with whom Jimi served in the Screaming Eagles and later scuffled with in Tennessee. The fat, loud, fun-loving drummer Buddy Miles came and went as he toured with his band, the Buddy Miles Express. Juma Sutan was a new arrival. He lived on forty acres near Woodstock, not far from Jimi's house, and played congas.

Jimi was also spending time now with Alan Douglas. Of all of Jimi's friends, eventually Alan would become the most disliked by Jimi's other friends. Nonetheless, when Jimi met Alan in New York, Alan's credentials were impressive. He was a tall, thin black man of Jewish background who had recorded some of the last words of both Lenny Bruce and Malcolm X. Jimi came to call Alan "A.D."—for Alan Douglas and also for "After Death."

"Jimi called him that because everybody he touched dropped dead right afterward," says Pat Hartley, whose best friend, Stella, was married to Alan at the time. "Alan Douglas did put good shit together, though. He was a black historian and all of that, so he seemed a good choice for Jimi."

When they met, Alan was working with a group of youngsters from Harlem called the Last Poets, and soon after that he went into the studio with Timothy Leary. Alan had his own record label at the time, Douglas Records, and he persuaded Jimi to provide tasty, improvisational backup guitar on both albums, *The Last Poets* (released by Columbia) and Leary's instantly forgettable *You Can Be Anything You Want to Be This Time Around* (eventually released by Capitol). The albums sold so poorly, lawyers for Jimi and Reprise Records decided not to sue but reprimanded Jimi severely.

Jimi didn't care. Whom he played with, or behind, mattered little, and so long as he was having a good time playing, he paid no attention to whether the jams were being taped. This was true in his scuffling days and it was no less true now.

"I feel guilty when people say I'm the greatest guitarist on the scene," he told a journalist. "What's good or bad doesn't matter to me. What does matter is feeling and not feeling. If only people would take more of a true view and think in terms of feeling."

For Jimi this "feeling" could most easily be expressed through music. In fact, it might have been the *only* way he could express himself with total honesty. Certainly it was the way in which he showed himself most candidly. Albums were "nothing but personal diaries," he said.

"When you hear somebody making music, they are baring a naked part of their soul to you."

Jimi jammed with everyone. Some he joined onstage in clubs. Others he took into the studio with him. Most of the memorable jams occurred in one place, at Steve Paul's Scene. It was there that Jimi eventually played with a *Who's Who* of musicians and singers, sometimes showing up three or four times a week to play guitar or, frequently, bass behind James Cotton, Johnny Winter, the Chambers Brothers, an early Fleetwood Mac, Spooky Tooth, the new Led Zeppelin, Richie Havens, Buddy Guy, Jim Morrison (who did little more than scream drunken obscenities as Jimi played the blues), the McCoys, and the young Rick Springfield.

In almost all of these jams Jimi participated with great enthusiasm but also modestly, never competing, soloing only when asked.

Socially, Devon Wilson was still in charge. "She wasn't there when it got bad for her and smack [heroin]," says Alvenia Bridges, a young black model who entered Jimi's New York entourage after knowing him slightly in Los Angeles. "She was a pretty wild lady, but she loved Jimi and he loved her and she ran the show. She told people where to sit at clubs."

Colette Mimram and Stella Douglas were usually around too, in the clubs at night, in their chic Manhattan boutique afternoons. Soon after Brian Jones's death, Jimi asked for and received permission from the Canadian court to go to Morocco with Stella and Collette to buy pillows and clothing and rugs. Friends say Jimi picked up all the bills, spending $10,000 on the trip and at least $20,000 more on the merchandise.

Few ever knew where, or when, Jimi slept. He had a sparsely furnished apartment on Fifteenth Street on the outskirts of Greenwich Village—really no more than three rooms, scattered with Moroccan pillows, piles of clothing and shiny guitars—but just as often he spent his nights somewhere else. He kept an apartment in a hotel in the East Fifties, vacated eventually when someone claiming to be his brother checked in and ran up a bill of more than $15,000. More often he stayed with one of his ladies in their apartments, strewn all over the city.

"He'd call in the middle of the night," says Alvenia Bridges. "He'd come over to sleep. There were too many people at his apartment. We'd go to Colony Records or go for a ride in a carriage in Central Park. He called one night when I was living on the West Side and he came over and he slept for eighteen hours straight. I never called him. Sometimes he'd just show up. I'd leave the key for him. He knew where I kept it.

"He shared his dreams with me. He had a dream to bring together all the creative people that he knew, to have his dreams come true. He thought he'd have enough money to make that happen. He really *believed* in his sky church music idea."

The idea of forming a musical commune was one that Jimi shared with everyone who would listen. His interviews of the time abound with talk of getting writers and musicians together to experiment, to jam, to "just see what happens." And as the Woodstock Music and Art Fair approached, many of the jams were moved to the Woodstock suburbs, to Jimi's big stone house at the end of Taver Hollow Road near a small village called Shokan.

"The house was rented in my name," Jerry Morrison says. "I'd known the owner and I told him I wanted the

JERRY HOPKINS

Jimi's Woodstock retreat

house for some clients. When he came up there and saw all those black musicians, he got uptight. But he was a nice man and backed off."

The house had eight bedrooms and was rented fully furnished, with many antiques, so it hardly looked like the average rock star's home. Certainly it didn't look like Jimi's. But Jimi seemed oblivious, unaware or uncaring about his environment. So long as there was electricity for his guitar, food and sex when he wanted it, a regular and varied supply of drugs, and companions with whom to play music, his wants were covered; he could just as easily have been in a Quonset hut in the Yukon Territory or a bamboo house in the Philippines.

Jerry Morrison remembers a call he got soon after renting the house. "We tried to keep the groupies away from the place," he says, "but Jimi went into Woodstock and brought a few girls back. That let it out, and after that they were always infiltrating. One night he called me at my house in Phoenicia Valley and said come right over."

"Hurry!" Jimi said, a note of panic in his voice. "I need help fast!"

Jerry ran to his jeep and drove as fast as he could the eight miles to the big two-story house in the woods. He rang the doorbell. The cook said Jimi was in his bedroom. Jerry took the steps two at a time and burst into the room.

"Jimi had a huge bed," Jerry says, "and there he was in the middle of it, covered by six or seven girls who were sucking on every orifice and protuberance."

Jimi looked up at Jerry and smiled and said, "You a friend?"

Jerry said, "Yes . . ."

Jimi said, "Well, do me a favor."

Jerry said, "Anything . . ."

Jimi said, "Well, take your clothes off and join me."

Jimi loved his Woodstock retreat. Although the property was not fenced, security was not considered a problem. The house was surrounded by miles of uninhabited hill country, and the region's longtime reputation as an artists' colony provided a hands-off attitude toward celebrities, even when they were of Bob Dylan's magnitude. Moreover, the house itself boasted several special amenities, including two caretakers, two live-in cooks, a fireplace so large it took two men to carry the logs for it, a pond, horses and—because the owner was an ice cream manufacturer—freezers full of Jimi's favorite dessert. The rent was $3,000 a month, but Jimi believed it was worth every penny.

The pasted-together *Smash Hits* album went onto the charts August 2—headed for the Number Six position—as Jimi prepared for the festival, jamming with a tightening group of percussionists who would appear with him. The festival was to begin in just two weeks, on the fifteenth, but already the audience was arriving, camping in the woods in tents and vans.

There were other signs that this would be more than just another rock festival. By late July, advertisements were promising appearances by (in the order listed) Joan Baez, Arlo Guthrie, Tim Hardin (then a Woodstock resident), Richie Havens, the Incredible String Band, Ravi Shankar, Bert Sommer, Sweetwater, Canned Heat, Creedence Clearwater (Revival), the Grateful Dead, Keef Hartley, Janis Joplin, Jefferson Airplane, Mountain, Quill, Santana, Sly and the Family Stone, the Band, Country Joe and the Fish, Blood, Sweat and Tears, Joe Cocker, Crosby, Stills & Nash, Jimi Hendrix, Iron Butterfly, Sha-na-na, Ten Years After and Johnny Winter. Clearly this was the most impressive collection of talent ever presented in one spot on a single weekend anywhere in the world.

The location and date added more promise. Although Bob Dylan never was booked to play, rumors of an appearance were rampant, and even if he didn't appear, the knowledge that he actually lived nearby was enough to make Woodstock and its environs "holy ground." How appropriate it was when, after local townspeople in Walkill, New York, objected, the festival site was moved to a 600-acre dairy farm fifteen miles away, outside a village called Bethel, whose name itself means "a hallowed spot, a place where God is worshiped."

It was as if the young people of America had taken the achievement of Apollo 11 as a challenge: Now that the older generation had put a man on the moon, the younger generation would have to do something impressive on earth.

Time magazine called it "history's biggest happening" and said it "may well rank as one of the significant political and sociological events of the new age." The *Village Voice* said it was a "hip version of Jones Beach transported to a war zone in Vietnam during the monsoon." Allen Ginsberg described it as "a major planetary event." *Newsweek* insisted it was both a picnic and an act of revolution, "Chicago without the politics . . . Fort Lauderdale with marijuana and LSD instead of beer." Max Lerner, the syndicated political columnist, wrote that the festival would be of interest to historians because it marked a "turning point in the consciousness the generations have of each other and of themselves." The New York *Post*'s pop reporter, Al Aronowitz, compared the whole thing to a "friendly monster with marijuana breath." *Life* put out a special edition and said "never before had a hippie gathering been so large or so successful, so impressive." *The New York Times* called it "essentially a phenomenon of innocence . . . they came, it seems, to enjoy their own society, to exult in a life style that is its own declaration of independence . . . with Henry the Fifth, they could say at Bethel, 'He that outlives this day, and comes safe home will stand a-tiptoe when this day is nam'd.' " Yippie leader Abbie Hoffman, who churned out a book called *The Woodstock Nation* in a week's time following the event, said it

[224]

marked "the birth of the Woodstock Nation and the death of the American dinosaur." Ellen Sander wrote in the *Saturday Review* that it was "nothing less than the ultimate pop experience, an event that completely transcended anything and everything hitherto considered pop." The list of writers and observers and their gargantuan appraisals was endless.

This was the reaction that came later. During the "Aquarian Exposition" itself, media attention was not so flattering.

The first two days Jimi stayed in his Shokan home listening to the radio. This upstate New York farming region was severely rocked by the event and it was all the local broadcasters could talk about. Highways were totally blocked for twenty miles in every direction. The fences went down almost immediately, permitting uncontrolled access to the festival grounds. By the end of the first day all the food concessions ran out of supplies and traffic problems made restocking an impossibility. The portable toilets overflowed and couldn't be emptied. It rained, turning the rolling pastureland into a muddy swamp, and more rain was predicted for the third day. Police reported seventy-five arrests for drugs and one death, caused when a tractor ran over someone in a sleeping bag. Local officials were appalled and asked Governor Nelson Rockefeller to declare the festival site a disaster area.

According to some sources, Jimi was freaked out by these reports and didn't want to perform, even though the musicians were being flown to the site in helicopters and offered private dressing rooms. The producers of the festival never talked with Jimi, remaining in telephone contact with Mike Jeffery, who told them not to worry.

The festival was scheduled to end sometime after midnight Sunday, but when midnight came, several acts hadn't performed, and the earliest Jimi would go on was projected for dawn. All that evening he and his fellow musicians, and

Jerry Morrison, remained in the house, consuming what Jerry describes as "considerable quantities of coke and grass."

One other thing was remarkable. "There was an argument," Jerry says, "between me and Mike Jeffery over whether or not Jimi should play 'The Star-Spangled Banner.' Mike said no. It'd caused a riot in Dallas, and he said he thought things were bad enough already here without making them worse. I disagreed. Because Jimi was going on as the final act, I thought he *had* to play the national anthem. It didn't matter. When Mike left the house, I told Jimi to go for it."

The audience was, in Jerry's words, "wasted and thinning fast," when Jimi was taken to a trailer about 1 A.M. The huge stage was well lighted, but aside from the banks of spotlights in front of it, the only lights the performers could see were those of small, flickering campfires. Everything else was lost in darkness. Only the hoarse roar coming at the end of a set or at the first appearance of a new band revealed the presence of an audience. By the time Jimi went on, at 10:30 Monday morning, there were about 60,000 left. Estimates of the crowd at its peak ranged from 250,000 to 400,000.

Jimi was resplendent in a white leather suit, the trouser legs flared at the bottom, the jacket cut short, just below the sternum, and hung with long fringe decorated with blue and white beads. A magenta scarf tied around his forehead and several gold chains completed the outfit.

Behind him were five musicians. Mitch Mitchell had returned and was sitting in his familiar position on drums and Billy Cox was playing bass. The other three were not so well known, and however much they continued to jam with Jimi, they never played publicly again with him in the same configuration. Larry Lee played rhythm guitar, Juma Sutan the congas, Jerry Velez the bongos.

Jimmy peered into the soggy distance, into what he had

called "the cave of despair" before he came to look at it. What he saw hardly changed his mind. It was, as one writer put it, "a solid body of mud held together by a mucilage of garbage and human excrement." But what Jimi *felt* was something else. Even after three long days the energy remained.

So he leaned back into his hips-thrust-forward stance and played the familiar notes that had all of them singing in their wasted heads: "Oh say, can you see . . . . . . by the dawn's early light?" And the dawn, or what was left of it, was his.

"Well, you gotta remember!" Jimi said. "Jesus, Jerry. This is important."

Jimi was seated across a table from Jerry Morrison in a bar in the Village, his expression a curious mix of amusement and irritation.

"Look, man," Jerry said, "I thought you'd be pissed off about the damage . . ."

Jimi looked at his friend. "Okay, maybe you'll remember if you tell me again. Start at the beginning."

Jerry sighed and told the story again. "There were a lotta people hanging around after the festival," he said. "And I guess some of them found out where you had your house. Or maybe one of the other guys took some people out there, and then they came back later with cans of paint. Whatever happened, somebody painted some of the walls black and the owner wants five thousand, six thousand dollars, to cover the damage."

"Yeah, yeah," Jimi interrupted impatiently. "And what was written on the wall in the bedroom?"

Jerry closed his eyes as if meditating. "Lemme think. Yeah. It said, 'Jimi, you shoulda been here. I give the greatest head.' And then it was signed—dammit, Jimi, I can't remember her name, I just can't."

Jimi looked at his friend with disgust. He shook his head. "Damn," he said, finally. "The girl says she's the best cocksucker in the world and you forget her name. Well, I tell you what—you drive back up there and find out. Got it?"

Jimi sat staring for a moment then said woefully, "Some kind of friend you turn out to be. I call you when I got a dozen girls with me and you can't even remember a simple name."

CHAPTER

13

Salvation, a discothèque at 1 Sheridan Square, in Greenwich Village, made quite a name for itself. First, it was one of New York's most fashionable nightclubs for the pop elite and the jet set, counting among its patrons Paul McCartney, who reportedly met his wife Linda there, and Jordan's King Hussein. One of the doormen was the actor Richard Roundtree, who later starred in the *Shaft* movies. When the club dropped its recorded-music policy and started featuring live performances, Jimi Hendrix played the first night.

Jimi was also kidnapped out of the club by the Mafia.

Until now this story has never been told—partly because it was covered up at the time and partly because the truth is so fantastic that it is almost unbelievable. It is, in short, reminiscent of Jimmy Breslin's book *The Gang That Couldn't Shoot Straight* or the story told about bumbling hoodlums in *The Pope of Greenwich Village*. Although, at the time, no one thought it was funny at all. Certainly not Jimi. Nor Mike Jeffery and the small handful of others close to Jeffery who knew about it. And least of all, Salvation's owner, Bobby Woods, who was found the victim of a gang-style murder only a few months later.

It began innocently enough. Jimi started frequenting the club sometime after it opened in 1968. According to Richie Rivera, bartender, and George Costs, doorman, Jimi usually entered the club alone around midnight and took a back table or sat at the bar and generally ordered Planter's Punch. As the evening wore on—Salvation was open until 4 A.M.—Jimi attracted his usual following. Sometimes he took one of the young women home with him. Richie says he favored one of the waitresses who was also a girl friend of Bobby Woods. Bobby told her to be friendly to Jimi, to soften him up so Bobby could ask him to perform in the club.

By now Bobby was in trouble, and the switch from canned music to live music was an attempt to dig out from under the problems he had. Bobby was forty-one, had made millions in a used-car agency in Queens and was an habitué of another "in" bar, when he decided to invest some of his money in a club of his own. He came to the cabaret business totally lacking in experience. Wisely, he bought Salvation, which was the third or fourth New York club started by Bradley Pierce, a scene-maker with the city's best celebrity mailing list. So when Bobby took over, there were lines running around the block and limousines pulled up in fleets.

His troubles began when Salvation was charged with liquor law violations and its sales license was revoked by the state liquor authority. The club continued to operate as an unlicensed bar, but its glamorous clientele moved on and was replaced by a much seedier element. As George Costa, who worked for both Pierce and Woods, puts it, "At first people who *used* drugs came in, and then it was people who *sold* it."

[230]

According to Richie, this group included a number-of "younger Mafia guys from Brooklyn who wanted to be paid protection money. There were four or five of them and they'd take turns hanging out at the club to keep track of how much business we were doing, what was going on. The way they worked, they figured out what it'd be worth to you not to be hassled. They didn't want to put you out of business, they only wanted all they could get without bankrupting you. These weren't 'made' men, by the way. They were younger guys out trying to earn their own 'bones.' Hustlers. Anyway, Bobby resisted them right to the end. He'd come to me when they showed up and take all the money from the cash register and leave the club with it. Next day they'd smack him around and he'd beg and make a deal and then he'd double-cross them again."

Because Jimi was a regular in the club, Bobby knew that he was rehearsing a new trio, with Billy Cox on bass and Buddy Miles on drums, and in early September he suggested that Jimi showcase the group at Salvation. Jimi didn't have to do anything special, didn't have to play his old hits. He could do anything he wanted.

The club held only 250 persons and there was no way he could be paid according to his normal fees, so he agreed to play without payment. Bobby then put the word out, invited the press, and charged $25 per person admission and instituted a three-drink minimum at $5 apiece. He also hired off-duty policemen because, according to Richie, he expected trouble.

"There were a couple of cops at the top of the stairs leading down into the club," Richie recalls, "and Bobby was at the door grabbing the money as people came in and stashing it away. He kept coming to the bar and taking receipts. He left early in the evening with most of the money."

As for Jimi, he was left alone to play as he wished, performing for fifty minutes. None of the songs was familiar. In fact, the set seemed more like an extended jam, and the audience was somewhat cool. Microphone problems made it worse, but at the end of the evening Jimi was pleased. In fact, according to George and Richie, Jimi was so pleased he began hanging out with Bobby, snorting a lot of coke with him and going for wild rides in Bobby's open motorboat on the East River. Richie says Bobby liked to shoot seagulls and pigeons on these outings, banging away at the birds with a .38 he usually kept in the bar.

"We'd try to snort coke in the boat, but the wind kept blowing it away," Richie says, laughing.

"One time," adds George, "we were water-skiing, and Jimi fell off the skis and hollered, 'Throw me a rope!' We were so stoned, we just threw the rope and forgot to hold onto one end."

The laughter died in October. That's when, according to Bobby in letters he turned over to his attorney shortly before his death, he met John Riccobono, who was related to Carlo Gambino's longtime *consigliere* (counselor) "Staten Island Joe" Riccobono. Don Carlo was known in New York as the "Boss of Bosses" and emperor of the underworld and was described by the chief of the New York City Police Department's Intelligence Division as "the most powerful of all the family bosses in the country." John Riccobono was hired by Bobby Woods at three hundred dollars a week to manage Salvation. Bobby was then persuaded to hire one of the friends of the Mafia man as doorman.

Almost immediately the new manager and doorman began reporting for work late and then began missing days altogether. Bobby tried to fire them but was informed that that would be impossible. Finally, he wrote in his letters, he "had to hire other men to do their jobs while continuing to pay their salaries."

It got worse. A few days later his manager and doorman entered the club with Staten Island Joe and several other

Mafiosi. "These men came . . . to sit in judgment on me," Woods wrote. "They decided I should pay John $4,000, keep Andy [the doorman] on the payroll at $200 per week and pay them an additional $400 per week for protection. I, of course, refused, at which time they proclaimed that the continued existence of the club and my very life were in danger."

Naturally Jimi knew nothing of this. He continued his late-night recording activities and periodically showed up at Salvation looking for female company or a little cocaine. It was the coke that led to trouble.

One night Jimi left the club with two of the young contacts he knew slightly, ostensibly to score some coke. The next thing he knew he was being held at gunpoint in an apartment in Manhattan's Little Italy. The next morning he was told to call Mike Jeffery. Bob Levine was in the office when the call came in, and after calling Mike to the office, Bob called Jerry Morrison, who was at home in upstate New York. He talked to Mike and said he would drive in. He said he knew some people who might be able to offer help.

"It was serious," Jerry recalls. "When Jimi called, he told Bob that he was being held by guys who wanted Jimi's management contract. Jimi said that if Mike didn't turn it over, the guys were going to kill him."

It didn't make much sense. Why would anyone want to strong-arm a personal manager into signing over his Number One act? And even if they did "buy" Jimi's contract, how could they be sure he would perform for them? Would they strap him to a cot, shoot him full of heroin until he was addicted and then hold him in narcotic captivity, providing drugs in return for recordings and concert dates? It sounded so antiquated, like something from the 1920s.

When I began checking the story with authorities, everyone shook his head in disbelief. The office of the New York City Police Department's Deputy Commissioner for

Information said a search of various files showed no reports of Hendrix being kidnapped. The FBI's Organized Crime Desk found nothing in its files, and two agents who were working there in 1969 said they don't remember ever hearing a thing about it. A copy of Jimi's FBI file in Washington reveals only the two car-theft charges from his teens in Seattle, which found their way to the FBI after he had been arrested for possession of heroin in Canada.

There were other convincing disclaimers, expressed by police and reporters. Kidnapping wasn't really one of the Mafia's interests, even though the Gambino family and several other New York families had had several of their own members kidnapped by the Mafia renegades during the same period. And even if the Mafia *were* so interested, Jimi wouldn't have been a logical target, because, as one Mafia watcher put it, "Every crazy nigger in Harlem would've come after the Italians once the word was out." Not only would the black community have been aroused—calling unwanted attention to the Mafia—but also Jimi was too sympathetic a target to the white public as well. The consensus was that if the Mafia were going to add kidnapping to their other fund-raising efforts, they would pick a rich non-entity, not a pop star.

Could it have been a practical joke?

Mike Jeffery and Jerry Morrison didn't think so. Still, Mike decided *not* to call police, accepting Jerry's advice to wait for his arrival in New York. Jerry walked into Mike's second-floor office about noon, and after getting a replay of the early telephone call, he made some calls of his own, finally reaching someone he identifies as "the son of a top godfather who owed me a favor." Jerry will not be any more specific than that, except to say that when you work in the music business in New York for twenty years, as he did, it is inevitable that you get to know and exchange favors with organized-crime figures.

"I asked him for help with a problem," Jerry says. "He asked me if my problem was black. I said yes. He asked me if my problem was a guitar player. I said yes. He said he was finishing dinner and to come over in half an hour. I asked if I could bring an associate and he said I could."

Jerry took Mike with him, and according to Jerry, Mike was greatly upset, ready to offer whatever money was necessary to ensure Jimi's release.

"How'd you know my problem was a black guitarist?" Jerry asked the young Mafia don.

The don didn't answer at first. Finally he said, "Look, I keep in touch."

In the silence that followed, Mike started babbling about giving anything—the contract, money, anything the gangsters wanted.

The young Mafioso looked thoughtful for a moment, then said, "I'll call you in the morning."

Jerry and Mike returned to Mike's office, where they spent a restless night.

Jerry says there were a number of calls the following morning before his friend finally told them where Jimi was being held.

"Who are these people?" Jerry asked. "How do we approach them?"

The Mafioso said, "Any way you want. They're jitterbugs. They don't know what they're doing and they don't have permission to do it."

"Well," said Jerry, "what can I do to them?"

"Anything you want."

Jerry says he called two friends—whom he won't identify—and with them he went to the address he was given. There he was told he was too late: Jimi had been taken away by two men and a driver only an hour and a half earlier.

"I asked myself where they'd take Jimi," Jerry says today, "and I figured they were renegades, with no protection in New York. The Mafia has a hundred 'safe' houses in the Catskill Mountains upstate, and I guessed they couldn't go to any of them. So I bet on a hunch they'd ask Jimi, and he'd say, 'Come to my place in the country.' I hopped in my car with my friends and ran back up to Woodstock."

It was sounding more and more like *The Gang That Couldn't Shoot Straight*. When you kidnap someone, you don't hide out in your victim's living room, do you?

Jerry and his friends drove out the long, narrow road to Jimi's big stone house. It was after midnight and cold. About half a mile from the gate Jerry stopped the car and said he was going ahead on foot.

"Give me half an hour to take out anyone they might have on guard. Then come on up to the house quietly, lights out."

Jerry set off through the woods, trying not to make noise as he trekked through the fallen leaves and brush. Ten minutes later he spotted a single figure lazing against one of the two stone pillars at the entrance to the estate.

"I walked up to him and put a gun to his head," Jerry says. "I told him to cool it. I frisked him, I took his gun."

His friends arrived moments later, and after tying the guard with rope and leaving him, the three men drove on to the house.

Jerry was passing along the new information the guard had given him: "He told me one of the cooks was asleep, the other was awake and the other two guys probably were in the kitchen drinking coffee."

Jerry says he sneaked up to the silent house and entered it through an unlocked cellar window, then stealthily crept up the steps to a kitchen door.

"I kicked the door open, rushed in with my gun, and sure enough, the guys were drinking coffee. They were both armed. We tied them up. I ran upstairs to find Jimi."

Jerry still had his pistol in his hand and he was out of

breath, adrenaline pumping, wondering if Jimi were alive or dead.

Jimi was in the master bedroom, sitting in the middle of his huge bed, apparently having a wonderful time. Near him was an ashtray containing several marijuana roaches and near that was an assortment of coke paraphernalia.

Jimi looked up at Jerry as he came through the door. "I knew you'd come," he said.

Jerry says he merely kicked the hoodlums out and sent them back to New York, where they got their just desserts from their Mafia chieftains. Jerry says today that he still does not know who masterminded the kidnap and doesn't want to know.

Some say it was Bobby Woods, who closed Salvation in November, publicly attributing his decision to a lack of ability, but telling friends that the real reason was the shakedown by the mob.

Three months later Bobby Woods was found lying in the middle of a street in Queens, his arms folded neatly over his chest. Bullets had been fired into his head behind each ear and into his jaw, another two into his chest. It was described in the newspapers as a "gangland rub-out" and when the letter he had written his attorney—"should anything happen to me"—surfaced, there was an investigation by police anxious to uncover Mafia links to nightclub ownership. Within a few weeks it was forgotten, and Bobby Woods was just another unsolved, violent death.

There was much left unexplained. Was Bobby Woods involved? Who were the young button men who abducted Jimi? And what happened to them afterward? Mafia watchers say renegades pulling stunts like this would be killed as an example.

Most remarkable, why hasn't there been so much as a whisper about the kidnapping among police and newspaper reporters, who devote so much of their lives to investigating organized crime? No field is more rife with rumor. So why, in a dozen years, hasn't even the flimsiest hint surfaced?

After this chapter of the book was completed, a copy was sent to a friend in New York, who took it to a high-placed policeman friend, who in turn showed it to several Mafia families. Before he was through he had strong denials of involvement or knowledge of the incident from all five organized-crime families in New York and New Jersey, as well as from the families in Buffalo and Philadelphia.

It was a lot of fun checking the story, he reported, because he rarely got to see big crime figures laugh. Not only was there no truth to the Mafia's being involved, the Mafiosi said, it was absolutely preposterous. The picture of Jerry Morrison creeping through the woods to disarm and then tie someone up, and then entering the house to disarm two more? Without anyone getting hurt or shot? Nonsense.

Everyone pretty much agreed that it could have been a setup, however—something arranged from beginning to end, perhaps by Jerry Morrison. What he probably did—if, in fact, he did it—they said, was hire two or three "broken noses" to fake a kidnapping so that Jerry could then ride in like a white knight or the cavalry—or Superman, as one of them put it—and emerge as the hero of the caper, without ever risking danger to anyone.

What would Jerry have gained by this? He could have gained some advantage certainly in future dealings with Jimi and his manager, Jeffery, who could have given Jerry something in return by way of a reward. What might that something be? Thirteen years later Jerry was still swearing the story was true.

For Jimi and Jeffery and others at the time, of course, it *was* true. Clearly *something* had happened, and it was very apparent that it wasn't comfortable. Once it was past, however, Jimi rarely referred to it, and when he did, he seldom shared much detail. It seemed to be an incident that he wished to forget.

CHAPTER

14

Jimi was tired of the cops-and-robbers scene.

The kidnapping was bad enough. Now everywhere he looked, there was drama. In Woodstock and in New York City there were cops and crooks crawling everywhere.

The first bad news came from upstate New York, where Jerry Morrison was arrested for possession of marijuana and cocaine. A young undercover narcotics officer had infiltrated the Woodstock music scene, trying to crack the network of dealers and smugglers known to service this community. In all, twenty-two persons were arrested, but none was considered a major trafficker. Jerry says the drugs in his possession had been purchased for Jimi, at Jimi's request, and when he went to Mike Jeffery, Jeffery said he would take care of it.

At the same time, in New York, the Scene closed. The official reason given by Steve Paul was that he wanted to devote his energies to his other interests, notably the management of guitarist Johnny Winter. The truth was that Steve was tired of hassling with the "junior Mafia" that kept trying to shake him down.

[239]

Organized crime was also reported unhappy about the Electric Lady Studios, still under construction on Eighth Street. Greenwich Village, which is adjacent to Little Italy, was a known Mafia stronghold, and it was believed that the family controlling the neighborhood objected to the media spotlight that might accompany the studio's opening. Another, more realistic theory had these crime figures worrying about competition from outside drug suppliers who would come in with the musical groups using the studio.

Most significant was Jimi's trial in Canada, now just eight weeks away. As the December 8 date approached, Jimi became preoccupied; some said obsessed.

"Jimi was panicked," says one friend who was around at the time. "There's no other way to put it. He *knew* he'd been framed on that heroin bust. Sure, he snorted the stuff ever' now and then. Christ, we all did. But he wasn't stupid. He *never* carried drugs when he had to cross customs. So Jimi believed somebody was out to get him. And he thought that somebody was his manager."

If this was imagined, other pressures applied by Mike Jeffery *were* tangible. By his own admission, Jimi had nearly forty songs in various stages of completion, with bits and pieces or completed rough tracks for all of them already recorded. In fact, Jimi had miles of tape sitting in hundreds of boxes—at the Record Plant, in his apartment, in the apartments of girl friends, in his manager's office, wherever he happened to go after one of his late-night sessions. Gerry Stickells did his best to keep things organized, but as Jimi kept recording, chaos began to creep in. Against this background, Mike was passing along demands from Reprise—which hadn't had any new material from Jimi in more than eighteen months—and also from Ed Chalpin, who was screaming for the album Jimi still owed him.

The press coverage of the time revealed more confusion. In the October 3 issue of *Life* magazine, both pictures and

Jimi's original text—from an interview— created an image that was shattered. Several pages of color photographs were shot through a kaleidoscope of mirrors. In one, dozens of heads and hands—Mitch's and Noel's as well as Jimi's—appeared disembodied against a background that looked like a geodesic dome. In others Jimi stood, unsmiling, with his guitar, his image reflected over and over and over, as if trapped in a psychedelic fun house with all the fun removed.

Accompanying the illustrations were some of Jimi's scattered thoughts: "Pretend your mind is a big muddy bowl and the silt is very slowly settling down—but remember your mind's still muddy and you can't possibly grasp all I'm saying. Music is going to break the way. There'll be a day when houses will be made of diamonds and emeralds which won't have any value anymore and they'd last longer in a rainstorm than a wooden house. Bullets'll be fairy tales." And on and on. "I don't think what I say is abstract," Jimi said. "It's reality."

Perhaps so. Surely it was Jimi's reality, a reality that seemed warped and turned inside out by the drugs that inevitably Jimi was soaring on at the time. This was made clear every time he talked to an interviewer now.

"If you revert back in time, there's Egypt," he told a writer for the Los Angeles *Free Press*. "It's very dusty now, but it used to be green. It's that they had a great flood and the world used to be flat, so they say, I mean, you know. And like they found memorandums on the moon, but no telling when they are going to get there, but when they do, they are going to find memorandums from other civilizations that have been there before and think nothing of it because the moon is there in the first place . . ."

When he talked about his music, however, Jimi's voice and thoughts emerged loud and clear. There was naiveté or innocence in his words but also a deep-felt reverence.

"A musician, if he's a messenger, is like a child who

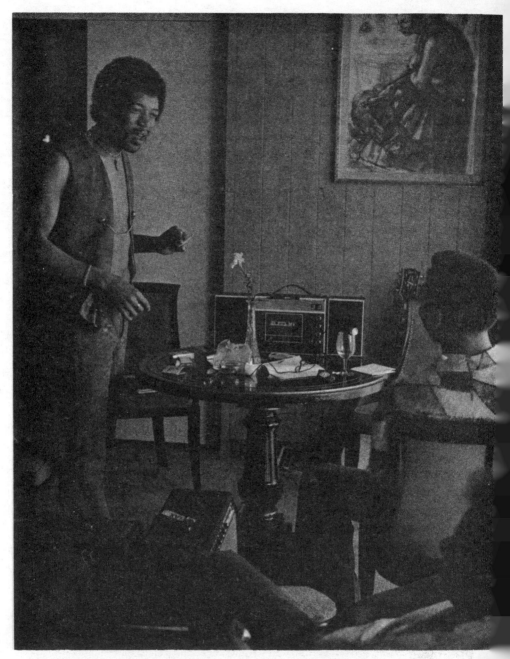

Jimi with his friends Billy Cox and Albert Allen, 1969

hasn't been handled too many times by man," he told *Life*, "hasn't had too many fingerprints across his brain. That's why music is so much heavier than anything you ever felt."

Then, in the November 15 issue of *Rolling Stone*, Jimi cried out: "I don't want to be a clown any more! I don't want to be a rock and roll star!"

He had had his hair cut short. He was dressing more conservatively—still wearing lots of jewelry and bright colors but fewer scarves; he even began to wear stylish suits. The groupie scene became less important to him. No longer was he a fixture in nightclubs.

It didn't matter. It was too late. Jimi was now rock royalty, daily grist for the insatiable media mill. In the same issue of *Life* magazine in which he made his impassioned statement about the musician as mesenger, *Life*'s editors called him a "rock demi-god." While *Vogue* called him "cinnamon to a generation short on spice . . . this year's personification of Flash, popsqueak for the elusive combination of grace and vulgarity forming the basis of the rock experience."

On November 27 Devon hosted a party for him in the Upper East Side apartment of producer Monte Kay. It was Jimi's twenty-seventh birthday. It was to be his last.

The party was not a big success. Devon tried, inviting the Rolling Stones—who opened that night at Madison Square Garden—and all of Jimi's closest friends. But then Devon flirted openly with Mick Jagger, and the drugs that were passed around freely seemed to get Jimi unusually "spaced." Then Devon left the party with Jagger, and Jimi retired to a downstairs room, where he sat alone in the dark. Finally he went home with one of his best friend's dates. She gave him a small present. They ate some ice cream. And then they went to bed.

Jimi flew to Toronto on Sunday, December 7. He had Jeanette Jacobs with him, as well as his friend Sharon

Lawrence, the UPI reporter who would testify for him. Meeting him in the hotel was Chas Chandler, who had flown in from London to offer his testimony. It was good to have friends giving such support, but Jimi was visibly nervous.

Jimi faced a possible seven years in jail, and the first day he entered the courtroom, Monday at 10 A.M., he was wearing a blue blazer and gray flannel pants purchased for the occasion.

Jimi sat with his attorneys for nearly ninety minutes before his case was called. Another two hours passed as a dozen jurors were selected, then, following a brief recess, the prosecution called the first witness, Marvin Wilson, the customs officer who had searched Jimi's flight bag at the airport in May. Wilson told his story much as he had told it before, at first to Canadian police, then to the prosecutor's investigators, and in between to friends and relatives. The answers came out as if rehearsed.

"When you called his attention to the vial of white powder," the prosecutor asked, "what did you say and do?"

"I looked at the defendant, Mr. Hendrix, and asked him did he know what it was."

"And what did, uh, Mr. Hendrix say?"

"He said, 'Oh no, I really don't know what it is. Someone must have put it in my bag.'"

The customs officer then told how his supervisor had arrived on the scene and invited the American musician to go to a nearby office. There, he said, Jimi was searched as the Royal Canadian Mounted Police conducted field laboratory tests on the white powder.

The second and third witnesses for the Crown were the supervisor and the lab technician, who supported Wilson's testimony. It was nightmarish. The facts as told were true, but Jimi was *innocent*. Later one of Jimi's friends said it was like one of those horrible movies on television where the innocent victim has car trouble and goes to a haunted house for help. In this case Jimi couldn't turn the movie off.

Finally in the trial it was Jimi's turn, as the defense began. Under questioning he told the jury and judge about himself—how old he was, where he was born, where he lived now, that he had served a year and a half in the paratroopers and had been discharged because of an injury. Now he was a musician, he said, and yes, it was true, he had been lucky enough to get four gold records that made a million dollars or more in retail sales.

Jimi's voice was characteristically soft and he looked into his lap when answering.

Jimi's lawyer asked him a question about his fans. Jimi said they were very generous. He said they gave him things all the time. He got a lot of scarves, clothes, jewelry, stuffed animals, cakes, poems and oil paintings.

"Do your fans ever give you drugs?"

Jimi looked up at the question and said matter-of-factly, "All the time."

On further questioning, Jimi said he was usually too busy when he got the gifts to look at them. Generally, he said, he just tossed them into his bags to examine later. And if ever the gift were dope, he got rid of it. Jimi admitted to the court that he had experimented with drugs, but he said he had given them up some time before. He had smoked marijuana four times, he swore; hash, three times; he had dropped acid five times; and he had sniffed cocaine two times. But he had never, ever used heroin.

Jimi's lawyer looked him in the eye and paused for dramatic effect.

"Mr. Hendrix," the attorney finally said, "do you mean that you've given up drugs entirely?"

Jimi said, "I've outgrown it."

It was all a lie, of course, but *mea culpa* followed by a denial of *current* guilt was a common defense in the 1960s and early 1970s. Juries seemed to like to "forgive" entertainers charged with possession of drugs so long as they seemed repentant and had cleaned up their acts.

Jimi returned to the stand Tuesday morning. This day he wore a brightly patterned shirt and blue patent leather boots, but otherwise he was conservatively dressed again. Through carefully rehearsed testimony he took the jury and judge and packed courtroom back to 6 P.M. on an evening in Los Angeles when he was being interviewed in his room in the Beverly Rodeo Hotel. The room was crowded, and he said he was feeling sick. He asked everyone to leave. He had a concert in three hours and he wanted to take a nap. He said that was when a young girl thrust a small bottle into his hand, saying, "Maybe this will make you feel better." Someone else had suggested he take some Bromo Seltzer, he said, so he assumed that's what it was. Without looking at the jar, he threw it into his flight bag. He said he performed in Detroit that night and the next night went on to Toronto, never giving the bottle of "medicine" a thought.

The Crown was relentless in its cross-examination, firing questions nonstop for more than an hour, mostly asking Jimi about drug use, terminology and availability. The idea was to make Jimi look like a practiced, habitual user. Jimi grew frustrated, then bored, and when the prosecutor asked how Jimi had acquired the aluminum tube that contained the hashish, Jimi sighed and said it was a gift.

"A gift?" the prosecutor said. "Come on now, Mr. Hendrix, what could such a tube be used for?"

Jimi looked up from his lap and smiled. "I dunno," he said, "maybe a peashooter?"

The courtroom exploded with laughter.

After lunch Sharon Lawrence was called to testify. She said she was one of the people in the hotel room with Jimi on May 1, and she confirmed Jimi's story to the last detail.

The prosecutor said he smelled a rat, finding Sharon's

memory a bit too good to be credible. Sharon disdainfully looked down at the prosecutor and said she was a trained observer. As a reporter for United Press International she often had to interview people and not take notes, so she had developed a sort of photographic memory that never failed her. She could even describe the person who had suggested that Jimi take some Bromo Seltzer.

Jimi's next witness was his friend Chas Chandler, who identified himself as Jimi's former manager. He also said that for several years he was a musician with a band called the Animals. He told the court that when he was touring and making records with that band, fans gave him gifts all the time.

"We had a policy," Chas said in a thick English regional accent that jurors strained to understand. "We never eat anything. Cakes, cookies—toss 'em in the roobish, 'cause you never knew what was in 'em. Usually drooooogs."

Chas went on to say that when he was managing Jimi, the guitarist was given drugs many times. That was a part of his image, Chas said. People believed—true or not—that Jimi used drugs, so they gave him bags and bottles of the stuff all the time. They wanted to turn him on.

At first both the judge and the Crown objected to Chas testifying. They said he was irrelevant. But they were persuaded, and when finally allowed, his testimony worked for Jimi, making it clear that in rock-and-roll circles, at least, it wasn't all that unusual for people to give drugs as gifts.

That night Jimi got very stoned.

On the third and final day Jimi entered the familiar courtroom in a gray pin-striped suit and a lurid purple shirt.

Jimi's lawyer made his final argument, resting his case on a technical bit of Canadian law that stipulated that true possession of something meant there had to be knowledge of that possession. In other words, if Jimi didn't *know* he had the stuff, he didn't legally have it. It was a philosophical

[248]

point and seemed, to some observers, rather vague as an issue on which to hang Jimi's future. But, said Jimi's attorney, the law was the law, and if there seemed to be a reasonable doubt that Jimi knew what he had in his flight bag, he could not be convicted.

The Crown's closing speech was brief. The prosecutor mentioned a few inconsistencies in Jimi's testimony and wondered aloud why Jimi had never tried to find the girl who gave him the jar, but that was about it.

The jury filed out.

The jurors filed into the courtroom eight hours later.

The jury foreman stood.

Jimi stood.

The foreman listened to the judge ask for the verdict and then he gave his nine-word finding: "We find the defendant, James Marshall Hendrix, *not guilty.*"

Jimi gulped and whooped. His lawyer congratulated him and then Jimi and Sharon embraced. For nearly twenty minutes people came up to him, shaking his hand and saying "Right on!"

On the way out of the courtroom Jimi told newspaper reporters, "It's the best Christmas present Canada could give me!"

Before getting on the plane to go home to New York Jimi got stoned, smoking some grass that was a gift from a Toronto fan.

In December 1969 Jimi's *Smash Hits* album was still near the top of the charts, and his first album, *Are You Experienced?*, remained on the same charts more than one hundred weeks after its release. Yet he hadn't appeared publicly in several months. Now there was an important "return" event: New Year's Eve at the Fillmore East, the funky auditorium in New York's Lower East Side operated by impresario Bill Graham.

Back in Manhattan the day after the trial, Jimi plunged into rehearsals and recording with an enthusiasm his friends hadn't seen in a long time. Rehearsals in a Greenwich Village loft with Billy Cox and Buddy Miles—now called the Band of Gypsies—took on the feeling of extended jams. Often friends joined them, playing late into the noisy New York night.

Jimi was relieved to hear Mike Jeffery's plan to provide Ed Chalpin with the album he was owed. Mike decided to give Chalpin a "live" album, to be recorded at the Fillmore East. Live albums were quicker and, in Jimi's case certainly, much cheaper to produce than studio recordings. At the same time, neither Jimi nor Mike wanted to give Chalpin any of the material already on tape; that was to be saved for later release.

So it was agreed that a mobile recording unit would be parked on the dark street next to the theater December 31 and January 1 and that Chalpin's album would come from whatever was recorded those two nights.

Jimi was contracted to perform two shows New Year's Eve, another two on the evening of the first, and the promoter, Bill Graham, wanted him to provide the most exciting shows of his career. So for the first show Jimi performed all his old tricks, humping his guitar, playing it with his teeth, doing everything but set it afire. He and Buddy and Billy all had played the chitlin' circuit in their early days, and that was the kind of show they did. The audience, either getting drunk or stoned or both, exploded with appreciation.

Backstage after the show, Jimi asked Graham what he thought.

"It was okay, Jimi, okay."

Jimi wanted more than that. He looked puzzled. He thought he'd put on a good show. The audience had loved him.

"Is that all?" Jimi asked. "Just okay?"

Jimi doing his thing

BARON WOLMAN

[251]

[252]

[253]

Graham looked at Jimi. His dark eyes flashed. "You want to know what I really think?" he asked.

Jimi said, "Yeah."

Graham nodded and turned on his heel, indicating that Jimi should follow him. He went to his office, where he said to the guitarist, "I thought the show sucked!"

Jimi was stunned and looked it. And then he was angry. "What the fuck do you mean, man? Those people ate it up."

"The show sucked, Jimi. You ask me what I think, I'm telling you. You did your coon act. Lemme tell you something: you can't play the guitar while you're fucking it! You're recording these shows, right? Well, when you listen to that first one, you're gonna fucking throw up. I bet you won't use a note of it. So why don't you go out there and *play* next show! You're a musician, Jimi. Play music!"

The next set Jimi played music, satisfying the audience, Graham, Chalpin and himself simultaneously.

Soon after the set started, Jimi stepped to the microphone and announced that "This next song is dedicated to all the troops fighting in Harlem, Chicago—and, oh yes, Vietnam—a little thing called 'Machine Gun.' "

What followed was unlike anything Jimi had played before. It was the end of a turbulent decade, one during which music and politics came together as never before. Initially Jimi claimed to be apolitical, and most of his early songs supported that position. His version of "The Star-Spangled Banner" represented a significant shift, but only a partial shift.

"Machine Gun" was something else. For more than twelve minutes the stage reverberated with feedback that sounded like dive-bombing planes and Vietnamese women shrieking at the sight of their children's deaths, while Buddy pounded out a jarring rat-tat-tat so loud and persistent that the audience recoiled as if physically struck.

[255]

Machine gun tearing my body [Jimi wailed]
Oh, machine gun tearing my buddies apart
Evil man make me kill you
Evil man make you kill me
Evil man make me kill you
Even though we're only families apart.

This song filled up most of one side of the album that was delivered to Chalpin the following week.

The second side of the album was less remarkable—largely blues-based songs delivered in straight 4/4 time with a slightly soulful bounce. Titles of the songs—"Power of Love," "Message of Love" and "We Gotta Live Together"—showed Jimi hadn't gone totally militant. The performance was excellent throughout but slightly repetitious, with Jimi falling back on familiar wah-wah patterns on almost every tune.

Jimi left the stage pleased, but soon his pleasure turned to anger, when he remembered for whom he'd performed: Ed Chalpin. For days afterward it was all he could talk about, and, according to friends, Jimi plunged into a deep depression.

This was aggravated by Mike Jeffery's insistence that Jimi get rid of Buddy Miles and Billy Cox.

"Look, I know you won't take this the wrong way," Mike said, "but it really isn't working with Buddy and Billy. They're good musicians and all that, but I think the audience wants Mitch and Noel."

Jimi sat slumped in the chair opposite Mike's desk. He said nothing.

Mike began to talk again, and for twenty minutes he filled the room with argument, pleading sweetly at first, ending his long rap with curses and shouts. Mike didn't like what he saw happening to Jimi's stage act and he made no secret of it. When Jimi had played the Woodstock festival,

Mitch was the only white musician present, and he was hidden behind his massive drum kit. And on New Year's Eve everybody in the band was black.

"Jimi, you know I have nothing against black musicians," Mike said, "but I do think I know what your audience wants. I talk to promoters every day and I know what they want. I don't care who you record with, but when you're onstage, everybody wants to see some white faces!"

Jimi said nothing, his face a mask.

There was a long silence, and finally Mike spoke. Now his voice was calm again and he was holding a single piece of paper toward the musician across from him.

"This is a letter of agreement," Mike said. "You and Noel and Mitch agree to get together, and I agree to book you on at least one tour of the U.S., with a gross of between seven hundred and fifty thousand and a million dollars . . . plus at least one tour of Western Europe, including the United Kingdom . . . plus a major tour of Japan. Just like before, you get fifty percent and Noel and Mitch split the other fifty."

Mike was still holding the letter toward Jimi. Jimi took it and glanced at it. He noticed that it was dated January ————, 1970. Only the day had to be filled in.

Jimi stood up, and after glaring at Mike, dropped the piece of paper on the floor and abruptly left the room, slamming the door behind him.

Jimi did next what he had done since his Seattle high school days when the pressure began to build: he sought refuge in music or drugs. This time especially in drugs.

"In those days he was out there," says Buddy Miles. "He just didn't care. He was under so much pressure. He didn't know where to turn. I never did acid but once. Jimi was into acid heavily at that time, almost every day. Grass, hash, acid, coke, booze, everything. He was a glutton. I hate to say that, but you have to be truthful. One time I talked to him. We had a fight. I picked him up by his collar. I said, 'Jimi, what are you doing? Is this all that life is—drugs?' He told me I was right, but he said he was afraid."

Jimi continued recording off and on at the Record Plant, using Mitch Mitchell on drums but still not committing himself to reuniting the old Experience. Friends say he was quiet, withdrawn and drinking heavily.

The next concert was scheduled for January 28, a benefit for the Vietnam Moratorium Committee, to be held in Madison Square Garden. Jimi's Band of Gypsies was to appear with more than a dozen big-name acts, including Harry Belafonte, Peter, Paul and Mary, Richie Havens, Judy Collins, The Rascals and the cast of the musical *Hair*.

It was depressing, and if what many of Jimi's friends say is true, it was tragic, awful, dangerous.

Everyone is in agreement: Jimi was given some LSD containing impurities, which put him on a massive "downer," one of those frightening bad dreams with lightning jolts and psychic rips. Acid, when it was "pure," or "clean," was incredibly intense. Impurities could render the soul, shatter all security.

Some of Jimi's friends, including Noel Redding, who attended the concert as a spectator and saw Jimi backstage, said it was a stranger who gave Jimi the LSD. Jimi was known to open his mouth when a fan walked up with his or her hand outstretched, offering unidentified drugs; he often gambled with drugs. David Henderson, the author of another book about Jimi, also said it was someone "unknown" who gave Jimi the ugly hit.

But others said it was Mike Jeffery who sent Jimi on his nasty trip. Buddy Miles, who was backstage with Jimi, swears that Mike gave Jimi a "couple" of acid tabs that "brought him to his knees" and "cramped up his stomach."

That was before Jimi went on, when he entered the backstage dressing room. The guitarist Johnny Winter, another performer on the bill, saw him and was shocked.

"When I saw him, it gave me chills," Johnny told *Guitar Player* magazine. "It was the most horrible thing I'd ever seen. He came in with his entourage of people, and it was like he was already dead. He just walked in—and even though Jimi and I weren't the greatest of friends, we always talked, always—and he came in with his head down, sat on the couch alone, and put his head in his hands. He didn't say a word to anybody, and no one spoke to him. He didn't move until it was time for the show. He really wanted to do that gig, but he never should have. It wasn't that it was bad, but his whole thing was inspiration, and there wasn't any. It was just completely uninspired.

"Finally, right in the middle of a song, he just took his guitar off, sat on the stage—the band was still playing—and told the audience, 'I'm sorry, we just can't get it together.' One of his people said he was sick and led him off the stage. He was just so unhappy that there was no way that he could play the show. It didn't have anything to do with the group. He had already died."

Was it true? Did Mike Jeffery really give Jimi bad acid? And did he do it accidentally or on purpose? Many say Jeffery controlled Jimi this way; they say that if he didn't actually give Jimi the drugs, he often gave Jimi important contracts to sign when Jimi was stoned.

To be fair to Mike, by now Jimi was stoned most of his waking hours and it would have been difficult to catch him "straight" at any time.

And to be fair to Jimi, it must be said that this wasn't particularly unusual in 1970 in rock-and-roll, where drug-taking was the rule rather than the exception. Coping while under the influence of ups, downs and psychedelics had become a way of life in the youth culture. The Beatles, just before receiving the queen's esteemed MBE (Member of the British Empire) awards, retired to the royal toilet to smoke a joint. A few years later Elvis Presley entered President Nixon's Oval Office to offer his services in an antidrug campaign while stoned out of his head on amphetamines.

And so it was with Jimi too. Cocaine or amphetamines started the day, barbiturates or heavy downers like heroin or Quaaludes ended the day, and in between came the recreational drugs: beer and wine and Scotch, LSD, pot, hash, peyote, soma, mushrooms, mescaline, and speedballs made of smack and coke.

This is not to say that Jimi was falling down. He was not. His capacity was great and his ability to maintain was phenomenal. Usually he seemed unchanged by drugs; stoned or not, he seemed, well, out there. He coped.

So long as the drugs were good. But what happened when the drugs weren't good? Did Mike Jeffery give him impure LSD on purpose?

Buddy Miles says yes. He says Mike gave Jimi the impure LSD to sabotage the group. "Jimi was so sick he had to stop the show," Buddy says. "Jeffery wanted to make us look bad. And so those were the only two gigs."

Buddy was fired peremptorily, Mike told Jimi the Experience was being reformed, whether he liked it or not, and the one-page agreement was brought out again. Noel and Mitch were already standing in the wings waiting for the call.

Noel Redding says the crucial meeting took place during the first week of February. He was present at the Madison Square Garden concert, he says, because Mike had called him to New York from his home in Britain. He was told then that the reunion was a certainty.

At the time, Jimi had no idea. And when Mike called him in, he resisted as he had a week before. Mike showed Jimi some financial statements he had worked up that afternoon. Mike said Jimi hadn't delivered an album to Reprise in almost two years, and, according to his contract, he was supposed to deliver two each year; that meant he owed Reprise four albums. Plus the $250,000 advance by Reprise to build the Electric Lady Studios.

There was more. Jimi still owed his lawyers for the Toronto trial defense. The current bill from the Record Plant was more than $15,000. He was hiring limousines and having them stand by around the clock while he partied or slept. This cost him another $5,000 a month.

The money wasn't coming in now. His European royalties were still frozen, thanks to Ed Chalpin's lawsuit. Jimi was paid well for his Fillmore East shows, but otherwise he hadn't worked once since Woodstock.

Mike held the heaviest blow until last.

"Jimi," he said, picking up the one-page agreement to reunite the original Experience, "there are a lot of unpaid taxes too."

Jimi panicked. Visions of Joe Louis on the ropes filled his head. So—stoned, of course—he signed on the dotted line.

CHAPTER

15

The same day, Mike called what he thought was the most important publication in the music field, *Rolling Stone*, and said Jimi was reforming the Experience and wanted to give an exclusive interview. Managing editor John Burks was not impressed. In his story he described news of the reunion as having "approximately the news value of a trial separation between Dick and Liz." He also acknowledged Mike Jeffery's graciousness as a host, remarking on the refreshments and alcohol served him when he arrived at Mike's apartment, where the interview was held.

However skeptical the reporter, the subject of the interview remained calm. Cool. John asked Jimi about his claim in the Toronto court that he had outgrown drugs. Was that true?

There was a long pause and Jimi said, "I don't know, I'm too . . ."

He paused again, serious.

"I'm too . . . *wrecked* right now."

He smiled, showing his long teeth in a grin that was reminiscent of Charlie Chaplin's: bigger than you expected after all that pantomime.

"This was Hendrix the comedian," wrote Burks. "This side of Jimi is the one people love. He does it all with split-second timing, a shrug, an eye cast downward, a slightly overaccented word. It's the essence of his charm, and figures, in many ways, in the way he makes music."

"I'll have to check into it," Jimi said, referring to his question about dope. "Oh yes, it's true, it's true. I don't take as much. That's what I was trying to tell them."

Jimi was goofing. Under the circumstances, he was having a very good time. It wasn't his idea to have a re-union, but once both Mitch and Noel were there, it was like old times. They laughed a lot together and told stories about the early days when they created "Foxy Lady" and "Voodoo Chile" in the studio almost spontaneously. Goofing then too.

Burks asked what the reunited Experience planned.

"Well"—Jimi grinned at Noel and Mitch—"I'll try to make it more of an up. We're going to go out somewhere into the hills and woodshed, or whatever you call it, to get some new songs and arrangements and stuff together. So we'll have something new to offer, whether it's different or not."

That said nothing, promised nothing.

The *Rolling Stone* writer felt used and said so in his article, implying that he was treated like a fan-magazine writer. Personally, he liked Jimi, and he admired him as a musician. But he didn't like the way Mike Jeffery kept tiptoeing around the room during the interview, offering wine and cognac as bracers against the winter chill, while wincing noticeably every time Jimi joked about his use of drugs. He also didn't like it when Jimi's publicist called two weeks later and said Jimi had a lot more to say and wanted to see him again.

Noel Redding (left), Mitch and Jimi being interviewed by Rolling Stone in 1970 following their "reunion"

John said it was too late—the story had been written and the issue of the paper was about to go to press. Was there anything really important to report?

Well, sort of. John was informed that Noel Redding wouldn't be rejoining the group after all, at least not right away. He was going on tour with Jeff Beck instead, and for the time being Billy Cox would stay.

It was a compromise Jimi could live with. A reunion with Mitch was acceptable. Jimi always liked Mitch and respected his drumming. But he and Noel fought, and Jimi thought he was an inadequate bass player. According to Mike Jeffery, there was also some disagreement with Buddy Miles.

[265]

"Musically it wasn't going down well between Jimi and Buddy," Mike said later that year. "Jimi was able to instill in his music all the four elements—water, air, fire, earth. When he played earth, Buddy was the best drummer in the world for him. But Jimi was getting less earthy, and when he got out there into air, Buddy just didn't make it. There were those large gaps that had to be filled by somebody with a different drumming technique than Buddy's. This is what I think, this is what I expressed to Jimi, and this is what he agreed with.

"So I had the difficult position of getting rid of, removing Buddy from Jimi. Jimi felt it, but Jimi could never say no. Buddy was a friend of his in a nonmusical sense. I told Buddy the trip was over. I did get the feeling that he took it very personally to me. We argued a bit and we shouted a bit. I think at that time he felt he wasn't getting his share from the group. He felt that he was a star too, and I regarded him as essentially a supporting man for Jimi."

Besides firing Buddy, Mike had much to do to regain the momentum lost by the diminished activity. With no new recordings in two years and only a handful of appearances the past six months, Jimi was becoming invisible.

Two things happened in February to make this very clear. First, *Rolling Stone* in its review of 1969 gave Jimi a special award. "Jimi Hendrix had a big year," the newspaper reported. "A pretty neat trick for a musician who made no music. He was busted for dope and got off, his Experience broke up with Hendrix starting a 'serious' new experimental group, he quit gigging except for a few festivals, and there were no new records. To Jimi Hendrix, the No News Is Big News Award."

That hurt. More painful was the reception given a 45-rpm single containing two new, original songs, "Izabella" and "Stepping Stone," typical Hendrix throwaway songs, heavy on the instrumental and inconsequential vocally and lyrically. The record never appeared on any chart anywhere, the first time since "Hey Joe" for one of his recordings to go completely belly-up in America.

The first thing Mike Jeffery did was fire Jimi's publicist, figuring he was an unnecessary expense, at least until the tour began in late April. He then began negotiating with a number of young filmmakers. So far his experience in putting Jimi into a movie had been disappointing. As early as 1968 the guitarist had been the subject of a thirty-minute film produced in Britain, but distribution was limited to a handful of European countries. A year after that several European concerts were photographed by Steve Gold, but Mike hadn't liked the film and, with added pressure from Warner Brothers, managed to halt distribution altogether. Jimi had appeared in *Monterey Pop* and by April would be on view in *Woodstock,* but in both documentaries he was just one of many acts. What Mike wanted now was a feature-length film, one over which he would have complete control.

A deal was made with Peter Pilafian, a sound engineer who worked closely with the Mamas and the Papas for a number of years and who was one of the producers of *Monterey Pop.* This was to be a simple in-concert film, photographed in May when Jimi played a theater in Berkeley, California. Mike made it clear that on this film he would be the executive producer.

A second film planned at the same time was more complex, and curious. This was *Rainbow Bridge,* conceived as a sort of cinematic phantasmagoria of psychedelic and occult philosophy and phenomena. The director of that film, Chuck Wein, previously had directed three puzzling films for the pop artist Andy Warhol, and when he walked into the Hendrix office, he was traveling at the speed of light and speaking what Jerry Morrison calls "fluent Tarot."

"I had known Jimi from the Scene and I was living with Pat Hartley and Devon," he later told *Rolling Stone.* "I was into reading Tarot cards, and I read the cards for Jimi and Mitch Mitchell and Billy Cox. Jimi started to tell me about being from an asteroid belt off the coast of Mars, so I said, 'Stop and I'll tell you about it because it's a place I've seen three or four times clear as a bell.' And that's the point that the deal got on, which was that there was something manifesting that had to be worked out. And that something eventually became *Rainbow Bridge*.

"A major purpose of ours was to remove the mass paranoia against the arrival of the Space Brothers, who are very universal beings, they're totally loving, they would rather disintegrate their own form than change anything by force on Earth.

"A group of people meditated together for many months and traveled out of our bodies to many people who we wanted to contact to support the venture, and we prayed that they would realize the purpose of it and join in the activity. And this worked on the inner plane and spiritual level. Then when we went to see them, we didn't have that physical plane and emotional opposition. Our lower selves seemed to be transmuted, and theirs did too. Things went smoothly; people just popped up all over the place."

The people who "just popped up all over the place," Chuck's way of describing financial backers, were Mike Jeffery and the president of Jimi's record company, Mo Ostin. Mike eventually contributed more than $500,000, Jerry Morrison says, because Mike was "enamored of the spiritual trip and liked investing in lost hippie causes." Mo went along for more practical reasons, pledging $450,000 toward the film's production in exchange for the rights to distribute a sound-track album, which he was told would be produced by Jimi.

The only problem was that when Jimi was told about the film, he said great, he really did want to make a movie with Chuck, but he didn't want to play his guitar in it. He said that to Mike and he told Chuck as well. Both said it was Warner-Reprise who wanted him to play, but not to worry, they'd take care of everything.

Chuck—and his partner, Barry Prendergast—were given the green light and told to expect to begin filming on the second largest island in the Hawaiian chain, Maui—which was becoming a popular gathering place for hippies—when Jimi played Honolulu while on tour, in July.

The pressures on Jimi continued in the weeks before the tour began. At the end of February twenty-one Black Panthers went on trial in Chicago, and once again he was approached by militant blacks to support his "brothers."

This was a recurring event in recent months. Jimi was criticized by blacks from the time he appeared at Monterey in 1967—either for performing like an Uncle Tom (eating his guitar) or for playing with white musicians. Even when Redding and Mitchell gave way to Cox and Miles, and Jimi made substantial contributions to black organizations, including a gift to the Martin Luther King, Jr., Foundation, the reproof continued.

Now, in March, he was approached by two old friends from Harlem who called themselves the Ghetto Fighters; they persuaded him to play in a 125th Street community concert. It was not a great success. The star of the show was Big Maybelle, one of the great blues shouters, and because Jimi was relatively unknown to the black audience, his performance was greeted perfunctorily.

Heavier pressure came from the ongoing insecurity Jimi felt about his management. For this reason, in the first week of April, he met with two young black lawyers to see what he could do about breaking his contract with Mike.

"We met Jimi down at the apartment he had in the Village," says one of them, Ed Howard, "and he outlined for us at that time a lot of the problems that he felt he had in his business relationships, and with the people around him, and

Jimi composing

he advised us that he wanted us to become his new counsel. I told him that I needed to review his contracts relating to his management and his music publishing, his songwriter agreement, and his recording contracts and all of the kinds of contracts that a musician like Jimi had. He didn't have any of them. Not one contract at all.

"He told me he would try to get these papers from the various people that had them and that he would make them available to me for my review and blah, blah, so that I could get a background in terms of what his rights, exposures and so forth might be. That was the last we heard from him for a little while."

If Jimi delayed the process of leaving his manager by failing to call the lawyers again, it was clear that the subject was obsessing him. All his close friends of the time report conversations that were shot with his discontent. Pat Hartley, still a member of his nightclubbing crowd, and her husband, the English filmmaker Dick Fontaine, both say Jimi announced his leaving as imminent, and Jimi described the tour, Pat says, as "the last go-round." Others, including Alan Douglas and Chas Chandler, say they were approached repeatedly to take over Jimi's affairs. However, Jimi's contract with Mike was ironclad.

Deciding to play a waiting game, Alan Douglas focused his attention on work with Jimi in the studio. By now Alan was spending many hours in the Record Plant every week that Jimi was in town and, since March, in Studio A of Electric Lady Studios, finished enough to record in but still overrun with workmen during the day.

Jimi was attracting a wide and impressive range of musicians to these sessions. Douglas explains that "basically, Jimi was a virtuoso, and it was my intention to deal with him in a way that if he felt like doing the blues, well, I would get a dynamite blues group behind him, and if he felt like playing Flamenco music, I would get some Spanish guys in, whatever it had to be. Jazz. He was getting into that, so I set up some jams with John McLaughlin, Dave Holland, Larry Young, people like that. Jimi was talking with Miles Davis on the telephone. We planned to record with Roland Kirk. Gil Evans was planning an album of Jimi's tunes after the original *Miles Ahead* album, which would be called *Voodoo Child Plays the Blues,* with Gil's big band and his arrangements and Jimi's lead playing over the top. There was a lot going on, being talked about."

Plans to work with some of the all-time jazz greats—notably Kirk, Evans and Davis—gave Jimi the excitement he needed during what otherwise were strenuous weeks. Although Douglas had Jimi's blessings, he did not have Mike Jeffery's, and according to Douglas, there was friction.

"I was pulling Jimi in another direction," he says, "and Michael was, ahhh, very paranoid about everybody and everything who got near to Jimi."

Soon there was more than "paranoia" as Mike began threatening to sue Douglas. And Chas Chandler withdrew when he heard that Jimi was asking others to do the same things he was asking him to do.

In the end Jimi repeated his inaction of the previous summer, complaining to friends about Jeffery but doing little else, preferring to keep the peculiar sort of "peace" that goes with backing down. Jimi was no coward. But he was not a fighter. And as Mike Jeffery knew, he was a man who couldn't say no.

Jimi couldn't say no to anything—and that included drugs. Friends say he was doping heavily again, or, perhaps, as one of them said, "just more openly." Jerry Morrison says he and Mike Jeffery tried to keep Jimi away from heroin especially, more or less letting the other, more "recreational" drugs go.

"I was in charge of the whole Band of Gypsies trip," Jerry says. "I was supposed to create an atmosphere where

[272]

no one could get to him, and I did. Coke was commonplace, plus psychedelics—grass, hash, psilocybin, that sort of thing. But I don't think he was using smack. Then after the Band of Gypsies broke up, when he began hanging out again in the studio, smack showed up. I don't think Jimi ever injected it, by the way. He and the others would go off and sniff it together."

On the twenty-fifth of April, Mike Jeffery and his girl friend, Lyn, began a vacation with friends in Woodstock, and Jimi began his tour.

The timing was perfect. Just two weeks before, the film *Woodstock* had gone into national release, giving Jimi important and widespread exposure. Because he and his music closed the documentary, just as he had closed the festival, the critics remembered him.

A reviewer for *The New York Times* called Jimi "black, hip and arrogant." Andrew Sarris in the *Village Voice* said he was the "most pornographic of all performers." Richard Schickel in *Life* spoke of his "strength and artistry." And nearly everyone mentioned Jimi's treatment of "The Star-Spangled Banner." It was, they said, daring, innovative, appropriate for the time—loud, ugly, treasonous. So naturally it was a featured song in almost every show on the tour. First stop: the 18,000-seat Forum in Los Angeles.

Tickets were reasonably priced—from $3.50 to $6.50—attracting a close-to-capacity audience. Jimi's friend Buddy Miles, leading a reformed Buddy Miles Express, was on the bill with him, and although Jimi hadn't performed publicly in six months, the crowd gave him what one reviewer called an "enormous opening response."

Critically, the show was not a great success, however. Although Jimi played several of his old hits, including "Foxy Lady" and "Purple Haze," and "The Star-Spangled Banner" got him a standing ovation that lasted several minutes, Robert Hilburn in the *Los Angeles Times* said Jimi was "more a personality than a musician," and Jim Bickhart wrote in *Entertainment World* that the concert was "deadly dull."

"Jimi's attempts to update too-familiar guitar solos became pure cacaphony," Bickhart said, "and [Billy] Cox was half asleep as he played bass runs first created by Noel Redding."

It didn't matter to Jimi. He seldom saw or read reviews, and by the time they were being written, he and Mitch and Billy were in Sacramento.

It was a tour of weekends—two- and three-concert bursts, usually spotted on Friday and Saturday nights—with the rest of the week free for travel or hanging out. From Los Angeles they flew to Milwaukee, Madison and Minneapolis, and the next week they went south, to Oklahoma City, Fort Worth and San Antonio. After that came Philadelphia, Cincinnati, St. Louis and Evansville, Indiana.

In every city the halls and auditoriums were mammoth in size to accommodate the demand for tickets. In Los Angeles reviewers generally focused on the phenomenon rather than on the music. Jimi was called innovative, a master of his instrument, but inevitably it was his image, or wardrobe, or, worse, his long-ago stage pyrotechnics that still made up much of the show review.

More disappointing was audience response to Jimi's new material. When the early hits or the national anthem were played, the halls exploded. But whenever he played songs like "Message of Love" or "EZY Rider," the crowd applauded perfunctorily. Not even the rhetorical and literal rat-tat-tat of "Machine Gun" made much of an impression.

Except in Berkeley.

Jimi arrived in the California university town on May 28, a day ahead of two shows scheduled for the Berkeley Community Theatre. Since 1964, when a "Free Speech" movement gained national headlines, Berkeley had been synonymous with the word "protest." Not long before Jimi's arrival a young man was killed and several others were wounded during riots over a "People's Park." A few months earlier, in February, when Judge Julius Hoffman sent the Chicago Seven—protesters at the 1968 Republican convention—off to jail for contempt, a thousand young people hanged the judge in effigy across from Berkeley police headquarters. In April, when 2,500 anti-ROTC demonstrators battled police, the University of California chancellor closed the campus down in the face of what he called "the most wanton destruction in UC's history."

The theater was small, holding only three hundred, but the evening was a major event, in part because seats were in such great demand, but more so because of the film crew. Everywhere Jimi looked were longhaired young people holding 16-mm cameras, getting ready to record the shows for a feature-length film that would be called *Jimi at Berkeley.*

This was the first of the two films authorized by Mike Jeffery. Mike was not present. He was back in Woodstock, arguing with his girl friend, Lyn. This was the night that they separated, permanently.

Things were not going perfectly for Jimi either. He was dressed splendidly for the film, wearing Indian moccasins and a beaded vest, a headband and a profusion of scarves. (His flirtation with more conservative dress during the time of his trial proved to be temporary.) Knowing this could be a film that made a difference in his career, he arrived at the theater with Devon—whom he flew in from New York for the occasion—full of optimism and excitement. That changed quickly.

More than a thousand frustrated fans gathered in front of the theater, unable to buy tickets. When the theater was opened, hundreds pushed forward, trying to force their way in, breaking the glass doors. Others scaled the walls and roamed the roof, looking for an entrance. Demonstrators

Jimi at a press conference

BARON WOLMAN

paraded the sidewalk, telling the filmmakers that they hoped this film wouldn't be like *Woodstock*.

"They're charging three-fifty for a movie *we* made!" the protesters said.

Jimi gave the people what they wanted. He went right into "The Star-Spangled Banner." The place erupted.

And then he revealed how he *really* felt. When he was finished with the national anthem and was ready to segue into "Purple Haze," he looked into one of the hand-held cameras in front of him and said, "Big deal!"

Jimi looked and sounded very bored.

Soon after that he went back in time. He waggled his long, thick tongue and played part of the Chuck Berry classic "Johnny B. Good" with his teeth. While playing another song he fell to his knees and then onto his back, then hunched along the stage on his knees, simultaneously playing the guitar with his tongue. Later he held his guitar between his widespread legs, the neck thrust toward his audience like a two-foot-long penis with tuning knobs. When the film *Jimi at Berkeley* was released a year after Jimi's death, in 1971, all these antics were included, and when Jimi played "Machine Gun" the filmmakers intercut scenes from some Berkeley demonstrations, including film of the tear gas and rifle confrontations over People's Park.

As Jimi continued the tour, going to Atlanta, Dallas, Houston, New Orleans, Kansas City, Baltimore, Pittsburgh and Boston in June, the album recorded at the Fillmore for Ed Chalpin, called *Hendrix: Band of Gypsies*, was soaring up the record charts. Appearing on the *Billboard* list the week it was released, May 2, it quickly went to Number Five, eventually remaining on the chart for sixty-one weeks and generally earning good reviews.

Gary Von Tersch, in *Rolling Stone*, compared Jimi's lyrics to the poetry of LeRoi Jones and said, "This album is Hendrix the musician. With just bass and drum support he is able to transfuse and transfix on the strength of his guitar work alone."

Robert Christgau, writing in the *Village Voice,* called the album flawed but said Jimi was "the music's nonpareil improviser" and described "Machine Gun" as "a peace-monger's long-overdue declaration of war . . . as powerful if not as complex as anything he's ever put on record."

It was Jimi's fourth authorized album and the last to be released in his lifetime.

In July, Jimi was back in New York, recording in his beloved new studio and arguing with Mike about his appearing in *Rainbow Bridge.* The way Chuck explained it later, Jimi was anxious to be in the film. Chuck even said it was at Jimi's insistence, finally, that he played his guitar in it. Everyone else around at the time remembers it differently.

When Jimi's old friend, the actress Pat Hartley, was asked to be in the film, she says she visited Jimi and Devon in New York and learned that Jimi hadn't even agreed to be in it. All he talked about, she said, was the pressure he felt to produce a quick album for his record company.

Jerry Morrison takes Jimi's resistance a giant step further, saying Jimi eventually was *forced* to participate.

"Jimi didn't even want to have *anything* to do with it," Jerry says. "He didn't even want to be *in* the film. So Mike Jeffery ordered Gerry Stickells and two roadies to go to Seattle where Jimi was performing at Sicks Stadium on July twenty-sixth. He told them to get Jimi loaded and physically take him to Hawaii. And they did. Jimi was shanghaied!"

Tempers continued to flare in paradise. Even Chuck admitted it. "We went through every kind of why-are-we-here riff until finally Jimi and Hartley got into an argument, and I said, 'Listen, the crew's been up there for eight hours! We have to do this now!'

"Jimi says, 'Well, okay, you do it then!'

"Hartley and I went upstairs ourselves, because we felt there was something crucial about it. We were really down, but we started the camera rolling, and Jimi comes walking down the aisle with a bottle of rosé wine in his hand."

In the end Jimi again went along, taking what little real direction was offered and agreeing eventually to perform in concert near the Rainbow Bridge Occult Center—for which the film was named—on the slopes of Maui's Haleakala crater. It would be this concert that formed the last half hour of *Rainbow Bridge* and much of the sound-track album.

The rest of the film was cinematic chaos, both in the filming and in the final cut. Nothing, absolutely *nothing,* seemed connected. Not even the people involved in the production of the movie were able to communicate.

Warners insisted that Chuck and his partner transport a full union crew from Hollywood, very few of whom could relate in any way to anyone they had to work with. As Pat Hartley said, "Chuck had rented the old Baldwin mansion, which was a girls' school, and there were about thirty of us living in the dorm together. Most of the crew thought all these vegetarians were trying to poison them."

Further damaging to communication was the abundance and variety of drugs. Members of the surfing community, some of whom appeared in the film, practically worshiped Jimi and brought him gifts of powerful, locally grown marijuana called Maui Wowee and sat around in the evenings sucking hashish smoke from elaborate water pipes. For a scene in a pasture near Makawao, a farm and ranch community, every hippie on the island showed up to romp in costume in the tall green grass and drink the Electric Kool Aid—LSD-laced punch—that was being served. That same day someone also showed up with a shoebox full of rolled marijuana cigarettes.

Plot was virtually nonexistent; improvisation was all. The way Chuck's vision ran, and the way the film began, three horsemen rode onto a beach, where a surfer was seen riding a wave. One of the horsemen raised a rifle and squeezed off a shot. The surfer froze mid-ride as Jimi's song "EZY Rider" came pounding in. Then the surfer spread wide his arms and rose like a Christ into the sky.

After that it got really confusing as the camera captured the wide range of the hip 1960s experience, from yoga and meditation and Zen to flying saucers, clairvoyance and ecology to encounter group Tai Chi Ch'uan and Polynesian girls spilling out of their bikini tops.

Finally came the concert, with approximately eight hundred to a thousand people arranged across the crater floor according to their astrological signs, so that, according to one of dozens of self-appointed "consultants," Jimi could play to the celestial "vibes."

Jimi was introduced by Chuck, who delivered a predictably spacey rap about humanity building a bridge between the heart and "the higher mental and spiritual centers of the planetary being."

Looking out at the astrologically organized audience, he implored them to participate.

"Instead of being like a reflective, groovy audience that we have at every love-in and concert forever and ever up to now," Chuck said, "if we just turn on *harmony,* so Jimi can stick to that and lead us across that bridge, and everybody all over the world is going to pick up on that."

Jimi played three forty-five-minute sets, wearing a Hopi Indian shirt and retiring after each show to a "sacred" Hopi-style shelter nearby. He was so stoned by the third set, his introductions to songs made little sense, and although the music itself seemed to engage the worshipful audience, when the "sound-track" album was released by his record company—after Jimi died—not a single note from Hawaii was used. Instead, other versions of the same songs, recorded in the studio, filled out both sides of the disc. This was not unusual. Often musicians went into the studio to "improve" on live recording. However, in this case Jimi's on-location music was horrible, and the audio was worse. For most of the second two sets Jimi wasn't even in tune.

Almost the entire time he was in Hawaii—escaping Maui once for a weekend in Honolulu with Pat Hartley— Jimi stayed very stoned. Perhaps in his sleep he "came down," but even that is uncertain, considering the quantity of grass and hashish he smoked and the number and assortment of pills he popped.

At one point during the filming Chuck asked him if he ever had an "out of body" experience, going to outer space, or Tibet, while leaving his body behind.

"Yes," Jimi answered matter-of-factly.

"Where do you go, when you go?" Chuck shot back.

"I don't know, man. It seems like there's this little center in space that's just rotating, you know, constantly rotating, and there's these souls on it, and you're sitting there like cattle at a water hole, and there's no rap actually going on, there's no emotions that are strung out, so you're just sitting there, and all of a sudden the next thing you know you'll be drawn to a certain thing, and the light gets bright and you see stuff, a page being turned, and you see yourself next to a Viet Cong, you know, a soldier being shot down, and all of a sudden you feel like helping that soldier up, but you're feeling yourself held in another vibe, another sense of that soldier. It seems like the soul of him, you know, and then you whisk back to the water hole or the oasis, and you're sitting there and you're rapping again or something, eating a banana cream pie and sitting on the gray hardwood benches and so forth, and all of a sudden somebody calls out again, but this is without words, that whole scene, and all of a sudden the next thing you know you see yourself looking down at the left paw of the Sphinx and the tomb of King Blourr and his friendly falcons and these all-night social workers with mattresses tied around their backs screaming 'Curb service! Curb service! Curb service!' You know, with a third eye in the middle of the Pyramid."

Was Jimi playing games? Was he having a religious experience? Was he merely stringing Dylanesque images like beads? Was he articulating unusual dreams? Was he merely stoned?

By the time Chuck and his expensive camera crew returned to Hollywood, they had more than forty hours of puzzling film and still more scenes to shoot. Warners was nervous. The original budget had been set at between $200,-000 and $300,000, and it was now clear that a million dollars was disappearing into the purple haze. Mike Jeffery went in and suggested that more of Jimi's future royalties be used, and when the record company objected, Mike pledged more of his own money.

CHAPTER

16

Back in New York by the
end of the first week of August, Jimi disappeared into Electric Lady Studios. A big press party was being planned for
August 28, the day before he was scheduled to leave for a
brief European tour, and he wanted to complete work on an
album he was calling, tentatively, *First Rays of the New Rising
Sun.*

It was hot in New York, humid and dirty and noisy,
and as Jimi loped the short five blocks from his apartment to
the studio, he found himself smiling. His friend Jerry Morrison was calling some of the jazz musicians he knew to
arrange meetings and schedule some possible jams. These
included the bebop trumpeter Dizzy Gillespie and the modern saxophonist Zoot Sims. With Alan Douglas working on
Miles Davis, Roland Kirk and Gil Evans, it was as if a *Who's
Who* of jazz were being assembled for him.

Descending the steps to the subterranean studio, entering the air-conditioned coolness, walking past a huge curving psychedelic mural, feeling his feet sink into red plush

The collage on the ladies' restroom wall at Jimi's Electric Lady Studio

carpeting, and knowing it all *belonged* to him; it was a high like no other he had experienced.

The men's room had a shower. There was a full kitchen. Soft, sprawling couches were built into each of the control rooms and covered with tie-dye silks and velvets designed according to Jimi's Indian/Morrocan/hippie tastes. The control rooms resembled spaceship interiors, like the cockpit of the Jupiter mission in the movie *2001: A Space Odyssey,* then in national distribution and massively popular with the stony set. Floating ceilings, multiramped floors, carpeted wall surfaces and complex lighting systems replaced the conventional shapes and colors and textures found in most recording studios.

It was partly twenty-first-century spaceship, partly psychedelic fantasy.

In this environment Jimi began finishing songs. Some were put aside for the *Rising Sun* album, others ultimately would be used in the *Rainbow Bridge* "sound-track" album, because he had played them in concert in the film. Among them was one of his most autobiographical, "Dolly Dagger," which took its inspiration and title from his girl friend Devon's attraction to Mick Jagger. ("She's so heavy, she'll make you stagger . . . she drinks her blood from the jagged edge.") Another, called "Earth Blues," featured background vocals by the Ronettes. And "Pali Gap" was a jazzy instrumental, recorded with his conga friend from Woodstock, Juma Sutan.

For Jimi music was still his great escape. When he was in the studio, time had no dimension or meaning. There was only sound and electricity. In a tangled nest of electronic gadgetry, with cables and wires running in all directions, Jimi was lost in ecstasy. Hours slipped by as if only a few moments had passed. And the spools of tape piled up.

One concert interrupted his orgy of recording. This was an August 19 date on Randall's Island, a small piece of land with a stadium situated in New York's East River. The producer of the show, a longtime jazz promoter named Don Friedman, said that at first the city refused him a permit, on the grounds that Jimi was too "volatile." When Mike Jeffery heard that, he said it was because Jimi was black and had played last in New York in Harlem for the Ghetto Fighters. He threatened to go to the city park commission and scream discrimination. All the necessary permits were approved.

Jimi arrived, stoned, with an entourage of his closest companions: Devon and her friend Betty Davis, who was Miles Davis's ex-wife, Alan and Stella Douglas, the farm-equipment heir Deering Howe and Colette Mimram. Jimi was to go on last, and technical problems, coupled with too many acts booked to perform in too little time, made everything run late. Jimi remained in his dressing room, getting completely stoned.

"He was consuming drugs nonstop," says Don Friedman. "He was mixing them. He was drinking. He was smoking grass and snorting coke. He may have had some heroin, because I know there was some in the room; several of those with him were heavily into it. I remember Mike Jeffery coming up to me over and over again. He kept saying, 'Put him on! Put him on or he won't make it!' "

Jimi went on at 5 A.M. He made it. Barely.

And then it was back to his beloved studio.

By now the recording machines were friends and he talked to them. His eyes reflected the rows of red and green and white lights as he spent hours adjusting the hundreds of switches and tuning knobs in search of the perfect mix. Once he called Les Paul. Jimi had never met the great guitarist but was aware of his knowledge of electronics and thought he might help him solve a problem.

"He called me up with several questions," Les said, "including an idea of miking a guitar amp from far away— across the room—while running the guitar directly into the board at the same time. He also wanted to know how I went into the board."

Les answered Jimi's questions happily, enjoying the talk. Then he told Jimi about the time he and his son had seen Jimi at the bar in Lodi, New Jersey, in 1965.

"We tried to find you for months after that," Les said. "We finally gave up. Then a couple of years later I saw one of your albums and recognized your picture on the cover. I was glad you found success."

Jimi shook his head as he heard the story. All he could say before hanging up was, "Just think . . . I came *that* close."

A lot of Jimi's past was coming back. Running into his long-ago friend Mike Quashie recalled the same scuffling days that Les Paul had. The limbo dancer's health was not good, and he asked Jimi for a loan.

Jimi accompanied the man he had once called "Jungle Bunny"—when Mike called Jimi "Jimmy Coon"—to his apartment on the edge of Manhattan's Little Italy. Quashie said Curtis Knight lived nearby; they were the "only blacks" in the neighborhood. It was a small cluttered apartment on the fourth floor on Bedford Street. Every surface was covered with bric-a-brac and kitsch. Everywhere Jimi looked there were posters and framed photographs of Quashie's exploits and friends. Eric Burdon's leather jacket hung on a peg. Mike told Jimi he collected clothing and Jimi began on subsequent visits to leave some of his hats. On one visit Jimi told Quashie he wanted him to host his press party for the opening of Electric Lady Studios, for which he would, of course, be paid. After spending the night on Quashie's couch, Jimi then left $2,000 in cash on the coffee table between the giant clam shell and the painted plaster Venus candle holder.

Quashie was resplendent the evening of the press party, a vision from his own Caribbean past. Standing at the door of Electric Lady Studios, he welcomed guests effusively.

Reporters and photographers and the "beautiful people" of New York were given elaborate press releases that said, "What makes Electric Lady unique is not its technical facilities (though they are among the most advanced anywhere), but the philosophy behind them: to create an environment in the New York area that would not only free the artist but actively encourage him to create his best work. The design, by John Storyk (designer of Cerebrum and many other multi-media facilities), promotes a feeling of casual comfort bordering on informal luxury."

Even the party was choreographed for maximum comfort. "We arranged it in two stages," says Pat Costello, Jimi's publicist. "We had the record business people come at five-thirty or six-thirty and the music press come an hour and a half, two and a half hours later, to be sure that the straight record biz suits and ties were gone, so the rock writers could light up [joints] at will."

Jimi remained in one of the second-floor offices most of the evening with friends. He stayed up all night, leaving with his road manager, Eric Barrett, for England in the morning without having had any sleep.

Eric says they were still "drunk" when they arrived at Heathrow Airport, but Jimi handled it well. It had been more than eighteen months since Jimi had played the Royal Albert Hall, and the London press was out in force. He agreed to talk with reporters in the airport lounge and then in the rooms he had booked at the Cumberland Hotel. At first he was most cordial, but he tired quickly because questions were, as usual, unimaginative.

"If I'm free," he told the London *Times*, "it's because I'm always running. I tend to feel like a victim of public opinion. They want to know about these girls, kicking people in the ass, doing the 'Power to the People' sign. I cut my hair. They say, 'Why'd you cut your hair, Jimi? Where'd you get those socks? What made you wear blue socks today?' "

All night he remained awake, and on the afternoon of August 30, exhausted from three days and two nights without sleep, he swallowed a handful of bennies for energy and flew by helicopter to the Isle of Wight.

The small island's economy was tourist-based, and in 1969 local authorities approved a three-day pop festival to boost the number of visitors. Bob Dylan headlined that show, and when 200,000 people came to hear him, the island's burghers approved a repeat performance in 1970. This time Jimi was the headliner, attracting 250,000 fans who paid $7 apiece for three days of music and squatter's rights at the 200-acre festival site.

The festival was two days old when Jimi arrived, and to him it looked like a repeat of Woodstock: thousands spread over a huge sloping field, with tents and banners and sleeping bags and everywhere the smell of sweat and hashish. Jimi was met at the helicopter landing pad by another clot of journalists but, thankfully, also an old friend, Vishwa, who taught transcendental meditation and yoga in Los Angeles. He cut through the crowd and led Jimi to a dressing room. He was worried because Jimi looked sick.

The speed Jimi took in London had run its course and now he was smoking hashish, crumbled and rolled with tobacco in the English style. Jim Morrison made his way through the crowd of hangers-on to say hello, and Jimi brightened briefly, then fell back in exhaustion. Finally it was time to go on. Jimi stubbed out his cigarette and headed for the stage, his beloved Stratocaster in one hand, a can of beer in the other.

It was a strange set. His welcome was enthusiastic. "It's been a long, long time, hasn't it?" he asked, and the crowd roared back its love. He then crashed into "God Save the Queen," giving it the same sort of distortion and improvisation he gave "The Star-Spangled Banner" in the United States, and next came another, more modern "anthem," the great Beatles hit, "Sergeant Pepper's Lonely Hearts Club Band."

It was all downhill after that. While playing "Machine Gun" he discovered that he and the festival security police were "broadcasting" on the same frequency. Because of the song, it was funny in a way, but it was annoying to be interrupted.

Jimi threw himself into his guitar and out came the voice of a cop: "Security force, come in . . . security force, come in . . ."

For forty-five minutes he played a concert of mostly familiar songs and hits, including "All Along the Watchtower" and "Red House" and his first hit in England, "Hey Joe." But he was not happy when he left the stage. Mitch and Billy hadn't stayed with him musically. Audience reaction seemed tentative. And he was so tired his ability to judge his own performance was crippled.

Vishwa accompanied Jimi to the waiting helicopter, wanting to go along. He looked at Jimi expectantly. In the past he had traveled with Jimi frequently.

Jimi stared coldly at his friend. Finally he said, dismissing Vishwa, "What are you—my old lady?"

He entered the helicopter, and with a great clatter of metal, chop-chopping blades, he disappeared into the morning sun.

The tedium of touring began again as Jimi moved from jet plane to limousine to dressing room to stage, ad nauseum, throughout Europe.

The rooms and jets and cars and huge concert halls swept past in a rush of speed and hash and beer. By the time he reached Arhus, Jimi was fading fast and just as he had stopped the show in the middle of the second song at Madison Square Garden, he did it again. His fingers were numb. His eyes were glazed.

Jimi looked at his Danish audience and said, "I've been dead a long time."

And then he walked off.

The next two concerts were okay, although in Berlin Jimi sounded fatigued in an interview he did with the U.S. Armed Forces Radio. His voice sounded like a frog's because he had sung so loudly, he said, and he was "nervous."

Then, on the Isle of Fehmarn, also in West Germany, it all came apart again. Jimi was scheduled to perform on Saturday night, the fifth, but when they arrived from Berlin, the festival was under attack.

"German bikers had robbed the box office and were charging outrageous parking fees," says one of Jimi's company. "They were drunk and shooting up the place. With guns! Half the crowd was drunk or zonked on reds [barbiturates]. A lot of that stuff is manufactured in Germany and it's real, real available. Hell, one of Jimi's off-and-on girl friends, Monika Danneman . . . her old man owned one of the largest pharmaceutical companies in Europe, in Düsseldorf. Everywhere you looked, people were nodding out. Or fighting."

Jimi remained sequestered backstage as the festival's master of ceremonies, the tiny British bluesman Alexis Korner, tried to keep the show on course. He spoke fluent German, and that helped. But it was hours before the crowd had settled enough for Alexis to finally introduce the headlined star.

Jimi ambled onstage. As Billy took his position to his left rear and Mitch sat down behind his big double drum kit, his long wavy hair blowing in a strong breeze, Jimi called out nervously to the audience:

"Peace . . . peace, anyway."

[291]

Half the audience cheered and applauded and the other half hooted and booed. Jimi looked startled. He booed back, thinking it might be some sort of joke. But now many of the audience began chanting: "GO HOME . . . GO HOME . . . GO HOME . . . GO HOME!"

Jimi waited for a moment, then, ignoring the continuing chant, he apologized for making everyone wait so long. It didn't make sense. After waiting so long, why were they shouting that?

"GO HOME . . . GO HOME . . . GO HOME!"

Jimi hurriedly introduced his band: "Mitch Mitchell on drums, Billy Cox on bass, and Jimi on public saxophone. Like to play some music for you."

"GO HOME . . . GO HOME . . . GO HOME!"

Jimi announced the first song in German and then in English, a fairly new composition called "The Killing Floor." And then he mouthed the first line of the song, "I should have quit you a long time ago." He paused and mumbled, "You motherfuckers!"

> I should have quit you a long time ago
> I should have quit you a long time ago
> Now you got me crying on the killing floor
> Lord knows I should have gone
> I just got here today y'all
> And now you got me crying on the killing floor

The set was brief, there were no encores, and after Jimi left, the bikers resumed the violence.

Worse was yet to come.

The press was told that Billy Cox had suffered a "nervous breakdown." It wasn't entirely a lie. Billy *did* break down and his nervous system surely was involved. The entire truth was that someone gave Billy some punch laced with

LSD. Billy never had taken acid before and the result was paranoid frenzy.

"They're coming to kill us!" he told Jimi. "Poison. Don't eat anything. They're after us!"

Jimi and just about everyone else nearby *had* had experience with LSD and they tried all the known ways to "talk him down," to calm Billy, to reassure him that he was safe.

"No, no, no! You don't understand! They are going to kill us!"

Finally Billy was taken to a hospital, where he was given Thorazine, the most widely used of all drugs against psychotic states, a downer so powerful it had largely replaced both electroconvulsive and insulin shock therapy and psychosurgery (prefrontal lobotomy) as treatment for the most severe mental disorders.

It seemed to make things worse. After the wildly hallucinatory rush, Billy now went the other way, turning into a human vegetable, a walking zombie, refusing, or unable, to talk or react to anyone or anything. The doctors and nurses couldn't get through to him, nor could Jimi.

The two final shows of the tour, in Rotterdam, were canceled, and Jimi checked Billy out of the Dutch hospital, taking him back to London, where he had friends who would look after him. Jimi believed it was just a matter of time before Billy recovered. He *had* to believe that.

Billy sat staring at the wall, smiling gently, saying nothing.

Jimi cried out.

"Oh, God! Oh, goddamn fuckin' God, please help!"

CHAPTER

17

Jimi was a gypsy in all of his "home" towns. London, where his career was reborn, was no different from New York, where his residences continued numerous and simultaneous.

Officially Jimi was back in his $40-a-day room at the Cumberland Hotel, overlooking Marble Arch, just off fashionable Park Lane. But he also had alternate homes, including an apartment taken by his sometime German girl friend, Monika Danneman, in the Samarkand Hotel, in the more bohemian Nottinghill Gate district.

Another flat available to him was that of Pat Hartley and Dick Fontaine, on Elvaston Place in Kensington, occupied at the moment by still another American friend, the model Alvenia Bridges. A fourth place was Danny Secunda's home in still another section of the city, an apartment whose occupants that week were Alan and Stella Douglas.

In the final week of his life Jimi slept in many beds.

He also gave several interviews to reporters from the London music press. Never did he reveal the concern he felt about Billy, who remained hidden in a friend's apartment, refusing to eat or speak. However, he did seem concerned about his image and the direction his music was taking.

"I've turned full circle, I'm right back where I started," he told *Melody Maker,* referring to his playing with a trio again. Now, he said, he wanted a big band, in which his guitar would take a diminished role. "I want other musicians to play my stuff," he said. "I want to be a good writer."

In all his interviews Jimi expressed worry about his image, said all the visual gimmickry was in his distant past, said it was something he'd used in order to get people to listen. The trouble was, the people had stopped listening.

"Everyone goes through changes," Jimi told Keith Altham of the *Record Mirror.* "I look around at new groups like Cactus and Mountain and they're into those same things with the hair and the clothes—wearing all the jewelry and strangling themselves with beads. I got out of that because I felt I was being too loud visually.

"I got the feeling maybe too many people were coming to look and not enough to listen. My nature just changed as well and I went and hid for a while.

"I started cutting my hair and losing jewelry, ring by ring, until I had none left. The freaky thing was never a publicity hype. That was just the way I was then. If I felt like smashing a guitar, I worked up some anger and smashed. The anger has dissipated, and I don't feel the need to dress up so much now I see others doing it."

A third music weekly, *Disc and Music Echo,* headlined on September 12: GENTLEMAN JIMI IS SETTLING DOWN! "I'd like to meet a quiet little girl . . . probably one from the country who doesn't know anything about my reputation," he told Mike Ledgerwood.

Jimi entertained the writers in his hotel room, usually with a number of unidentified young women present— women who weren't quiet little girls from the country—

while drinking his favorite wines, most often Chablis or rosé. According to some of the girls, he was also smoking thumb-thick joints. One of them, Lorraine James, who was then living in a London commune, said he had a lot of marijuana with him, rare for England, where hashish was the popular and cheaper smoke. Many of his companions say they also saw Jimi swallow a number of pills, which were unidentified.

It is said that just before you die, your life passes in parade before you. For Jimi this grim cliché came true as his old friends and adversaries arrived in London to participate in his final days.

Everywhere he went he saw his past. He had drinks at the Speakeasy with Alvenia, then let Monika cook a meal for him. He met with Alan and Stella and Devon, then disappeared long enough to meet with his English girl friend from 1966, Kathy Etchingham.

The "enemies"—people Jimi perceived as enemies, anyway—seemed to be arriving on the same flights from New York. One of them was Ed Chalpin. Flushed with his success in America, he was in London now to push his claims against Jimi's European record companies. Affidavits were being taken. A court date was imminent.

In addition, there were reports that Mike Jeffery was in town, or coming to town, to check on Billy and to meet the London solicitors about the Chalpin lawsuit. If he was in town, he did not call Jimi. But Jimi was concerned.

"He had an anxiety attack at Elvaston Place," Alvenia says. "He told me a story about being kidnapped and taken to upstate New York. He got really intense about his management. He said, 'Man, they'll just do anything with you.' He was real unhappy in London. He didn't seem like his old self. He needed a lot of love. I'm a kisser, so we'd hug and kiss. But it wasn't enough. I thought, What can I do? He was so unhappy! There was so little time . . ."

Lorraine Jones says Jimi was calm and good-natured one moment and downstairs on the street the next, in a telephone booth, talking—to whom? to whom?—about how his manager was stealing all his money and he didn't know whom he could trust.

On the evening of September 16 Jimi was on a "roll," careening from flat to flat, from club to club. At one stop it was reported that a man Jimi and his friends had been talking with suddenly leaped over a railing and plummeted to the floor below, breaking his legs.

Eventually they went to a popular jazz club on the edge of Soho, Ronnie Scott's. Eric Burdon and his new band were performing there. Eric's manager met Jimi at the door. This was Steve Gold, who hadn't seen Jimi since he filmed him at the Royal Albert Hall.

"He was ripped," Steve says, "and I told him he couldn't come in. I told him to come back the next night."

On the morning of the sixteenth Jimi's hairdresser, Finney, appeared to do Jimi's hair in the apartment occupied by Billy Cox. Billy was still a vegetable, staring dumbly as Finney pressed curl after curl, making Jimi's hair seem fuller than it was in front.

Suddenly Billy said, "That was a good one!"

Finney and Jimi rushed to Billy's side. Slowly they coaxed a few more words from him, and a few hours later they put him on a plane home to the U.S.

That night Alvenia Bridges and Finney were at Ronnie Scott's, along with Alan and Stella and also Devon, who was angry with Jimi because she had been looking for him for two days unsuccessfully. Making matters worse, Jimi entered the dark club with Monika Danneman.

"Is that your blonde of the week?" Devon asked.

Jimi laughed, then said, "Where's Mick?"

Devon glared for a moment, then gave Jimi an oh-what-the-hell look and moved her chair to make room for the couple to sit down.

Eric Burdon was on the stage, and when Eric saw Jimi, he invited him to sit in. "At first he played like an amateur, real bad, using stage tricks to cover up," Eric said. "Then he came on with a solo which was up to scratch, and the audience dug it. He went offstage and came back and played the background to 'Tobacco Road.' He wasn't just freaking. He was jelling nicely with the band."

Afterward Jimi told Monika he would see her later; he had to talk with Alan before he returned to New York the following day. He then spent the night in the Secunda flat with Alan, Stella and Devon. Then, on the morning of the seventeenth, he accompanied Alan to the airport.

"Jimi told me he wanted me to talk to Mike Jeffery," Alan says. "He wanted out of his contract, but he didn't know how he could do it. We talked about it half the night, and we finally decided that Jimi could offer to pay Mike his percentage for however long the contract was, on top of whatever he paid his new manager. I don't know if Mike would have gone for it. I never got the chance to ask."

At 11 A.M., soon after Alan's plane took off, Gerry Stickells called Jimi's British agent, Dick Katz, saying Jimi wanted to do another tour of Britain and the Continent. Dick got on the phone and in a matter of hours booked several dates in England and Germany.

Jimi spent what remained of his final day with Monika. Jimi took her drawing pad and drew the number nine nine times, linking the figures into each other, saying "nine consciousness" was the highest form of consciousness. He then drew a Christian cross, decorating each of the four lines with sketches of the faces of famous people. Martin Luther King, Jr., and other black faces formed the left horizontal line, John Kennedy and Hitler and other Caucasian faces the opposite. Geronimo and other "red" faces formed the lower vertical, Buddha and Genghis Kahn and other "yellow" faces the upper vertical.

Monika Danneman

"Monika," Jimi said, "remember this. This is the grand design. Remember all I say. You are a painter. Put this in your paintings. Nine. Remember the number nine. There are nine planets. And remember the number four. Four colors. Remember."

Jimi and Monika went shopping after that, to the Kensington Market, where they ran into Devon and Stella, who invited Jimi and Monika to accompany them to a party that night. Jimi accepted immediately, leaving Monika to drive her little blue Opel home alone, and went with Stella and Devon back to the Secunda apartment. After the women had changed clothes, the three took a cab to the party.

Jimi scanned the room as he entered with the two strik-
ing women. He met three of the men present—the financier
Bert Kleiner, the music publisher Pete Cameron, and David
Salmon, heir to a British fast-food chain. There was plenty
to drink but no evidence of any hash or other drugs, so in a
bathroom, Devon produced some "black bombers," capsules
containing an amphetamine and a sedative. Jimi took one.
He also snorted a small quantity of powdered LSD.

After a time Monika arrived. By now Devon was nodding, too drugged to move. Stella said she wanted to remain,
so Jimi went off with Monika. Monika said later that they
collected Alvenia and had a drink at a club in Soho, soon
leaving Alvenia at Ronnie Scott's, where she wanted to meet
one of Eric Burdon's musicians. Monika and Jimi then returned to Monika's flat. Monika says that it was 8:30 P.M.
when they arrived, but it could have been later.

"I cooked a meal and brought out a bottle of wine
about eleven P.M.," Monika says. "He drank more of the
bottle than I did. He had nothing to drink other than the
wine. He had a bath and washed his hair and then we talked
and listened to music until about one-forty-five A.M., when
he told me he had to go to some peoples' flat. They were not
his friends and he did not like them. He told me he did not
want me to go with him, so I dropped him off there, and
picked him up an hour later, just after three."

What happened during that hour is not known. No one
has come forward to fill the gap and Monika does not remember the address of the mysterious flat, nor did Jimi say
anything about the visit afterward.

Monika continues her story: "When we came back, we
were talking. I took a sleeping tablet at about seven A.M. [the
morning of the eighteenth]. I made him two fish sandwiches.
We were in bed, talking. I woke about ten-twenty A.M. He
was sleeping normally. I went round the corner to get cigarettes. When I came back, he had been sick. He was breath-

ing and his pulse was normal, but I could not wake him. I saw that he had taken sleeping tablets. There were nine of mine missing."

The tablets, a prescription drug called Vesparax, came ten to a package. Monika had taken one. Now the package was empty.

Monika looked at Jimi, vomit drying around his mouth and nose. She tried again to awaken him. He failed to respond to her calls and touch. She wanted to send for help but feared that Jimi would be angry if she had him taken to a hospital and nothing was really wrong. So she telephoned Eric Burdon for advice. Alvenia was in the hotel room with Eric.

"I can't wake up Jimi!" she cried.

Eric said, "Call an ambulance! Now!"

Monika said she would and hung up. Alvenia told Eric she would run the short distance to Monika's hotel, leaving Eric free to go to a photo session that was scheduled.

"I arrived just as the ambulance pulled up," Alvenia says. "Monika said she had hidden Jimi's guitar. She didn't want anybody to know who he was. She had Jimi's passport and other identification and when we got to the hospital she checked him in, using a false name. She was afraid he would get mad at her."

Apparently Jimi was still alive. Alvenia says that the ambulance attendants assured her that Jimi "was going to be all right." While waiting outside one of the emergency rooms, Alvenia made several calls—to Eric Burdon and then in an attempt to find Eric Barrett and Mitch Mitchell.

Finally someone in white appeared to tell the women that Jimi was dead.

"We didn't believe it," Alvenia says. "We didn't want to. I said I wanted to see him and finally they agreed to let us go in. We asked for his possessions and they gave us what he had in his pockets. Then Monika became hysterical. She curled up on the floor and began crying. I ran to a phone and called Eric and he sent someone to take us back to his hotel."

Eventually the body was identified by Gerry Stickells, after which it was moved to the morgue.

In Mike Jeffery's office in New York there was chaos. Jerry Morrison was there when the call came in from Gerry Stickells, and he says Jeffery couldn't be found, so he, Bob Levine and Kathy "synchronized everything. We ran to get a locksmith friend to unlock Jimi's apartment in the Village to rescue the guitars and tapes, because we knew the leeches had keys, we knew they'd clean the place out. We got there first and took the guitars and everything of value back to the office."

Jerry says four days went by before they found Mike in Majorca, where he still had his nightclub. Jerry believes Mike was in London on the eighteenth, when Jimi died, but when Bob Levine told Mike on the telephone that Jimi was dead, Mike "gasped as if he were surprised."

Jeffery flew to London, remaining there for several days, telling Levine to see what could be done about organizing a musical tribute, either at Bill Graham's Fillmore East, or if it could be held down in size, at the Electric Lady Studios.

In the meantime the press vented its inky spleen. Albert Goldman, who would go on to write sensationalistic books about Lenny Bruce and Elvis Presley, fairly oozed in *Life* magazine: "If you were drawn even for a moment into Jimi Hendrix's breathless quest for life, his urgent headlong pursuit not simply of pleasure but of the most elusive and exotic states of mind and soul, you would know that his death was an inevitable product of his life. Hendrix once sent someone a bag of cocaine with a high-flown note inscribed in flowery script: 'Within I grace thee with wings. O lovely and true Birds of Heavenly Snow and Crystals. Fly my love as you have before. Pleasures are only steps and this . . . just one more.' That was the rhetoric of his life and it swept him along heedless of dangers that made his mere existence a daily miracle. It sent him flickering among the candles and bottles and fuming incense of his nocturnal day, it moved him to sniff cocaine and drop acid and drink wine all in a row, like the chord changes in a tune on which he was improvising."

Hubert Saal in *Newsweek* was briefer: "Who's next? Who else is good at handling drugs until he isn't good at it?"

Other writers took a far different tack. Yes, it was a shame, perhaps even stupid, and clearly a terrible waste, but what of the ones who drank and smoked themselves to untimely deaths because of cancer and cirrhosis and traffic accidents? These writers chose to consider Jimi's contribution and not his disappointing, early demise.

Michael Lydon wrote in *The New York Times* that "Jimi Hendrix was more than a star. He was a genius black musician, a guitarist, singer, and composer of brilliantly dramatic power. He spoke in gestures as big as he could imagine and create; his willingness for adventure knew no bounds. He was wild, passionate, and abrasive, yet all his work was imbued with his personal gentleness. He was an artist extravagantly generous with his beauty."

Noting his place in contemporary musical history, *Downbeat* magazine said; "Hendrix's excitingly eclectic guitar playing, combining classic blues elements with psychedelic freak-out effects (he was one of the main popularizers of the fuzz box and the wa-wa pedal), and his dynamic stage manner, highly erotic, charged with energy and featuring eccentric dress and hair style, made him one of the few black rock performers able to compete in popularity with the top white groups."

Those who appreciated Jimi were pulling out all the stops. John Burks in *Rolling Stone* said, "The amazing thing is how rich a musical legacy Hendrix left in so short a time."

Al Aronowitz in the New York *Post* called Jimi a "flashing, graceful black giant." *Good Times,* a weekly published in California, said he served as "an inspiration for thousands during his tornado journey through the public psyche." *Rags* magazine described Jimi as "the most other-worldly and muscially inventive of all the rock and roll guitarists—*the* best cat there was at taking us to that place beyond the stars." Carmen Moore in the *Village Voice* said, "A fuse in the new-world love machine has gone out and cannot be replaced."

As much as this prose was being rushed into print, death stories and theories were the talk of London. One British newspaper called Jimi a "cocaine addict" and another headlined its story DRUGS KILL HENDRIX AT 24 [*sic*], although which drugs were not specified. Others described him as "a victim of the pop-and-drugs culture he helped perpetuate" and "prophet-in-chief of the drug generation."

On the street the talk was most specific, and divided. Some, including the singer Marianne Faithfull, said Jimi unknowingly heaped a lot of heroin-laced sugar into a cup of coffee. Other, wilder accounts had him the victim of an FBI plot to eliminate black radicals, or had him flown to Hollywood, where he was murdered and then returned to London in a chartered jet.

Eric Burdon had another hypothesis. He said yes, it was drugs, but more than that, it was intentional: Jimi committed suicide. This was a theory he took to the BBC forty-eight hours after Jimi's death.

"He made his exit when he wanted to," Eric said. "His death was deliberate. He was happy dying. He used a drug to phase himself out of his life and go someplace else."

There was some circumstantial evidence to back this claim. The day of his death Jimi was expected in a London court in the ongoing Ed Chalpin case. Jimi's European royalties had been tied up in this lawsuit for more than a year, and he feared another humiliating loss. He also remained confused and frustrated by his record production, the direction of his music and his management. Burdon hinted that such matters made Jimi depressed, although he admitted that generally Jimi was a happy soul, always smiling.

There was also the matter of Jimi's belief in reincarnation, often spelled out in his song lyrics and interviews. This would make death seem not an end but a door that opened onto another birth.

However, the real "proof," Burdon said, was in a poem that Jimi wrote at Monika's flat only hours before he died.

> The story of Jesus
> so easy to explain,
> after they crucified him,
> a woman, she claimed his name.
>
> The story of Jesus
> the whole Bible knows
> went all across the Desert
> and in the middle, he found a rose.
>
> There should be no questions
> there should be no lies
> He was married ever
> happily after
> for all the Tears we cry.
>
> No use in arguing all
> the use to the man that moans
> when each man falls in Battle, His
> soul it has to roam
>
> angels of heaven
> flying Saucers to some,

made Easter Sunday
the name of the Rising
Sun

The story is written
by so many people who dared,
to lay down the truth
to so very many who cared
to carry the cross
of Jesus and beyond

We will guild the light
this time with a woman in
our arms

We as men
can't explain the reason why
the woman's always mentioned
at the moment. That we die.

All we know
is God is by our side

and he says the word
So easy yet so hard
I wish not to be alone
So I must respect my other
heart

Oh the story
of Jesus is the story
of you and me
No use in feeling lonely
I am you searching to be free

the story
of life is quicker
than the wink of an eye.

the story of love
is hello and good-bye
until we meet again.

Most convincing of all was the actual overdose—the apparent consumption of nine potent sleeping pills when the prescribed dosage was half of one. Can anyone make that big a mistake? Apparently the answer is yes, he can. Especially if he has learned from experience that his capacity is greater than that of the average individual, as Jimi's must have been. The cliché about some people "holding their liquor" better than others has scientific backing, and it is the same with drugs.

Did Jimi actually think he was able to handle that much Vesparax? Hadn't he already consumed a significant quantity of alcohol and a number of barbiturates? Again the answer is yes, but that may explain why he swallowed nine more. It is possible he was so stoned he didn't remember how much he had taken. Surely his judgment was damaged, his memory muddled.

What was it, then? Suicide? Or an "honest" but unfortunate accident?

Her Majesty's coroner had the final word. An autopsy was performed September 21, three days after Jimi's death, by Robert Donald Teare, a practicing physician and a pathologist in the department of forensic medicine at St. George's Hospital. He found Jimi to be a "well nourished and muscular young adult man" and said there were no signs of drug addiction (no needle marks). However, several drugs were found in his liver, blood and urine. These included a popular tranquilizer, Seconal; an unidentified am-

phetamine, which along with a commercially available de-
pressant called Durophet made up the "black bomber" he
took at the party; two other depressants, allobarbital and
quinalbarbitone; enough alcohol to fail a drunk-driving test
(in the U.S.); as well as the Vesparax.

. An inquest was ordered, in part because of the public
furor caused by Eric Burdon but mostly because of Jimi's
notoriety and the presence of so many drugs. Four witnesses
appeared at Westminster Coroner's Court on September 28:
the pathologist, the policeman who investigated the case,
Gerry Stickells and Monika Danneman.

Her Majesty's coroner Gavin L. B. Thurston ruled that
on the basis of the pathologist's findings, Jimi had died "as a
result of inhalation of vomit due to barbiturate intoxica-
tion." What this meant was that Jimi had so depressed his
central nervous system, he had "paralyzed" his gag reflex.
Then, as his stomach rejected the poisonous overdose, the
vomit was caught and couldn't be fully expelled. And because Jimi was unconscious and unable to move, some of
what *was* expelled was inhaled into his lungs. Literally, he
had drowned in his own vomit.

The coroner then reviewed the testimony of Gerry and
Monika, who said Jimmy was "happy . . . even-tempered . . .
not a man to have moods" and definitely not the suicide
type. The coroner concluded that there was "insufficient
evidence" to call the death intentional or accidental. Closing
the inquest with an "open verdict," he said, "The question
why Hendrix took so many sleeping tablets cannot be safely
answered."

Plans for a tribute in New York subsequently were canceled, and Jimi's body was returned directly to Seattle,
where preparations for another public memorial service
were dropped, partly because of a lack of time to organize
properly, partly because the city authorities blanched at the
idea, fearing the problems caused by crowds.

Nonetheless the musicians began arriving in Seattle on Tuesday the twenty-ninth—first Noel Redding and Mitch Mitchell, along with Gerry Stickells and Eric Barrett, then Johnny Winter and his manager, Jimi's old friend who ran the Scene, Steve Paul. John Hammond, Jr., joined the others at the Hilton Hotel, accompanied by the writer Al Aronowitz. Miles Davis checked into another hotel downtown, and the entire Buddy Miles band took rooms at the Holiday Inn.

By Wednesday there were many more, some of them Jimi's closest associates: Mike Jeffery with the publicist Michael Goldstein; Jimi's favorite engineer, Eddie Kramer; the filmmaker Chuck Wein—who still hadn't finished editing *Rainbow Bridge*—along with a sound man who had done two Hendrix tours, Abe Jacob.

These friends and relatives gathered on October 1 at the Dunlap Baptist Church, where Patronella Wright, a family friend, sang three spirituals, accompanied by a gospel piano, and Mrs. Freddie Maye Gautier, another family friend, delivered a brief eulogy that included one of Jimi's last poems, recorded only a few months before in New York:

> Angel came down from heaven yesterday.
> She stayed with me just
> Long enough to rescue me.
> And she told me a story yesterday
> About the sweet love between the
> Moon and the deep sea.
> And then she spread her wings
> High over me.
> She said she's gonna come back tomorrow.
> And I said fly on my sweet angel,
> Fly on through the sky.
> Fly on my sweet angel.
> Tomorrow I'm gonna be by your side.

Sure enough this woman came back to me
Silver wings silhouetted against a child's sunrise.
And my angel said to me,
Today is the day for you to rise.
Take my hand,
You're gonna be my man,
You're gonna rise.

She took me high over yonder,
And I said fly on my sweet angel
Fly on through the sky.
Fly on my sweet angel,
Forever, I will be by your side.

The pallbearers were friends from Jimi's childhood, with one exception, Herbert Price, who had worked for Jimi as a valet and chauffeur. From the church the procession of perhaps one hundred cars—most of them driven by fans, who remained outside during the service—made the twenty-minute drive to Greenwood Cemetery, in nearby Renton. There the Reverend Harold Blackburn said a few words, and following a chorus of "When the Saints Go Marchin' In," Jimi's casket was lowered into the grave.

Jimi's father, Al Hendrix, at the funeral

Last rites. Jimi's brother, Leon, is standing directly behind the funeral directors in the first row

Jimi's coffin is carried from the church

The gravestone

FOREVER IN OUR HEARTS
JAMES M.
"JIMI" HENDRIX
1942 ———— 1970

EPILOGUE

Jimi Hendrix had been dead less than a month when his father, Al Hendrix, was approached by a Seattle lawyer, William Lockett. The elder Hendrix knew Lockett, trusted him. Lockett said he had some friends who wanted to start a nonprofit memorial foundation in his son's name.

The friends included two local attorneys who were supposed to put up some of the seed money, Gary Culver and Buck Austin. Others were the owner of a small chain of skin-flick movie houses in California, Harold Greenlin, who lived in Los Angeles, and a bearded, balding fat man called Tiny Becker, one of Greenlin's theater operators, who came from San Francisco to run the foundation.

Mr. Hendrix, accompanied by a family friend, Mrs. Freddie Mae Gautier, attended a meeting at which photographs of some land outside Seattle were produced. Mr. Hendrix was told that rock festivals would be held there, a museum would be erected, and a campground would be established where underprivileged black children could come without charge. All Mr. Hendrix had to do, they said, to make this dream come true, was sign a document giving the foundation the right to use Jimi's name.

Mr. Hendrix was nodding his head, saying it all sounded good to him, when Mrs. Gautier interrupted. "What's in it for Mr. Hendrix?" she asked.

Mr. Hendrix said the lawyers then produced "more cash money than I ever saw before. There was ten hundred-dollar bills. And they said something about a salary after the money started to come in."

Mr. Hendrix signed a contract and a receipt for the cash. The contract sold "to the Jimi Hendrix Memorial Foundation, Inc., a Washington corporation to be formed at once by Raymond Becker, the exclusive right to use the name of his deceased son, Jimi, in the promotion of a permanent memorial to him and/or any other use whatsoever deemed necessary or advantageous to the aforementioned corporation."

As part of the agreement, Mr. Hendrix was named vice president and Mrs. Gautier was named a director. But the foundation's operation was given totally to Tiny Becker, the president. Soon after that, a suite of six offices was rented in downtown Seattle, and a Portland, Oregon, carnival booking agent named Ted Coates was brought in to run the phone room.

"They had about a dozen, fifteen telephones in one of the rooms," Mr. Hendrix recalled. "They had people to sell advertisements in a Jimi Hendrix Picture Book." William Lockett had Mr. Hendrix sign a sworn affidavit stating that Coates and his boys weren't being compensated, a requirement for the foundation to get a city permit to operate a charity. It wasn't true. Later, Coates said the pitchmen were working on a 25 percent commission, while he and another room manager were splitting an additional 20 percent.

The pitch was direct. The Official Jimi Hendrix Memorial Foundation Souvenir Photograph Album offered a half-million guaranteed circulation. The foundation was said to own 146 acres of land that was to be dedicated to the state within three years as the Jimi Hendrix Memorial Park. Half a dozen music scholarships were promised.

Not surprisingly, Becker and his foundation attracted attention in the Seattle newspapers. But when Becker was asked about the mysterious 146-acre parcel of land, no one challenged his answer: "We can't disclose the location at this time, because we're trying to buy the adjacent land and don't want to drive the price up." Later Walter Wright, an investigative reporter for Seattle's *Post Intelligencer,* exposed all the sordid details.

It was clear that the foundation was being run with big money in mind, but first Becker had to learn his job. The first benefit show was staged in Seattle's Phoenix Club, a second in the much larger Eagles Hall, which held about 2,500 uncomfortably. This one ran nonstop for two days and offered more than twenty bands. Most bands were not paid, having been talked into appearing either in tribute to the dead guitarist or for the "valuable exposure" the performances would provide. The shows were well attended. Teenagers hired by Becker sold buttons and pillows and bumper stickers that said JIMI HENDRIX LIVES—FOR THE JIMI HENDRIX MEMORIAL FOUNDATION. Memberships were sold for $10 or $20.

Mr. Hendrix attended both shows. Each time he was led on-stage by the three-hundred-pound Becker and introduced to the audience. It was quite an experience for the quiet, golf-loving gardener. Still, what he remembered most vividly was the lack of backstage organization, the friction between his "partners." "They were squabbling over the money," he said. "It was a mess."

Indeed it was. Ted Coates had a fight with Becker, quit, and went to the police. Another bitter employee told the state Department of Labor that the foundation was breaking minimum-wage laws. The city permit to conduct a charitable fund-raising operation was canceled. About the same time, city license inspectors discovered Becker's police record, which included an arrest for trying to exchange $785 worth of stolen airline tickets, an arrest made in Seattle the same week that Becker was named president of the Jimi Hendrix Memorial Foundation.

Lockett asked Mr. Hendrix to sign another affidavit and told officials he had fired Tiny Becker. Mr. Hendrix, he said, was the new president. That wasn't true, either, but he was given a temporary permit anyway.

The benefit shows continued, and so did the telephone calls to area businessmen, seeking advertisements for the souvenir book. A third concert was held in the Tacoma, Washington, Sports Arena, a fourth in another Seattle club. But the last one wasn't advertised, and attendance probably was insufficient to pay costs.

When Mr. Hendrix went to the office a few days later, everything was gone, even the unsold candy bars and the little rubber stamps of Jimi's face that were used to mark concertgoers' hands as they entered the halls and clubs. Next day, he and Mrs. Gautier went to city hall and solemnly withdrew their application for a fund-raising permit.

And what of the money? No one knew. A $267 check written by Becker for city taxes bounced, and Lockett had to make it up in cash. No one even knew how much money was taken in. Records simply were not kept. Austin and Culver said they never got their initial investment back. Lockett was later indicted in connection with eight armed robberies and killed himself. Becker was shot to death by his wife.

This particularly sad operation is one of the things that drove Mr. Hendrix into the arms of another attorney, a black man of his own age, Leo Branton Jr. of Los Angeles. Branton came highly recommended. Initially, he was suggested by Herbert Price, who worked for Jimi as a man Friday during the filming of the documentary *Rainbow Bridge* and was in London when Jimi died, accompanying his body to Seattle. Price had worked for the singer Nat "King" Cole when Branton was Cole's attorney. Mr. Hendrix told Price that Jimi's manager, Michael Jeffery, said there wasn't much left of Jimi's legacy—all they'd found so far was less than $25,000 in cash. Worse, there was an outstanding debt of $200,000 owed to the IRS, and as time passed, other large debts to recording studios and to Warner Bros. emerged. In brief, Jimi Hendrix's career after his death was in as much chaos as it had been before it.

Branton told me he started his legal career litigating personal injury cases, but left a Los Angeles law firm to study entertainment and tax law because "I was going to break the stronghold that white lawyers had on business from black entertainers." One of his first clients was the actress Dorothy Dandridge, a friend of his wife's, who was maid of honor at their marriage. In time, he said, he represented a number of entertainers, black and white, among the latter Inger Stevens, negotiating her contract for the television series *The Farmer's Wife*. Then, in 1968, after eight years in the business, he decided to retire and with his wife go to Sweden "to try their style of socialism." Before he could do that, he was asked to help a dozen members of the Black Panther party who'd been arrested in Los Angeles, and soon after that he joined the legal team defending black activist Angela Davis. He remained in the United States.

Branton said he listened to Al Hendrix's story, then went to New York to meet with Jeffery and the estate's legal administrator, Henry Steingarten, returning to California with fire in his eyes. How, Branton puzzled, could Steingarten, a lawyer, represent the Hendrix estate properly when Jeffery was being represented by Steingarten's partner, Steve Weiss?

Branton also learned the details of Jeffery's original management deal with the Jimi Hendrix Experience. "Mike got Jimi in 1966 to sign an agreement with him and Chas Chandler, on the basis of 40 percent of his gross income to them. Within a day or so, he got Jimi to sign an exclusive recording agreement, and he agreed to pay Jimi 3 percent of whatever those records earned. Which 3 percent Jimi had to share with Mitch Mitchell and Noel Redding. He then took that same piece of paper to Track and Polydor Records in London and gave them the right to distribute Hendrix records for 10 percent. So with an exchange of a piece of paper, he made 7 percent of the record earnings and Jimi made only 3 per cent, which he had to share with two other people. Then, after doing that, Jeffery turned right around and told Jimi he wanted his 30 percent commission on the 3 percent."

Branton met again with Al Hendrix, who gave him permission to do whatever he thought best. Branton said he went straight to Steingarten and threatened to take him to the Bar Association on a conflict of interest charge unless he resigned as the estate's administrator. For whatever reason, Steingarten resigned. Branton meanwhile engaged two young black attorneys in New York, Ed Howard and Kenny Hagood, who had met with Jimi about four months before he died; Jimi had been, they said, seeking new legal representation, but when they asked to review his existing contracts, he told them that he didn't have any copies, and although they subsequently talked on the phone, they never met again. The deal with Branton was that Hagood would administer the estate, being probated in New York; Howard would be the attorney of record; and Branton would mastermind the strategy and argue the Hendrix cause in court.

"I took the Hendrix estate case because there were issues that I thought I could do some good in," Branton told me. "I took the Angela Davis case for the same reason. Every case that I take, there's a reason for my taking the case aside from the fact that I'm a lawyer and anybody could come and have my services. [There was the] great exploitation of an artist during his lifetime, and what appeared to be an effort to continue that exploitation after death. It had to stop."

On the job by February 1971, under six months from

the time of Jimi's death, Branton knew that the first thing he had to do was put the estate in a better cash position, so he decided to sell Jimi's interest in the Electric Lady Studios. Jeffery agreed to pay the estate $240,000, the figure he and Hendrix had originally invested. He also agreed to assume responsibility for what remained of a $300,000 loan from Warner Bros. However generous this may have seemed on the surface, in a short time the investment was repaid and the studios were operating profitably.

Simultaneously, Jeffery and Eddie Kramer were going through whatever tapes they could find, sending new material to Warner Bros. as quickly as possible to take advantage of the posthumous market that developed following the publicity attached to Jimi's death. Warner Bros. accepted three albums and rejected the fourth, apparently deciding there was nothing else worthy of release, and the remaining tapes were returned to the Hendrix estate.

Meanwhile, in the Ed Chalpin trial, pending in London when Jimi died, Chalpin complained that the *Band of Gypsies* album, released in 1970, wasn't as good as he'd been promised, a claim that seemed laughable since it was the second biggest Hendrix album up to that time. At the conclusion of the trial, the judge said Chalpin had no credibility and ordered him to pay the Hendrix estate's legal fees (the loser always does so in Britain, unlike in the United States) promptly. Chalpin agreed to pay Branton $150,000. In addition, Chalpin was required to deliver to the Hendrix estate all unreleased tapes in his possession. However, he was permitted to continue to exploit the albums already on the market. (While the trial was in progress, Mike Jeffery was killed in a plane crash on a weekend trip to Majorca, simplifying and complicating matters simultaneously. In time he became only a name in the proceedings, and rarely was his estate involved in litigation or sale of property.)

A rift between the Hendrix estate and the musicians in Jimi's past occupied more of Branton's time. Noel Redding and Mitch Mitchell sued the estate, claiming an oral agreement with Jimi whereby Jimi kept half of the record earnings and personal appearance fees, and they would split the other half. "There was nothing written," Branton said. "It was all oral. And they sued for all of Jimi's earnings in the past and in the future. Another interesting thing is that who shows up as Mitch Mitchell's lawyer but Steve Weiss, who used to be one of Jimi's attorneys. So here's Steve Weiss suing his former client. And all of the people who were around Jimi at the time of Jimi's existence, the attorneys and accountants, all of them were going to come into court and testify on behalf of Mitchell and Redding. Faced with losing half of the income, we decided to settle rather than go all the way through the litigation."

Redding won $100,000 and Mitchell $265,000, because he had appeared on more recordings.

What happened, or didn't happen, next depended on who you believed. Branton insisted he kept Mr. Hendrix well informed and that the elder Hendrix understood what he was told and understood the documents that were presented for his signature regarding the disposition of what came to be called "the legacy"—the rights to all unreleased tapes as well as Jimi's original compositions. In 1974 Branton sold all of these rights—with Al Hendrix's legal authorization—to Presentaciones Musicales S.A. (PMSA), a Panamanian corporation founded in the 1950s for his former client, Nat Cole, and a Los Angeles jazz promoter named Norman Granz. At its founding, as in 1974, the corporation had served American companies as a tax haven. When I asked Branton why PMSA got the world rights to the legacy, he said, "Because they offered us the best deal. It's that simple." (At the time, PMSA also owned world rights to Werner Erhardt's est teaching program.) The selling price: a reported $500,000.

That's Branton's version of the story. Twenty years later, in 1993, in what turned into a protracted and ugly lawsuit against Branton, Mr. Hendrix said he didn't understand, and possibly wasn't told, what he was signing, and certainly wasn't told that Branton had a financial interest in PMSA. But that was a long way off. In 1974 Branton was not only Al Hendrix's meal ticket, he had become a trusted family friend. Branton told me that although he had sold the tapes and copyrights at what, in retrospect, might be called "distressed" or undervalued prices, he still had hopes of salvaging some of the music and generating new material to keep the legacy alive.

As a foreign corporation, PMSA could not do business in the United States, so Branton had to find a company that would enter into an agreement with PMSA to make masters from the tapes that Warner Bros. had rejected. The firm that got the contract was Depaja Inc., a New York company formed just three weeks following the sale to PMSA. Depaja was designed to carry on a variety of activities in entertainment, from production to management to marketing, but specifically to make masters from the Hendrix tapes and make a deal for U.S. distribution, retaining foreign distribution for themselves. The officers? The two lawyers Branton had hired in New York, Ed Howard and Kenny Hagood, and Branton himself. When pressed for details, Branton clammed up, while Hagood and Howard claimed that the money "passes right through." Branton did admit, however, that he negotiated Depaja's new contract with Warner Bros.

Branton also began negotiating with someone to sort through the hundreds of unreleased tapes, a selection by now far larger than that available to Jeffery and Kramer. This was Alan Douglas, who also was in London when Jimi died and who had in fact been with him in various studios off and on for several months prior to his death, serving as an unofficial producer. Like Branton, Douglas boasted an excellent résumé. Today an aging hipster who still favors Nehru jackets, he got his start in the 1950s with Roulette Records, a jazz label. In 1962 he took over the jazz line for United Artists, producing sessions for Duke Ellington, Charlie Mingus, Art Blakey, Eric Dolphy, and John McLaughlin. Getting caught up in the hippie scene, he also worked with such diverse characters as the Last Poets, Lenny Bruce, and Timothy Leary.

Branton then formed another company, Are You Experienced? Inc.—naming himself chief executive officer and his son Chip Branton chief financial officer—and hired Douglas, who in turn hired Tony Bongiovi to wade through an incredible 800 hours of tape pulled together from all over New York. (In some cases, outstanding studio charges had to be paid before the tapes were surrendered.) The first two album releases, *Crash Landing* and *Midnight Lightning*, were planned for release in 1975. What only Douglas and Bongiovi and a few others knew was that Douglas was taking liberties with the tapes, stripping away all the tracks but Jimi's from some of the unmixed, unbalanced, and usually unfinished songs. He then hired New York studio musicians and backup singers and overdubbed new parts. This would cause a bitter division among Hendrix purists that lasts to the present day.

Douglas eventually turned away some tapes he was offered, including sixty boxes of tape from Chas Chandler. "I offered Chas a fifty-fifty deal with the estate," Douglas said, "and Chas came back and told me through his representatives that Mike Jeffery never paid him his $300,000, so he wanted us to pay that, and he also wanted 2 or 3 percent, retroactive, of every record that's ever been sold. He also wanted to have control of the distribution and give the estate 25 percent. The deal was so stupid that we just rejected it, and I haven't discussed it with him since then. The stuff is on the street now anyway [on bootleg tapes and CDs], so his sixty boxes of tapes don't mean anything now as far as I'm concerned."

In a related incident, one of Jimi's early girlfriends, Kathy Etchingham, now nearing forty and married to a

British physician, in 1981 approached Leo Branton with tapes she said the guitarist brought home from various studio sessions. Branton confirmed they were genuine, then informed Etchingham that they belonged to the estate and demanded their return. Etchingham declined, taking them to the Sotheby's auction house, where they sold a year later for about $2,250, a low figure because it was admitted that copies probably had been made by Branton and Douglas when they reviewed the tapes.

In time such a figure would come to seem ludicrous as the market for pop music memorabilia blew up like a huge balloon and became one of the big moneymaking categories at major auction houses. For example, Jimi's peacock feather waistcoat sold for $15,000; his much-photographed black hat for $21,000; and, drawing probably the highest price of all, the white Stratocaster guitar he used at Woodstock was sold at Sotheby's in London in 1990 by Mitch Mitchell for $297,000. (It then was resold for an undisclosed figure to a museum being planned in Seattle.)

In time, life calmed somewhat for Al Hendrix and all the lawyers involved in the posthumous Hendrix industry. Back taxes were paid and kept current. Lawyers were hired to explore a Bahamian company formed by Mike Jeffery, through which apparently at least a million dollars had flowed, but in the end everyone threw up their hands and walked away from it. Two paternity suits in the United States were dismissed on the grounds that you can't sue a dead man, and when a woman in Sweden actually won her paternity case in Stockholm, the decision was turned away by a court in Los Angeles. According to Hagood and Howard, in the first five years alone fifty-four different legal matters passed through the courts, right down to giving one of Jimi's distraught ex-girlfriends $169 for telephone calls she made after the guitarist's death.

As the years passed, new material appeared as predictably as the seasons. Many of the issues were bootlegs, unauthorized tapes traded largely within the growing Hendrix cult underground. Others included soundtracks from *Rainbow Bridge,* the in-concert documentary filmed in Berkeley, and from a Jimi Hendrix documentary produced by Warner Bros. Films. After *Crash Landing* and *Midnight Lightning,* both commercial successes, were attacked by both fans and critics, Alan Douglas packaged *Nine to the Universe,* which presented edited sections of studio jams, with the original backing musicians retained. When Douglas was asked by an interviewer why he had altered the guitarist's tapes on previous releases, he said, "Why do you want to hear Jimi's mistakes?"

At the same time unauthorized T-shirts and souvenir posters were being sold worldwide by anyone with access to a silkscreen press. Fans started publishing magazines. (The lawyers ignored the fanzines and when they had time went after the bootleggers, but that was like chasing ghosts.) Several books about Jimi were published, including one by Curtis Knight and my own, which was published in 1983.

Then, in March of that year, PMSA sold the legacy to three other offshore companies. Bureau Voor Muziekrechten Elber B.V. (Elber), a Netherlands corporation, acquired the rights of exploitation and distribution of Jimi's music in the United States and Canada. Another Netherlands firm, Auteursrechlenmaatschappij B.V. (ARM), got Jimi's music publishing firm, Bella Godiva Music Inc., which controlled most of his song copyrights. A third company, Interlit, B.V.I. (Interlit), a British Virgin Islands corporation, gained the rights to exploit and distribute Jimi's music outside the United States and Canada. At the time, Al Hendrix would say later, he thought he still owned everything; it would be another ten years before he learned that that was no longer true.

The value of the estate continued to grow during this time, as did Jimi's status, both in the music community and in his hometown, Seattle, where one of the city's wealthiest and most reclusive businessmen developed an interest in opening a museum dedicated to Jimi's music. This was Paul Allen, a bearded, bespectacled man who had cofounded Microsoft with his grade-school friend Bill Gates. The second largest shareholder in the company, in 1995 he was reckoned by *Forbes* magazine to be worth $6.5 billion, making him the fourth richest man in the United States.

Following a cancer scare in 1982, Allen left Microsoft—retaining a seat on the board—and began focusing more of his attention, and wealth, on his love of basketball and rock guitar, purchasing the National Basketball Association's Portland Trail Blazers and collecting Jimi Hendrix memorabilia, including several of Jimi's guitars. Allen was a guitar player himself, and everyone who knew him frequently heard him say how much Jimi had changed his life.

According to Jim Fricke, the chief curator of the museum-in-progress and also a guitarist who sometimes jams with his boss, Allen—who hates to be interviewed and enjoys being described as "the nicest billionaire you'll never meet"—first approached the Hendrix family about the museum in 1992. As a result of this meeting, Mr. Hendrix appeared at a public hearing in Seattle in September, when Allen went before the city council to generate support for opening the museum at the Seattle Center, location of the 1962 World's Fair, a site owned by the city. Mr. Hendrix endorsed the effort, and while some public opinion ran against Jimi because of his drug-abusing image, Allen began hiring an interim staff. A month later the council cleared the way for construction of the project by authorizing negotiation of a long-term lease.

It was no accident that this happened in 1992; this would have been Jimi's fiftieth birthday had he lived, a year that turned into a celebration in the guitarist's name. According to *Billboard* magazine, in a story that started on the first page and filled up two pages inside, twenty-two years after the guitarist's death his catalog generated annual album (and CD and tape) sales of 2 to 3 million units worldwide. At the same time, Warner Bros. announced plans to release a tribute album of Hendrix songs as played by other bands; photographic exhibitions toured the United States and Europe; several new books were published; and *Rolling Stone* put Jimi on a cover, calling him "The Greatest Guitarist of All Time." This was also the year when he was inducted into the Rock and Roll Hall of Fame—Neil Young made the presentation, and Al Hendrix was there to accept—and was selected for a Lifetime Achievement Award at the Grammy Awards ceremony.

Against this backdrop of adoration, in January 1993—one month after the U.S. license to distribute and exploit Jimi's records held by Warner Bros. expired—the Hendrix picture shifted like underground tectonic plates, leading to a powerful quake. That was when Al Hendrix learned that two companies he had never heard of—Elber and Interlit—were offering everything he thought *he* still owned to one of the world's largest music companies, MCA Music Entertainment, part of a wide-ranging conglomerate that also produced television shows and motion pictures (from *Jaws* to *Jurassic Park*) and operated the popular Universal City theme parks.

There is no agreement regarding the proposed buyout figures, but initial reports ranged from $30 million to $75 million, with most accepting the higher figure. Al Hendrix had been rewarded nicely in the twenty years since his son died. A man who once stared goggle-eyed at ten hundred-dollar bills when they were thrown onto the table for the right to his son's name for a phony Jimi Hendrix memorial foundation, Mr. Hendrix had received over the ensuing years as much as $4 million, or an average of $200,000 a year. Surely this was a fortune compared to Mr. Hendrix's earnings as a gardener, but later his attorney would point out that while Mr. Hendrix had received $4 million, the estate had been generating $3 million to $4 million a year for the better part of twenty years. Besides, according to everyone who knew Mr. Hendrix, it wasn't the money, it was the legacy. He swore to everyone that he thought he was still the only heir, and as such the legal owner. He was confused; he said he felt cheated, deceived.

Paul Allen had asked to buy certain rights that now seemed threatened by the MCA deal. He needed the rights to use the Jimi Hendrix name as well as some of his songs, and MCA likely would not be willing to share anything. No one will say openly that this is what motivated Allen to make his next move. They say he really is a nice man, and that his business interests often seem tempered by personal ones. David Coursey, editor of *P.C. Letter*, a computer industry newsletter, compares him to the Tom Hanks boy-in-a-man's-body character in the movie *Big:* "You can almost see him dancing on the big piano like Hanks does in F. A. O. Schwarz." The Trail Blazers have practiced on the regulation-size basketball court on Allen's six-acre estate—once staging, for his and his friends' amusement, a private game with the Seattle Supersonics—and Allen still plays guitar with friends; in 1996, he jammed on stage at the prestigious computer trade show in Las Vegas.

Whatever his motivation, Allen went to Mr. Hendrix and said he wanted to help him stop the sale to MCA and, if the legacy actually had been lost to the offshore companies, to do everything possible to get it back. Putting his money where his mouth was, Allen offered an interest-free loan that would eventually rise to $5.8 million to underwrite the legal fight. Allen told Mr. Hendrix that if he won, he had to pay him back. If he lost, there was no obligation.

The gauntlet had been thrown down; a nasty two-year court battle followed, involving virtually everyone who'd ever had anything to do with Hendrix during his life and after his death. Even journalists who hadn't written about Jimi Hendrix in a decade or more got calls from investigators seeking some elusive truth that might help turn the legal tide. (I was called several times in Bangkok, where I now live.)

The first action taken, once Mr. Hendrix had hired the Seattle law firm of Hendricks and Lewis—with Paul Allen's guarantee of payment of fees—was to fire Branton. Then, on April 16, 1993, one of the new attorneys, O. Yale Lewis, filed a lawsuit on behalf of James A. Hendrix in the U.S. district court in Seattle, charging that Branton had concealed the true nature of various agreements regarding Jimi's recordings and copyrights, and had often acted in direct conflict of interest—the same charge that, twenty years before, Branton had levied against the administrator of the Hendrix estate. "It was Al Hendrix's expressed desire that he retain ownership of and control over the Jimi Hendrix legacy," the suit claimed; Branton "did not act to preserve Al Hendrix's ownership," but instead assisted in the transfer of ownership of Jimi's recording and song catalogs to other companies.

Jimi's father was described in the lawsuit as "a gardener with a seventh-grade education [who] was and is unsophisticated about the entertainment industry" and who relied on Branton as his sole source of information regarding his son's work and posthumous exploitation. The suit further charged that Branton had negotiated deals in which the elder Hendrix received from PMSA an undervalued sum for all the unmastered recordings and all of Jimi's song copyrights—property now being sold for perhaps $75 million—as well as subsequent deals that transferred these rights to ARM, Elber, and Interlit. Mr. Hendrix said he had not been informed of these transactions.

It went on. The action charged that Branton had shared in profits as a shareholder and director of Depaja, which earned a 2 percent royalty on sales of Jimi's recordings; that he profited from the operation of Are You Experienced? Ltd., the production company that hired Alan Douglas and in which Branton served as CEO and his son Chip as CFO; that he used $25,000 of Al Hendrix's money to purchase a condominium in Hawaii in his own name; and that he invested $200,000 of Mr. Hendrix's capital in a Seattle office property and $550,000 in a California limited partnership—all without his client's knowledge or consent. Mr. Hendrix asked the court to put any prospective sale of the legacy on ice. He also asked for damages for what the lawsuit called "more than twenty years of abuse of his trust, misrepresentations, mismanagement, unjust enrichments, and self-dealing by his former attorney."

It was hardly a surprise when, three days later, Branton filed a countersuit, charging Mr. Hendrix and the attorney Lewis with defamation of character. In interviews, Branton denied the charges that the guitarist's father had signed documents "with little or no explanation." He said Al Hendrix was well informed of every action taken, transactions that made him a "millionaire many times over."

"The man is not incompetent," Branton said. "He can read, and he signed them [the documents] himself."

Al Hendrix never denied that. He admitted that the signatures on the papers of transfer were his. What was at question, according to U.S. district court judge Thomas Zilly, was the "disparity in education and sophistication between plaintiff and defendant Branton." This was made clear in Mr. Hendrix's deposition, where he testified that when Branton first introduced the subject of selling the legacy to PMSA, the former gardener told the attorney, "Now, I want Jimi's music. I mean, if they want to use it more or less like on a loan basis or something of that sort, that's the way I looked at it. I said, I'm going to keep—I want all of Jimi's things, I mean his music. I wasn't going to sell or anything of that sort. And at the time he told me that this company was—I had taken it as a loan where they would use the music and I'd get a—oh, an annual fee from them for the use of Jimi's music. But I'd still be master of the—I mean in control of all his music."

Zilly's ruling came in 1994, leaving Branton and Douglas "restrained and enjoined, until further order of the court, from selling, abandoning, licensing, transferring, liquidating, encumbering, pledging, assigning, extending, or otherwise disposing of or concealing any asset or property of, or asset or property derived from, the Hendrix legacy." In other words, Branton and Douglas and others opposed by Mr. Hendrix were frozen dead in their tracks. They also were ordered to make a quarterly accounting of all royalties and other income generated from the "distribution and marketing of Hendrix Artistic Properties."

By then the MCA deal had gone through, giving the company distribution rights for a period of five years in the United States. (Alan Douglas said that many other companies had shown an interest in acquiring the Hendrix catalog, but MCA had offered the most money and the most freedom.) However, after receiving a letter from the Hendrix estate's lawyer, MCA agreed to put the brakes on their own expectations and to work with the court, giving Mr. Hendrix full approval rights in any planned product release, hoping for a peaceful resolution that would eventually end in their favor.

For the next year the various parties continued to jockey back and forth. Alan Douglas, who was claiming copyrights to all the recordings in which he served as the producer or engineer, made his legal moves, and Branton's attorneys made theirs, as did lawyers representing the various offshore companies. One observer said that there was no way of telling exactly how many attorneys were involved, "but at least fifty."

In the midst of all this, MCA released one of the best of Jimi's posthumous albums. Produced by Alan Douglas, :Blues—the colon is part of the title—was a carefully harvested collection of just what the title promised, studio jam sessions that demonstrated Jimi's roots in black music, from the Mississippi Delta to Chicago rhythm and blues. There had been many other official releases since his death, along with countless bootlegs, but this album was the one that made the fans and critics happiest. Also during this period, in a move unrelated to the lawsuit, MCA acquired the distribution rights to Jimi's Woodstock performance and released a CD subtitled "Jimi's Greatest Performance"—an exaggeration, although it was his most famous, because of his radical arrangement of the U.S. national anthem. Both CDs went onto the best-selling music charts.

1994 brought another bizarre twist: Britain's attorney general, Sir Nicholas Lyell, finally ruled on a request to re-open the inquiry into Jimi's death, made a year before by Kathy Etchingham, Jimi's early girlfriend. In 1993, believing that the woman with Jimi when he died, Monika Danneman, had delayed in calling for an ambulance, Etchingham had commissioned a private investigation and submitted her findings to Lyell. There also were some who believed medical staff had been negligent—although Etchingham's examination held them innocent—while others entertained a theory that the guitarist committed suicide.

"Jimi deserves the dignity of truth in death," Etchingham said. "And the fact that new witnesses had just given statements that give a rather different account of his last night made me decide that people should know that the circumstances leading up to his death were not entirely as they appeared to be at the time." The attorney general accepted Etchingham's dossier and an application to reopen the inquiry, but after consideration he turned it down, and the open verdict was left in place. "Although the whole story might never be revealed," Etchingham said later, "at least I have helped to remove any suspicion hanging over the medics who tried to save him by tracking them down."

(Etchingham also sued Danneman for libeling her in a book. She won, and the court ordered Danneman not to repeat an allegation about Etchingham's truthfulness. When in 1996 Danneman repeated the charge, Etchingham asked the High Court in London to jail her. The judge found

Danneman in contempt of court but released her. Two days later Danneman committed suicide.)

As the legal fight in Seattle neared its second anniversary, Paul Allen approached the Hendrix family once more, seeking assurance that once the battle was won, he would be given the rights he needed to operate a museum bearing Jimi's name. The Hendrix family reportedly told him no, and Allen said that further funds would not be forthcoming; he had reached his stated $5 million limit. The Hendrix family's attorney, O. Yale Lewis, told the *Seattle Weekly*, "That's not why he stopped lending the money. The museum decided they needed more extensive rights than had originally been planned . . . [and they] pressed the family for fairly substantial, very expansive, and aggressive dedications of the family." Lewis said Allen now wanted a ninety-nine-year, exclusive worldwide contract to use not only Jimi's likeness and name but also many of the copyrights and master recordings.

"They wanted too much, too hard, too fast," said Janie Hendrix-Wright, the daughter of Al Hendrix's second wife, adopted by him and by now becoming a family spokesperson. As it turned out, a further $800,000 was paid by Allen, taking the loan total to $5.8 million, but after that the spigot was turned off. Lewis denied that he and Allen had agreed on a ceiling, but he also admitted that there was no guarantee that the funds available were unlimited. Lewis also expressed gratitude publicly, as did the Hendrix family, for Allen's support of the lawsuit so far.

However, with the anticipated trial still a year away, the loan cutoff put Lewis's law firm in a shaky position, forcing him to lay off many employees. It also led Paul Allen to change the direction of the museum, expanding it to include other music personalities from the Pacific Northwest—including Bing Crosby, Paul Revere and the Raiders, the Kingsmen (whose song "Louie Louie" is one of the all-time rock classics), Nirvana, and Pearl Jam—

and renaming it the Experience Music Project.

Through the early months of 1995 the two sides continued to take shots at each other, in the courts and in the press. When Alan Douglas released still another remastered, overdubbed compilation, *Voodoo Soup,* for instance, Janie Hendrix-Wright told the press that she hated it. She also objected to a flyer inserted in the package for a Hendrix foundation set up by Are You Experienced? Inc. without the family's knowledge or approval, a foundation believed by some to be no more than a public relations stunt, although several scholarships apparently had been granted legitimately.

By now attorneys for all sides had begun negotiating an out-of-court settlement under the guidance of U.S. District Court judge William Dwyer, a liberal Democrat who established his reputation in Washington as a lawyer in the 1960s when he won a libel judgment against John Birch Society leaders. Before becoming a judge he had also been credited with keeping baseball in Seattle in a court fight opposing the American League's attempt to move the league's expansion team, had won multi-million-dollar judgments from juries in complicated cases, and had persuaded an all-white jury to acquit a Seattle Black Panther leader on charges of stealing a typewriter.

Finally, on July 25, 1995, after meeting with Judge Dwyer for two days, attorneys for all sides agreed that all motions would be stricken "without prejudice." The trial, scheduled for the following month—and expected to last at least three months—was canceled, and it was stated that all claims and counter-claims were settled. At last, an agreement had been reached.

(By way of a footnote, the Hendrix family attorney had planned to bring into court several prominent musicians who were expected not only to testify about the value of Jimi's contribution to music but also to say that Douglas was ruining it. These included Carlos Santana and Stan Gossard and Mike McCready of Pearl Jam.)

Many of the details of the settlement were sealed, but it was clear that, while Branton and Douglas were not left holding an entirely empty bag, Al Hendrix had won. According to Lewis, Mr. Hendrix was to be paid an undisclosed "significant" lump sum. But when the annual royalties, which had been exceeding $5 million, started rolling in again, Mr. Hendrix was to make payments to a group of five companies, who relinquished any further claim to the Hendrix music rights. Lewis said that the intent was that the Hendrix family eventually would pay out more than it received in the initial payment, but he emphasized that the difference was not important when compared with the long-term value of the estate.

Branton gained ownership of two real estate properties—it was not specified which—and Alan Douglas was given court permission to finish a new recording, *On the Road,* and a documentary then in production, *Room Full of Mirrors,* but was told that after that he was out of the Hendrix business, and the Hendrix family would retain ownership of both those properties. Douglas further was allowed to receive a producer's royalty on recordings he had supervised, but he gave up his copyright claims to the songs.

Most important, all rights of ownership of the legacy—the unmastered recordings, the song copyrights, the publicity rights, the exploitation rights, the royalties, the photographs and other visual images, the films and videotapes, the manuscripts, and other personal property—were returned to Al Hendrix, his daughter Janie Hendrix-Wright, and a nephew, Bob Hendrix, who then rented a suite of offices in one of the toniest buildings in Seattle's Pioneer Square and hired a secretary who answered the phone, "Good morning, Experience Hendrix."

Unprepared to administer a multi-million-dollar rock and roll estate, and after so many years of exploitation, Janie Hendrix-Wright quite naturally seems defensive today. Reportedly, she panicked as well as celebrated when the case was won and quickly called the administrators of the Elvis

Presley estate for guidance. Determined to gain control of everything associated with Jimi, in 1996 she went so far as to go after one of Jimi's most loyal followers, whose fan magazine (published in Seattle) had always been deferential to the family. Why? Apparently, there were some blind ads in it offering unauthorized Hendrix T-shirts. The Presley estate by now had a reputation for being unbending, and the Hendrix estate was following suit. Record companies in the United States, Europe, and elsewhere were urged to pursue and prosecute bootleggers to clear the marketplace for further authorized merchandise.

"As far as merchandise is concerned," she said, "we are very particular of how his face is portrayed. I like him smiling and looking like he enjoyed life, because that's what he did, he enjoyed life. On a lot of the merchandise that went out, he looked so serious."

What Hendrix-Wright said about the music pleased the fans. Taking a swipe at Alan Douglas, she said she and the family would be "doing it the right way—not bringing in karaoke-style musicians to overdub what he's done. A lot of things we've come across were overlooked, and we're very pleased that they were overlooked because they arc gems, they are jewels." By mid-1996, however, there were no announcements of plans to release any of this, nor had anyone been named to oversee its production.

Meanwhile Paul Allen was continuing with his plans for his museum, which now had a $60 million budget, and in May 1996 he was ready to display the architect's plans. Bolstering his interest in entertainment, Allen also by now had invested $1.8 billion of his fortune to buy an 80 percent interest in Ticketmaster, a national ticket sales organization believed to overcharge for tickets, and threw another $500 million into a new movie company owned by Steven Spielberg, Jeffrey Katzenberg, and David Geffen, getting in return an 18 percent interest in the company and a seat on the board. In addition, he was well known as a philanthropist, funding several AIDS programs, and was rumored to be a possible buyer for the Sea Hawks, a hockey team moved from Seattle to Los Angeles (he wanted to move them back), and a Seattle franchise for the National Football League.

The Jimi Hendrix machinery, well oiled for so long by Leo Branton and Alan Douglas and others, had been dismantled. Yet as this book goes to press, filings continue to arrive in the U.S. district court. My brother, Jack Hopkins, a longtime court reporter for Seattle's *Post Intelligencer*, told me that when he asked to look at the file, the court clerks remarked:

"It is very popular, they say. The file is still growing, by the way. They are fighting over distribution of assets, etc."

As for the guitarist who started all this, his grave is still a site of pilgrimage and his music continues to sell on millions of tapes and CDs, coming a close second to Elvis Presley in posthumous sales. In *Guitar Player* magazine's 1995 annual readership poll, *:Blue* was voted Best Historical Reissue Recording, and in 1996 readers named both *Voodoo Soup* and *Band of Gypsies* in the same category. Also in 1996, in *Guitar* magazine Jimi was voted Best All-Time Guitarist. "Maybe we don't even need this category anymore," the editors said, "because Hendrix wins by a landslide every year."

Who's buying all the tapes and CDs, casting votes, and trekking to the grave? Let me tell you a short story. In 1995 I went on a four-day kayaking trip in Thailand's Phangna Bay, where I met a family from the United States. Their daughter was happy to learn I had written for *Rolling Stone* for several years (she was a subscriber), and I was happy to hear her answer to my question, "Who do you like? You got any favorite groups?" She first named one of the alternative bands. "But then," she added, "I also like Jimi Hendrix. He's cool." Fourteen years old, she had been born more than ten years after Jimi's death.

As any of the lawyers in this story might say, "I rest my case."

DISCOGRAPHY

Prepared by Steven Szep

Author's Note: The following albums, cassettes, and compact discs represent only official releases, most of which are still available commercially. Hundreds of bootleg recordings also have been slipped into the marketplace. They are not included in this discography because they are hard to find or unavailable to the general audience.

The albums, tapes, and CDs are arranged here in an order that generally follows Jimi's career chronologically, not by their release time. For example, the pre-Experience material was marketed after the early Experience albums, but in the listing that follows, it precedes it. Because the posthumous material zigzags all over the place chronologically as well as musically (with many overdubs and other changes), it has been placed at the end of the discography.

g = guitar   ts = tenor sax
vo = vocals   or = organ
d = drums   p = piano
b = bass   bk vo = background vocals
fl = flute   vbs = vibes
xyl = xylophone   perc = percussion

PRE-EXPERIENCE

Jimi Hendrix-Little Richard, Friends from the Beginning
RECORDED: 1963
RELEASED: 1972
Jimi Hendrix (g), Black Arthur (g), Henry Oden (b), Little Richard (p, vo), Bumps Blackwell (d), brass and bk vo group are unidentified

1. "Whole Lotta Shakin' Goin' On"
"Goodnight Irene"
"Keep A Knockin'" (Instrumental)
"Goin' Home Tomorrow"
"Belle Stars"
"Tutti Frutti" (Instrumental)

2. "Lawdy Miss Claudie"
"Why Don't You Love Me?"
"Lucille" (Instrumental)
"Hound Dog"
"Money Honey"
"Funky Dish Rag"

RELEASED BY: ALA, Stateside
Portions of album released as: *Together* (Pickwick); *Roots of Rock* (Everest).

The Isley Brothers and Jimi Hendrix, in the Beginning
RECORDED: 1964
RELEASED: 1972
Jimi Hendrix (g), Ronnie Isley (g, vo), Kelly Isley (d, vo), Rudy Isley (b, vo), brass and other percussion are unidentified

1. "Move Over, Let Me Dance"
"Have You Ever Been Disappointed"
"Testify" (Parts I and II)
"Move Over, Let Me Dance" (Instrumental version)

2. "Wild Little Tiger"
"The Last Girl"
"Simon Says"
"Looking for a Love"

RELEASED BY: T-neck, Polydor

Birth of Success
RECORDED: 1965
RELEASED: 1972
Jimi Hendrix (g), Curtis Knight (g, vo), other personnel not credited

1. "I'm a Man"
"Sugar Pie, Honey Bunch"

2. "Last Night" (Instrumental)

"Get Out of My Life, Woman"
"Ain't That Peculiar"

"(I Can't Get No) Satisfaction"
"Land of a Thousand Dances"
"U.F.O."*

RELEASED BY: Music for Pleasure
Recorded live at George's Club 20, Hackensack, NJ, 12/26/65.
*Studio song, recorded in 1966.

What'd I Say
RECORDED: 1965
RELEASED: 1972

Jimi Hendrix (g), Curtis Knight (g, vo), other personnel not credited

1. "Drivin' South"
"California Night"

2. "Killing Floor"
"What'd I Say"
"I'll Be Doggone"
"Bright Lights, Big City"

RELEASED BY: Music for Pleasure
Recorded live at George's Club 20, Hackensack, NJ, 12/26/65.

Mr. Pitiful
RECORDED: 1965–66
RELEASED: 1981

Jimi Hendrix (g), Curtis Knight (g, vo), other personnel not credited

1. "Woolly Bully"
"Left Alone (Bleeding Heart)"
"Have Mercy"
"Something You've Got"
"Itsy Bitsy Teenie Weenie Yellow Polka Dot Bikini (Just a Little)"

2. "Stand By Me"
"Hold On to What You Got"
"Mr. Pitiful (California Night)"*
"I Should've Quit You (Killing Floor)"*

RELEASED BY: Astan
Album contains live material previously unreleased, location unknown.
*Recorded live, possibly at George's Club 20, Hackensack, NJ, 12/26/65.

20 Golden Pieces of Jimi Hendrix
RECORDED: 1966–67
RELEASED: 1980

Jimi Hendrix (g), Curtis Knight (g, vo), other personnel not credited

1. "You Got Me Running"*
"Money"*
"Let's Go, Let's Go, Let's Go"*
"You Got What It Takes"*
"Sweet Little Angel"*
"Walkin' the Dog"*
"There Is Something on Your Mind"*
"Hard Night" (Instrumental)*

2. "Ballad of Jimi"
"No Business"
"Gotta Have a New Dress"
"Don't Accuse Me"
"Flashing" (Instrumental)
"Hang on Sloopy"*
"Twist and Shout"*
"Bo Diddley"*
"Tutti Frutti" (Instrumental)†

"Hush Now" (Instrumental version)   "Lucille" (Instrumental)†
"Knock Yourself Out" (Instrumental)

Liner notes are misleading.

    RELEASED BY: Bulldog

*Recorded live, possibly at The Cheetah Club, New York, NY, 2/14/66.
†Studio material recorded with Little Richard in 1963.

Get That Feeling
    RECORDED: 1965–66
    RELEASED: 1967

Jimi Hendrix (g), Curtis Knight (g, vo), other personnel not credited

1. "How Would You Feel?"
   "Simon Says"
   "Get That Feeling"

2. "Hush Now"
   "Welcome Home"
   "Gotta Have a New Dress"
   "No Business"
   "Strange Things"

    RELEASED BY: Capitol

Flashing
    RECORDED: 1966–67
    RELEASED: 1968

Jimi Hendrix (g), Curtis Knight (g, vo), other personnel not credited

1. "Gloomy Monday"
   "Hornets Nest" (Instrumental)
   "Fool for You Baby"
   "Happy Birthday"
   "Flashing" (Instrumental)

2. "Day Tripper"
   "Odd Ball" (Instrumental)
   "Love, Love"
   "Don't Accuse Me"

    RELEASED BY: Capitol

My Best Friend
    RECORDED: 1966–67
    RELEASED: 1981

Jimi Hendrix (g), Curtis Knight (g, vo), other personnel not credited

1. "Get That Feeling"
   "Happy Birthday"
   "Hush Now"

2. "Day Tripper" (Instrumental version)
   "Odd Ball" (Instrumental)
   "Sleepy Fate (No Business)" (Instrumental version)
   "My Best Friend (Ballad of Jimi)" (Instrumental version)

    RELEASED BY: Astan

Roots of Hendrix
    RECORDED: 1966
    RELEASED: 1971

Jimi Hendrix (g), Herman Hitson (g), Lonnie Youngblood (ts, vo), Lee Moses (b), other personnel not credited

1. "Wipe That Sweat" (Instrumental)
   "Sequel I" (Instrumental)
   "Sequel II"
   "Goodbye, Bessie Mae"
   "Two in One Goes"
2. "All I Want"
   "Under the Table" (Instrumental)
   "Sequel I" (Instrumental)
   "Sequel II" (Instrumental)
   "Psycho" (Instrumental)

RELEASED BY: Trip, Phoenix, Musidisc, Joker, Music Distributor
Recorded at Abtone Studios, New York, NY.
ALSO RELEASED AS: *Two Great Experiences Together* (Maple)

Rare Hendrix

RECORDED: 1966
RELEASED: 1972
Jimi Hendrix (g), other personnel not credited
1. "Good Feeling"
   "Voice in the Wind"
   "Go Go Shoes, Part I"
   "Go Go Shoes, Part II"
2. "Suspicious"
   "Good Times"
   "Bring My Baby Back"
   "Hot Trigger" (Instrumental)

RELEASED BY: Trip, Enterprise, Explosive, Phoenix, Musidisc, Audio Fidelity, Joker, Fantasy
Recorded at Abtone Studios, New York, NY.
This album does not list the song titles in their playing order.
ALSO RELEASED AS: *Hendrix 66* (Enterprise)

In the Beginning

RECORDED: 1966
RELEASED: 1972
Jimi Hendrix (g), other personnel not credited
1. "Hey Leroy"
   "Free Spirit"
   "House of the Rising Sun" (Instrumental)
2. "Something You Got"
   "Let the God Sing"
   "She's a Fox"

RELEASED BY: Shout
ALSO RELEASED AS: *Free Spirit* (Phoenix)

Moods

RECORDED: 1966
RELEASED: 1973
Jimi Hendrix (g), other personnel not credited
1. "A Mumblin' Word"
   "Miracle Worker" (Instrumental)
   "From This Day On" (Instrumental)
   "Human Heart" (Instrumental)
   "Feel That Soul" (Instrumental)
   "All Alone" (Instrumental)
2. "Get Down"
   "So Called Friend"
   "Girl So Fine" (Instrumental)
   "Every Little Bit Hurts" (Instrumental)
   "You Say You Love Me"

RELEASED BY: Trip, Phoenix, Accord, Musidisc, Music Distributor

The Genius of Jimi Hendrix
> RECORDED: 1966
> RELEASED: 1974

Jimi Hendrix (g), other personnel not credited

1. "Red House"*
   "Sweet Thing"
   "Blues Blues"*
   "Groove Maker"

2. "Peoples Peoples"*
   "Fox (She's a Fox)"
   "Whoa' Ech"*
   "Gonna Take a Lot"
   "Lime Lime"*

> RELEASED BY: Trip, Phoenix, 51 West, Musidisc, Music Distributor

Recorded at Abtone Studios, New York, NY.

> ALSO RELEASED AS: *Flashback* (Trip)

*This material is from a different source, and is part of the *Sky High* recording session.

Kaleidoscope
> RECORDED: ?
> RELEASED: 1982

Jimi Hendrix (g), other personnel not credited

1. "Everything (Wake Up This
      Morning and You Find
      Yourself Dead)"*
   "You Got It" (Instrumental)
   "Nobody Can Change Me
      (Under the Table)" (In-
      strumental)
   "Everything You Get"

2. "Night Life" (Instrumental)
   "Edda Mae" (Instrumental)
   "Find Someone" (Instru-
      mental)
   "By My Baby"

> RELEASED BY: Nutmeg

Previously unreleased material, dates and locations unknown.

*This material is part of the *Sky High* recording session.

EXPERIENCE

PERSONNEL: Jimi Hendrix (g), Noel Redding (b), Mitch Mitchell (d)

Are You Experienced?
> LABEL: Barclay, MCA, Polydor, Reprise, Track
> RECORDED: 11/1966–3/1967
> RELEASED: 5/1967

"Hey Joe"
"Stone Free"
"Purple Haze"
"51st Anniversary"
"The Wind Cries Mary"
"Highway Chile"
"Foxy Lady"
"Manic Depression"

"Red House"
"Can You See Me"
"Love or Confusion"
"I Don't Live Today"
"Fire"
"Third Stone from the Sun"
"Remember"
"Are You Experienced?"

Note: Different releases will include some but not necessarily all of these tracks. This complete listing is for the MCA CD release.

Axis: Bold as Love
LABEL: Barclay, MCA, Polydor, Reprise, Track
RECORDED: 3/1967–9/1967
RELEASED: 1/1968

1. "E X P"
   "Up from the Skies"
   "Spanish Castle Magic"
   "Wait Until Tomorrow"
   "Ain't No Telling"
   "Little Wing"
   "If 6 Was 9"
2. "You Got Me Floatin'"
   "Castles Made of Sand"
   "She's So Fine"
   "One Rainy Wish"
   "Little Miss Lover"
   "Bold as Love"

Electric Ladyland
LABEL: Barclay, MCA, Polydor, Reprise, Track
RECORDED: 6/1967–5/1968
RELEASED: 9/1968
ADDITIONAL PERSONNEL: Mike Finnigan (or), Steve Winwood (or), Al Kooper (p), Chris Wood (fl), Freddie Smith (ts), Jack Casady (b), Larry Faucette (perc), Buddy Miles (d)

1. ". . . And the Gods Made Love"
   "Have You Ever Been (to Electric Ladyland)?"
   "Crosstown Traffic"
   "Voodoo Chile"
2. "Little Miss Strange"
   "Long Hot Summer Night"
   "Come On (Part 1)"
   "Gypsy Eyes"
   "Burning of the Midnight Lamp"
3. "Rainy Day, Dream Away"
   "1983 . . . (A Merman I Should Turn to Be)"
   "Moon, Turn the Tides . . . Gently, Gently Away"
4. "Still Raining, Still Dreaming"
   "House Burning Down"
   "All Along the Watchtower"
   "Voodoo Child (Slight Return)"

Smash Hits
LABEL: Polydor, Reprise, Track
ORIGINAL RELEASE: 6/1969
A hits package from the three Experience LPs.

1. "Purple Haze"
   "Fire"
   "The Wind Cries Mary"
   "Can You See Me"
   "51st Anniversary"
   "Hey Joe"
2. "Stone Free"
   "The Stars That Play with Laughing Sam's Dice"
   "Manic Depression"
   "Highway Chile"
   "Burning of the Midnight Lamp"
   "Foxy Lady"

Historic Performances Recorded at the Monterey International Pop Festival
LABEL: Atlantic, Reprise
RECORDED: 6/18/1967
ORIGINAL RELEASE: 9/1970

1. "Like a Rolling Stone"
   "Rock Me Baby"
   "Can You See Me"
   "Wild Thing"
Note: Side 2 presents a performance by Otis Redding.

Experience
   LABEL: Ember, Ariola, Sonet, Jimco, others
   RECORDED: Royal Albert Hall, London, 2/24/1969
   RELEASED: 8/1971
   ADDITIONAL PERSONNEL: Dave Mason (g), Chris Wood (fl), Rocky
Dzidzournu (perc)
1. "Sunshine of Your Love"   2. "Bleeding Heart"
   "Room Full of Mirrors"   "Smashing of Amps"

More Experience
   LABEL: Ember, Sonet, Kaleidoscope, Jimco, others
   RECORDED: Royal Albert Hall, London, 2/24/1969
   RELEASED: 3/1973
   ADDITIONAL PERSONNEL: Dave Mason (g), Chris Wood (fl), Rocky
Dzidzournu (perc)
1. "Little Wing"   2. "Fire"
   "Voodoo Child (Slight Re-   "Purple Haze"
      turn)"   "Wild Thing"
                                    "Bleeding Heart"
Note: Some releases contain the same tracks as the previous two com-
bined: *The Final Experience, The Last Experience,* etc.

Jimi Plays Monterey
   LABEL: Polydor, Reprise
   RECORDED: Monterey Pop Festival, 6/18/1967
   ORIGINAL RELEASE: 2/1986
   "Killing Floor"   "Can You See Me"
   "Foxy Lady"   "The Wind Cries Mary"
   "Like a Rolling Stone"   "Purple Haze"
   "Rock Me Baby"   "Wild Thing"
   "Hey Joe"
Note: This is the entire performance.

Live at Winterland
   LABEL: Ryko, Polydor
   RECORDED: Winterland, San Francisco, 10/12/1968
   RELEASED: 5/1987
   ADDITIONAL PERSONNEL: Herbie Rich (or), Jack Casady (b)
   "Fire"   "Tax Free"
   "Manic Depression"   "Foxy Lady"
   "Sunshine of Your Love"   "Hey Joe"
   "Red House"   "Purple Haze"
   "Killing Floor"   "Wild Thing"

Radio One
   LABEL: Ryko, Castle Communications
   RECORDED: Various BBC performances, 1967
   ORIGINAL RELEASE: 1969
   ADDITIONAL PERSONNEL: Jimmy Leverton (vo), Trevor Burton (vo),
Alexis Korner (g)

"Stone Free"
"Radio One Theme"
"Day Tripper"
"Killing Floor"
"Love or Confusion"
"Drivin' South"
"Catfish Blues"
"Wait Until Tomorrow"
"Hear My Train a Comin'"

"Hound Dog"
"Fire"
"Hoochie Koochie Man"
"Purple Haze"
"Spanish Castle Magic"
"Hey Joe"
"Foxy Lady"
"Burning of the Midnight
   Lamp"

GYPSY SUN & RAINBOWS

PERSONNEL: Jimi Hendrix (g), Billy Cox (b), Larry Lee (g), Mitch
Mitchell (d), Juma Sutan (perc), Jerry Velez (perc)

Woodstock
   LABEL: Cotillion, Atlantic
   RECORDED: Woodstock Music and Arts Festival, 8/18/1969
   RELEASED: 6/1970
   "Star-Spangled Banner"
   "Purple Haze"
Note: The rest of this recording contains performances by other artists.

Woodstock II
   LABEL: Cotillion, Atlantic
   RECORDED: Woodstock Music & Arts Festival, 8/18/1969
   RELEASED: 4/1971
1. "Jam Back at the House"   "Getting My Heart Back To-
   "Izabella"   gether Again"
Note: The rest of this recording contains performances by other artists.

Woodstock
   LABEL: MCA, Polydor
   RECORDED: Woodstock Music & Arts Festival, 8/18/1969
   RELEASED: 2/1994

"Fire"
"Izabella"
"Hear My Train a Comin'"
"Red House"
"Jam Back at the House"

"Voodoo Child (Slight Re-
   turn)"/"Stepping Stone"
"Star-Spangled Banner"
"Purple Haze"
"Woodstock Improvisation"
"Villanova Junction"

BAND OF GYPSIES

PERSONNEL: Jimi Hendrix (g), Billy Cox (b), Buddy Miles (d)

Band of Gypsies
LABEL: Barclay, Capital, Polydor, Track
RECORDED: Fillmore East, New York, 1/1/1970
RELEASED: 4/1970

1. "Who Knows"
   "Machine Gun"

2. "Changes"
   "Power of Soul"
   "Message of Love"
   "We Gotta Live Together"

Band of Gypsies 2
LABEL: Capital
RECORDED: First three tracks, Fillmore East, New York, 12/31/1969
and 1/1/1970; last three tracks, Atlanta Pop Festival, 7/4/1970
RELEASED: 10/1986

"Getting My Heart Back To-
   gether Again"
"Foxy Lady"
"Stop"

"Voodoo Child (Slight Re-
   turn)"
"Stone Free"
"Ezy Rider"

RE-FORMED EXPERIENCE

PERSONNEL: Jimi Hendrix (g), Billy Cox (b), Mitch Mitchell (d)
Note: No recordings were released before Jimi's death.

Isle of Wight
LABEL: Barclay, Polydor
RECORDED: Isle of Wight Festival, England, 8/30/1970
ORIGINAL RELEASE: 11/1971

1. "Midnight Lightning"
   "Foxy Lady"
   "Lover Man"

2. "Freedom"
   "All Along the Watchtower"
   "In from the Storm"

The First Great Rock Festivals of the Seventies
LABEL: Columbia, CBS
RECORDED: Isle of Wight Festival, England, 8/30/1970
RELEASED: 9/1971

"Message to Love"
"Midnight Lightning"
"Foxy Lady"

Live Isle of Wight '70
LABEL: Polydor
RECORDED: Isle of Wight Festival, England, 8/30/1970
RELEASED: 1991

"God Save the Queen"　　　　　"Dolly Dagger"
"Message to Love"　　　　　　"Red House"
"Voodoo Chile"　　　　　　　"In from the Storm"
"Lover Man"　　　　　　　　"New Rising Sun"
"Machine Gun"

POSTHUMOUS RELEASES

You Can Be Anyone This Time Around
LABEL: Douglas, Ryko, etc.
RECORDED: 5/1969
RELEASED: 4/1970
PERSONNEL: Jimi Hendrix (g), Stephen Stills (g), John Sebastian (g),
Buddy Miles (d), Timothy Leary (vo)
　　"Live and Let Live"
Note: Jimi appears only on this track.

The Cry of Love
LABEL: Barclay, Polydor, Reprise
RECORDED: 3/1968 to 8/1970
RELEASED: 3/1971
PERSONNEL: Jimi Hendrix (g), Billy Cox (b), Mitch Mitchell (d),
Arthur Allen (vo), Albert Allen (vo), Juma Sultan (perc), Buzzy Linhart
(vbs), Buddy Miles (d), Jerry Velez (perc), Paul Caruso (ha), Stephen
Stills (p), Kenny Pine (g), Emeretta Marks (vo)
1. "Freedom"　　　　　　　2. "Straight Ahead"
　"Drifting"　　　　　　　　　"Astro Man"
　"Ezy Rider"　　　　　　　　"Angel"
　"Night Bird Flying"　　　　　"In from the Storm"
　"My Friend"　　　　　　　　"Belly Button Window"

Rainbow Bridge
LABEL: Reprise
RECORDED: 10/1968 to 7/1970
RELEASED: 10/1971
PERSONNEL: Jimi Hendrix (g), Mitch Mitchell (d), Billy Cox (b),
Arthur Allen (vo), Albert Allen (vo), the Ronettes (vo), Buddy Miles (d),
Juma Sultan (perc), Noel Redding (b)
1. "Dolly Dagger"　　　　　　2. "Look Over Yonder"
　"Earth Blues"　　　　　　　　"Hear My Train a Comin'"
　"Pali Gap"　　　　　　　　　(Community Center,
　"Room Full of Mirrors"　　　　Berkeley, 5/30/1970)
　"Star-Spangled Banner"　　　"Hey Baby"

Hendrix in the West
LABEL: Barclay, Polydor, Reprise
RECORDED: 2/1969 to 8/1970
RELEASED: 1/1972
PERSONNEL: Jimi Hendrix (g), Mitch Mitchell (d), Billy Cox (b), Noel Redding (b)

1. "The Queen" (Isle of Wight Festival, 8/30/1970)
   "Sergeant Pepper's Lonely Hearts Club Band" (Same)
   "Little Wing" (Sports Arena, San Diego, 5/24/1969)
   "Red House" (Same)

2. "Johnny B. Goode" (Community Center, Berkeley, 5/30/1970)
   "Lover Man" (Same)
   "Blue Suede Shoes" (Same)
   "Voodoo Child" (Sports Arena, San Diego, 5/24/1969)

War Heroes
LABEL: Barclay, Polydor, Reprise
RECORDED: 1968 to 1970
RELEASED: 10/1972
PERSONNEL: Jimi Hendrix (g, b), Mitch Mitchell (d), Buddy Miles (d), Juma Sultan (perc), Jerry Velez (perc), Noel Redding (b), Billy Cox (b)

1. "Bleeding Heart"
   "Highway Chile"
   "Tax Free"
   "Peter Gunn"/"Catastrophe"
   "Stepping Stone"

2. "Midnight"
   "3 Little Bears"
   "Beginning"
   "Izabella"

Note: "Stepping Stone" had Buddy Miles's drum part removed and replaced by Mitch Mitchell's in 1972.

Soundtrack Recordings from the Film: Jimi Hendrix
LABEL: Polydor, Reprise
RECORDED: 1966 to 1970
RELEASED: 6/1973
PERSONNEL: Jimi Hendrix (g), Mitch Mitchell (d), Noel Redding (b), Billy Cox (b), Buddy Miles (d)

1. "Rock Me Baby"
   "Wild Thing"
   "Machine Gun"

2. "Johnny B. Goode"
   "Hey Joe"
   "Purple Haze"
   "Like a Rolling Stone"

3. "Star-Spangled Banner"
   "Machine Gun"
   "Hear My Train a Comin'"

4. "Red House"
   "In from the Storm"

Loose Ends
LABEL: Barclay, Polydor
RECORDED: 7/1967 to 7/1970
RELEASED: 2/1974

1. "Coming Down Hard on Me Baby"
   "Blue Suede Shoes"
   "Jam 292"
   "Drifter's Escape"

2. "Burning Desire"
   "I'm Your Hoochie Coochie Man"
   "Electric Ladyland"

Crash Landing

LABEL: Polydor, Reprise

RECORDED: Most original tracks wiped in 1974–75; new musicians added in their place

RELEASED: 3/1975

PERSONNEL: Jimi Hendrix (g), Buddy Miles (d), Billy Cox (b), Jeff Mironov (g), Alan Schwartzberg (d), Bob Babbit (ba), Jimmy Maeulen (perc), Linda November (vo), Vivian Cherry (vo), Barbara Massey (vo), Mitch Mitchell (d)

1. "Message to Love"
   "Somewhere"
   "Crash Landing"
   "Coming Down Hard on Me Baby"

2. "Peace in Mississippi"
   "Power of Soul"
   "Stone Free"
   "M.L.K."

Midnight Lightning

LABEL: Polydor, Reprise

RECORDED: Most original tracks wiped in 1975; new musicians added in their place

RELEASED: 11/1975

PERSONNEL: Jimi Hendrix (g), Mitch Mitchell (d), Noel Redding (b), Jeff Mirov (g), Alan Schwartzberg (d, perc), Bob Babbit (b), Lance Quinn (g), Jimmy Maeulen (perc), Maeretha Stewart (vo), Hilda Harris (vo), Vivian Cherry (vo), Buddy Miles (d), Billy Cox (b), Buddy Lucas (ha), Juma Sultan (perc)

1. "Trashman"
   "Midnight Lightning"
   "Getting My Heart Back Together Again"
   "Gypsy Boy (New Rising Sun)"

2. "Blue Suede Shoes"
   "Machine Gun"
   "Once I Had a Woman"
   "Beginning"

Nine to the Universe

LABEL: Polydor, Reprise

RECORDED: 1969

RELEASED: 3/1980

PERSONNEL: Jimi Hendrix (g), Buddy Miles (d), Billy Cox (ba), Devon Wilson (vo), Dave Holland (b), Jim McCarty (g), Larry Young (or), Larry Lee (g)

1. "Message from Nine to the Universe"
   "Jimi/Jimmy Jam"

2. "Young/Hendrix"
   "Easy Blues"
   "Drone Blues"

The Jimi Hendrix Concerts

LABEL: CBS, Douglas, Media Motion, Polydor, Reprise, etc.

RECORDED: 10/1968 to 7/1970

RELEASED: 8/1982

PERSONNEL: Jimi Hendrix (g), Mitch Mitchell (d), Noel Redding (b), Billy Cox (b)

"Fire" (Winterland, San Francisco, 10/10/1968)
"I Don't Live Today" (Sports Arena, San Diego, 5/24/1969)
"Red House" (New York Pop Festival, Randalls Island, 7/11/1970)
"Stone Free" (Royal Albert Hall, London, 2/24/1969)
"Are You Experienced?" (Winterland, San Francisco, 10/1/1968)
"Little Wing" (Same)

"Voodoo Child (Slight Return)" (Same)
"Bleeding Heart" (Royal Albert Hall, London, 2/24/1969)
"Hey Joe" (Community Center, Berkeley, 5/30/1970)
"Wild Thing" (Winterland, San Francisco, 10/10/1968)
"Hear My Train a Comin'" (Same)
"Foxy Lady" (Forum, Los Angeles, 4/26/1969)

Doriella Du Fontaine
LABEL: Celluloid, Restless, etc.
RECORDED: 11/1969
RELEASED: 7/1984
PERSONNEL: Jimi Hendrix (g, b), Buddy Miles (d), Lightnin' Rod (vo)
"Doriella Du Fontaine"
"Doriella Du Fontaine (Radio Edit)"
"Doriella Du Fontaine (Instrumental)"
"O.D."

Johnny B. Goode
LABEL: Capital, EMI
RECORDED: 5/1970 to 7/1970
RELEASED: 6/1986
PERSONNEL: Jimi Hendrix (g), Billy Cox (b), Mitch Mitchell (d)
"Voodoo Chile" (Atlanta Pop Festival, 7/4/1970)
"Johnny B. Goode" (Community Center, Berkeley, 5/30/1970)
"All Along the Watchtower" (Atlanta Pop Festival, 7/4/1970)
"Star-Spangled Banner" (Same)
"Machine Gun" (Community Center, Berkeley, 5/30/1970)

Gloria
LABEL: Polydor
RECORDED: 10/1966 to 10/1968
RELEASED: 1988
PERSONNEL: Jimi Hendrix (g), Mitch Mitchell (d), Noel Redding (b)
"Gloria"
"Hey Joe"
"Voodoo Child (Slight Return)"
"Purple Haze"

:Blues
LABEL: MCA, Polydor
RECORDED: 12/1966 to 5/1970

RELEASED: 4/1994

PERSONNEL: Jimi Hendrix (g), Buddy Miles (d), Noel Redding (b),
Billy Cox (b), Mitch Mitchell (d), Jack Casady (b), Steve Winwood (or),
Lee Michaels (or)

"Hear My Train a Comin'"

"Born Under a Bad Sign"

"Red House"

"Catfish Blues" (Vitus, Bus-
    sum, Holland, 11/10/1967)

"Voodoo Chile"

"Mannish Boy"

"Once I Had a Woman"

"Bleeding Heart"

"Jelly 292"

"Electric Church Red House"

"Hear My Train a Comin'"
    (Community Center,
    Berkeley, 5/30/1970)

COMPILATIONS

Re-experienced
LABEL: Polydor
RELEASED: 1972

The Essential Jimi Hendrix, Volume 1
LABEL: Polydor, Reprise
RELEASED: 7/1978

The Essential Jimi Hendrix, Volume 2
LABEL: Polydor, Reprise
RELEASED: 7/1979

The Singles Album
LABEL: Polydor
RELEASED: 1983

Kiss the Sky
LABEL: Polydor, Reprise
RELEASED: 10/1984

The Ultimate Experience
LABEL: MCA, Polydor
RELEASED: 11/1992

Legacy
LABEL: Polydor
RELEASED: Unknown

The Story of Jimi Hendrix
LABEL: Polydor
RELEASED: Unknown

Voodoo Soup
LABEL: MCA, Polydor
RELEASED: 1995
Note: Some more track erasures and overdubs.

"The New Rising Sun"	"Night Bird Flying"
"Belly Button Window"	"Drifting"
"Stepping Stone"	"Ezy Rider"
"Freedom"	"Pali Gap"
"Angel"	"Message to Love"
"Room Full of Mirrors"	"Peace in Mississippi"
"Midnight"	"In from the Storm"